The Atkinson Family
Imprint in Higher Education

The Atkinson Family Foundation has endowed this imprint to illuminate the role of higher education in contemporary society.

The publisher and the University of California Press Foundation gratefully acknowledge the generous support of the Atkinson Family Foundation Imprint in Higher Education.

Being-Moved

RHETORIC AND PUBLIC CULTURE: HISTORY, THEORY, CRITIQUE

Series Editors: Dilip Gaonkar and Samuel McCormick

1. *High-Tech Trash: Glitch, Noise, and Aesthetic Failure,* by Carolyn L. Kane
2. *Being-Moved: Rhetoric as the Art of Listening,* by Daniel M. Gross

Being-Moved

Rhetoric as the Art of Listening

Daniel M. Gross

UNIVERSITY OF CALIFORNIA PRESS

University of California Press
Oakland, California

© 2020 by Daniel M. Gross

Library of Congress Cataloging-in-Publication Data

Names: Gross, Daniel M., 1965– author.
Title: Being-moved : rhetoric as the art of listening / Daniel M. Gross.
Other titles: Rhetoric and public culture (Oakland, Calif.); 2.
Description: Oakland, California: University of California Press, [2020] | Series: Rhetoric and public culture: history, theory, critique; 2 | Includes bibliographical references and index.
Identifiers: LCCN 2019030104 (print) | LCCN 2019030105 (ebook) | ISBN 9780520340459 (cloth) | ISBN 9780520340466 (paperback) | ISBN 9780520974548 (ebook)
Subjects: LCSH: Heidegger, Martin, 1889–1976. | Listening (Philosophy) | Rhetoric—Philosophy.
Classification: LCC B105.L54 G76 2020 (print) | LCC B105.L54 (ebook) | DDC 808.001—dc23
LC record available at https://lccn.loc.gov/2019030104
LC ebook record available at https://lccn.loc.gov/2019030105

Manufactured in the United States of America

29 28 27 26 25 24 23 22 21 20
10 9 8 7 6 5 4 3 2 1

CONTENTS

Acknowledgments vii

Introduction to the Art of Listening
1

1. Martin Heidegger on Listening c. 1924
28

2. Being-Moved: A Disciplinary Prehistory
57

3. Face-to-Face Communication, Disfigured
95

4. Passive Voices, Active Listening: A Case Study in Rhetoric and Composition
122

Appendix: The Art of Listening in Select English Manuals and Sermons, 1582–1665 139

Notes 183

Works Cited with Additional Suggested Readings 219

Index 241

ACKNOWLEDGMENTS

I have benefited tremendously from conversations at the following institutions: UC Berkeley, the École Pratique des Hautes Études (Paris), the Seminar für Allgemeine Rhetorik (Tübingen), the University of Pittsburgh, the University of South Carolina (Conference on Rhetorical Theory), the University of Southern California (National Communication Association Summer Honors Doctoral Conference), the Carnegie Mellon–University of Pittsburgh–Duquesne University Consortium for Rhetoric and Discourse Studies, the University of Illinois at Chicago, the University of California–Irvine, and Stanford University. Professional organization audiences for portions of this work include the Modern Language Association (MLA), the National Communication Association (NCA), the Conference on College Composition and Communication (CCCC), the International Society for the History of Rhetoric (ISHR), and the Rhetoric Society of America (RSA).

I am grateful for a DAAD (German Academic Exchange Service) Annual Grant research fellowship that allowed me to do archival work in the Tübingen University library, and for an Andrew W. Mellon Postdoctoral Fellowship at the University of California, Los Angeles (Center for 17th- and 18th-Century Studies) which facilitated work at the Clark Library. UC Irvine Humanities Commons provided publication support.

In each case I thank the original publishers for letting me draw material from the following pieces: "Martin Heidegger's SS 1924 Lecture Course on Aristotle's *Rhetoric* and the Destruction of the Corpus Aristotelicum," in *Commenting on Aristotle's Rhetoric from Antiquity to the Present / Commenter la Rhétorique d'Aristote de l'antiquité à la période contemporaine*, ed. Frédérique Woerther (Leiden, Netherlands: Brill, 2018); "Rhetoric and the Origins of the Human Sciences: A Foucauldian Tale Untold," *Quarterly Journal of Speech* 102, no. 3 (2016): 225–44; "Active Listening, Passive Voices: Gendered Legacies in the History of Rhetoric," in Special Issue: "Rhetorik und Subjektivität," *Rhetorik: Ein internationales Jahrbuch* 30 (2011): 17–29; "Listening Culture," in *Culture and Rhetoric*, Berghahn Books Studies in Rhetoric and Culture I, ed. Ivo Strecker, Stephen Tyler, and Robert Hariman (New York: Berghahn, 2009), 59–73; "The Art of Listening: A Course in the Humanities," *The International Journal of Listening* 21 (2007): 72–79; "Melanchthon's Rhetoric and the Practical Origins of Reformation Human Science," *History of the Human Sciences* 13, no. 3 (2000): 5–22. Some material for chapter 3 was originally drafted for the collection *Responding to the Sacred: An Inquiry into the Limits of Rhetoric*, ed. Michael Bernard-Donals and Kyle Jensen (University Park: Pennsylvania State University Press, 2020).

Feedback on the writing at various stages came from John Durham Peters, Nancy Struever, Samuel McCormick, Barbara Biesecker, David Marshall, Don Bialostosky, Deirdre N. McCloskey, Michael Bernard-Donals, Kyle Jensen, Jerry Hauser, Frédérique Woerther, Ivo Strecker, Stephen Tyler, and Robert Hariman, among others. Fabulous editorial support has been offered by my graduate research assistant Allison Dziuba, who was assisted with classical material by Michael Berlin. Thanks to all.

This book is dedicated to the memory of my father, Philip Gross—a child psychiatrist of the practical Freudian variety, who would like a book of mine winding up so close to home.

Introduction to the
Art of Listening

I. THE PROBLEM

The erosion of public debate is one of the great concerns of the twentieth and twenty-first centuries, and "voice" stands in for what has been lost on the order of political subjectivity: Welsh Tories have no voice, conservatives have no voice in the media, the poor have no voice, the people have no voice.[1] Alternatively, in free speech we like to imagine the correspondence between personal voice and the voice of democracy: secure the first and the second should follow. But who is listening? The ear of democracy is an uncanny figure despite the fact that one is impossible without the other. Explain this disfigurement, moreover, and we address some important puzzles of our political age, including the basic vulnerability that lies at the heart of political agency itself. Though we sometimes like to imagine otherwise, political formations, including democratic ones, require passive dispositions such as apathy, ignorance, subjectification, adherence, obedience, suggestibility, accountability, attentiveness, open-mindedness, and sensitivity, as well as the related, middle-voiced experiences of *appearing* apathetic or ignorant, listening, learning, belonging, obeying, changing one's mind, being subject to this or that, being oriented, being addressed, being held accountable, being responsible, being obliged, being moved.[2] What follows will be, in part, a phenomenology of these passive dispositions by way of the rhetorical tradition where the ear of democracy is latent, instead of political philosophy that traditionally proceeds by way of the theoretical eye (θεωρία from θεωρός, "spectator," literally "one looking at a show").[3]

Apart from sound studies, which is relevant, though it frames inquiry differently, what kind of attention has listening received in the humanities and in the interpretive social sciences? Writing at the end of her life, the eminent political theorist Hannah Arendt returned to hearing as she worked against some philosophical distortions in *The Life of the Mind*. Noting how each major category of mental activity draws its metaphor from a different bodily sense, she links formal philosophical thinking to sight, aesthetic judgment to taste, and Jewish faith to hearing, because the Jewish God is heard but not seen.[4] The Hebrew word *shema* traditionally translated as "obey" literally means "to hear": שְׁמַע יִשְׂרָאֵל = Hear, [O] Israel.[5] "Metaphors drawn from hearing are very rare in the history of philosophy," Arendt concludes, "the most notable modern exception being the late writings of Heidegger, where the thinking ego 'hears' the call of Being." This parenthetical passage continues with a condensed history that tells of the ear's demise:

> Medieval efforts to reconcile Biblical teaching with Greek philosophy testify to a complete victory of intuition or contemplation over every form of audition, and this victory was, as it were, foreshadowed by the early attempt of Philo of Alexandria to attune his Jewish creed to the Platonizing philosophy. He was still aware of the distinction between a Hebrew truth, which was heard, and the Greek *vision* of the true, and transformed the former into a mere preparation for the latter, to be achieved by divine intervention that had made man's ears into eyes to permit greater perfection of human cognition.[6]

And though Arendt is in good company as she critiques the theoretical disposition of philosophy, she remains thereby tied to a philosophical orientation that makes Heidegger seem thoroughly anomalous and forecloses critical paths, like rhetoric, that do not run directly through philosophy. No doubt Arendt's critique of theory allows her to pick up rhetorical phenomena along the way. She notes how Hans Jonas disqualifies hearing as the only possible competitor to sight for preeminence because it "intrudes upon a passive subject" or in her own words because "the percipient is at the mercy of something or somebody else," and she reminds us of the German cluster of words indicating a position of "non-freedom from *hören*, to hear: *gehorchen, hörig, gehören*, to obey, be in bondage, belong" (112). But these fundamentally political considerations appear only distantly from the philosophical perspective; in fact, rhetoric offers much more detail because it is the traditional domain where subjection is both theorized and practiced. That's one goal of this book. In broad strokes and in some carefully selected detail composing a critical narrative, I rediscover rhetoric at the heart of political and other forms of modern human subjectivity as they appear in the human sciences broadly conceived. As a scholarly project, then, I do talk in terms of disciplines. But as we have learned most notably from Michel Foucault (chapter 2), disciplines are not just a matter of scholarship, as they speak to basic forms of subjectivity and its transformation across a social field. Obedience, for instance, is something I might be called to, which sounds one way coming from Arendt's Jewish God, and another way coming from that cluster of German words that she pointed out in her projects on evil. I take seriously and study disciplinary formation in this book, as disciplines are ways to live.

In fact, following Arendt's close colleague Leo Strauss, political philosophy has recently returned to persuasive rhetoric for assistance, most notably in Bryan Garsten's *Saving Persuasion: A Defense of Rhetoric and Judgment*, where the title of this book indicates how it is more about the active dispositions of judgment than it is about the virtues of passivity. If only rhetoric were not detached from the Ciceronian tradition of practical judgment, Garsten argues, perhaps a more robust republican tradition might have persisted even now, as political reason in the liberal tradition seems exhausted.[7] Garsten is not alone, moreover, when it comes to mining rhetoric for a critique of enlightenment philosophy and its limiting rationality. Though inspired by Martin Heidegger, who never left rhetoric behind completely, ear work in Arendt, Jonas, Don Ihde, David Michael Kleinberg-Levin, and Gemma Fiumara reverts, in the end, to the philosophical paradigm and thus loses its grasp on the aural history and phenomenology that runs *directly* through rhetoric.[8] In contrast, my focus remains on rhetoric throughout this project, while I explain at key instances why it regularly reverts to philosophy, as witnessed, for instance, in Arendt. Chapter 2 explains how the disciplinary structure of the human sciences detaches from its practical origins in rhetoric as the art of moving souls, instead making the sciences primarily the support of state reason. And not surprisingly this historical detachment from rhetoric, designed to shore up a new type of political subjectivity less vulnerable to exogenous persuasion—hence reason over passions of the soul, management over movement, eye over ear and so on—could never succeed in principle, producing instead a whole set of painful approximations legible most readily through the field of psychology and in the related twentieth-century subfield of psychoanalysis (chapter 3).

No doubt in democratic formations we can also make reasonable judgments, express ourselves conscientiously, and act decisively. But these favored activities occupy us less often than we like to think. What's more, we already have relatively sophisticated schemes to describe them because, in part, these activities appear where we would like to imagine ourselves, for reasons I will try to explain in this book. Starting with the philosopher Martin Heidegger—a figure through whom Western democratic traditions were strangely refracted in his Summer Session (SS) 1924 lecture course on Aristotle's *Rhetoric*—I reconsider the history of rhetoric not as the art of speaking, but rather as the art of listening. What is sometimes called the "other side of language" will confirm a basic corollary to the democratic equation: out of the inevitable slippage between speaker and auditor emerges a political imaginary where the subject must be sutured in more or less satisfactory terms (for example the "good man speaking well") while rhetorical failure takes the form of a phantasm—the classical specter of rhetorical effeminacy, for instance, or the modern specter of the disembodied voice: Gothic rhetoric. At the same time SS 1924 inadvertently helps generate a different genealogy of the human sciences that puts this now familiar critical discourse in new perspective and renders phantasmagoria not so strange after all. Indeed, we've been listening quite attentively all along.

How can we begin to understand the renunciation of listening, which seems to have a modern flare? In *The Psychology of Clothes* (1930) it would seem British psychoanalyst J. C. Flügel provides some clues, as he explains "The Great Masculine Renunciation" of another subjectification, namely flamboyant dress, which appears for Flügel under the Ovidian dictum *"Forma viros neglecta decet*—neglect of appearance becomes men."[9] "Greater uniformity of costume has really been accompanied by greater sympathy between one individual and another, and between one class and another," speculates Flügel. "Take any ordinary social function. The men are dressed in a dull uniformity of black and white, 'the very embodiment of life's prose,' as one writer has it.... But if there is a lack of romance, there is also absent the envy, jealousy, the petty triumphs, defeats, superiority, and spitefulnesses engendered by the—doubtless more poetical—diversity and gaiety of the women's costumes" (114).[10] In *The Acoustic Mirror*, Kaja Silverman situates classic Hollywood cinema in this same psychohistorical trajectory, where passive exhibitionism is transformed into active scopophilia (erotic pleasure in the use of vision); more broadly, the desire to be seen is transformed into the desire to see and to know, which includes for Silverman mastery not just of the visible world, but also the audible world via cinema (24–26). When it comes to the art of listening, psychoanalytic theorists like Silverman and Mladen Dolar have useful reminders if we want to examine the apparatus, such as classic cinema, whereby the male voice gains fragile authority over "the voice of the mother" that speaks volumes to masculine vulnerability, as figured in the open ear.

For example, it is no accident that the virtuoso ear in classic cinema such as *Touch of Evil*, or for that matter in the listening technologies of the psychoanalyst or the stethoscope, gain authority by way of a distinction from the female body offering up its truths. Consider respectively Jonathan Sterne's groundbreaking work on what he calls mediate auscultation, or Sigmund Freud's *Dora*, which I will situate in chapter 3.

Likewise, the ideal orator after Cicero insists upon a virility that would mask our dramatic subjection to language, a subjection that threatens to return in the form of logorrhea traditionally known as "mere ornamentation" or its opposite: passive listening imagined as the catatonic condition suffered when one finally stops talking in the plain style. By what mechanisms, then, does our imaginary identification so consistently line up with the agent of an utterance rather than the patient? One goal of this book is to answer this psychoanalytic question by way of a history of the human sciences, which turns out to be essential if we are to understand both how we got here and what we can do about it. To understand, that is, how we have come to a pointed anxiety about maintaining ourselves in the public arena—finding our voice and expressing ourselves reasonably—we need to know a lot more about the disciplinary structures that normalized the rational actor in the middle part of the twentieth century, while all sorts of alternatives consolidated under the countervailing term *irrational*. Indeed, it is time to approach some of the famous pathologies of the middle twentieth century differently—Nazism most prominently—by bringing to bear a longer history of rhetoric as the art of moving souls.

Like Flügel, we can begin symptomatically with the observation that a certain sort of male subject proves his symbolic potency through the repeated demonstration of the symbolic impotence of those subject to speech. In the spirit of Flügel's analysis of visual dissociation, we observe that the male subject dissociates himself from the audible world, attempting thereby to align himself with a symbolic order within which power has become more and more dispersed and nonmaterial. For Flügel, such is life's prose: male subjectivity is better unseen, and I would add unaddressed. At about the same time, in the 1920s Walter Benjamin and Siegfried Kracauer on the Continent, Walter Lippmann, John Dewey, and Herbert A. Wichelns in the United States, are among those concerned with the decline of "face-to-face" communication in mass media: just as the eye is dispersed and dematerialized as a facial feature, so is the ear.

We should not be surprised that the efforts to recuperate visual power analyzed by Flügel and later psychoanalytic theorists is accompanied by similar efforts to recuperate vocal power in the face of mass media. When in 1925 Wichelns famously warns in "The Literary Criticism of Oratory" that propaganda and publicity in the guise of public education threaten the public mind, we witness one such effort at the inception of communication studies as an autonomous discipline. Although we know how to judge timeless literature, we don't know how to judge oratory because, according to Wichelns, oratory is a vehicle for statecraft and therefore it is bound up with the things of the moment difficult for the critic to reconstruct. "Yet," urges Wichelns in a striking counterfactual, "the conditions of democracy necessitate both the making of speeches and the study of the art. It is true that other ways of influencing opinion have long been practiced, that oratory is no longer the chief means of communicating ideas to the masses.... But, human nature being what it is, there is no likelihood that face to face persuasion will cease to be a principal mode of exerting influence, whether in courts, in senate-houses, or on the platform."[11] Moreover rhetorical criticism according to Wichelns has a recuperative power for the agent of speech earned, characteristically, at the expense of a pliable audience (from the Latin *audire*, to hear): "The scheme of a rhetorical study includes the element of the speaker's personality as a conditioning factor; it includes also the public character of the man—not what he was, but what he was thought to be. It requires a description of the speaker's audience, and of the leading ideas with which he plied his hearers" (212). Again, the male subject proves his symbolic potency by demonstrating the symbolic impotence of those subject to speech; whereas the soldier conquers with an art exogenous to the life affected, the "effective wielder of public discourse" conquers with an art indigenous to the life affected (215). But to Wichelns's credit, this analogy does not resolve so easily: the speaker's character and thus the force of his speech relies, ultimately, upon public opinion.[12] Rhetoric as a life science depends upon those lives affected. And how are those lives affected? Rhetoric has to think about this too, though traditionally it has done so in fits and starts, as we will see in an excursus on rhetorical anthropology (chapter 2). Concluding this book, I will take Flügel's dictum literally, exploring how prose pedagogy also sutures the writing subject around the figure of vocal agency. How do we learn to speak and listen, read and write—how do we learn to communicate—through different regimes of fragmentation? Why do we so animate our rhetorical theories and handbooks?

My use of psychoanalytic theory thus has some affinity with Friedrich A. Kittler, who in *Discourse Networks 1800/1900* analyzes a sensual regime—of the eye, the ear, the hands of children—as it takes shape, for instance, in a particular pedagogy like that of the Bavarian school official Heinrich Stephani, who oralized the alphabet around 1800.[13] I will track how historically specific formations of psyche depend in part upon "rhetoric" as it is positively manifest in handbooks, pedagogies, and in theories of rhetoric and communication, focusing for example in chapter 4 on the figure of vocal agency in contemporary writing pedagogy. Methodologically like Kittler, my point here is that fantastic forms of subjectivity can be read off of the handbooks and other practical material given to young people and others who are not fully formed, which is to say everyone. The specifically psychoanalytic insight is that such subject formation never produces a seamless transition to subject and then to citizen, relying as it must upon the phantasm of the finishing school and thus ultimately the consummately finished and then polished, whose fragile formation stands still under erasure: the good man speaking well (or not), the best and the brightest (not to mention everyone else)—flickering stars in what Ngũgĩ wa Thiong'o famously called the "general bourgeois education system" with its global reach.[14]

One type of recuperative project in politics and public culture pays special attention to phantasmagoria, including the forms of failed subjectivity that rail against a political norm just by being bent or broken: voices noticeably strained, or lapsed, or missing, from the models that might show up in handbooks and how-to's.

At about the same time that Heidegger was lecturing on Aristotle's *Rhetoric*, Walter Lippmann in the United States published *Phantom Public* (1925) which marks, in the words of one critic, a transition from agora to phantasmagoria. Indeed much can still be gained by measuring the distance between particular ideologies of rhetorical agency and the promising symptoms of their failure in the incomprehensible (Bachmann), the deficient (Lea and Street), the inscrutable (Lee), the inarticulate (Mazzio), the eccentric (Nicholson), the undisciplined or unruly (Alexander, Jarratt, and Welch), the excessive (Al-Kassim), the silenced (Glenn), the unheard (Spivak).[15] But what recourse do we have along with listening more attentively to the previously unheard, for instance?[16] Critical pedagogues on this short list and beyond have a useful set of strategies; in what follows my strategy is distinctly historiographic.

Operative binaries including masculine/feminine, agent/patient, active/passive, and especially in our case eye/ear, only do so much when reversed. Since, for example, reading Silverman and Laura Mulvey the masculine eye dominates important forms of high modernism, one might think we should validate the ear instead. Perhaps an experimental film like Mulvey's *Riddles of the Sphinx* does this by eschewing a conventional voiceover and by disidentifying a woman's voice and a character who appears on screen.[17] But perhaps it is also not accidental that Mulvey is a theorist and historian of film. Without knowing how these related binaries came to bear, and took hold consequentially, the reversals themselves can't do much and might even wind up reinforcing the very structures under scrutiny. Instead, as feminist historiographers have taught us most consequentially—Gerda Lerner on private property and the creation of patriarchy, Evelyn Fox Keller on technology and mother nature, and Susan Jarratt plus many others on the very idea of rhetoric in the public sphere—it is only when pernicious binaries are denaturalized by way of a detailed history that we learn where exactly the weakest points are in our current system of givens, thereby destabilizing most effectively the system in its extension.[18]

Psychoanalysis-as-theory is itself a particular formation with built-in limitations due, in one crucial instance, to its increasingly obscure history as a human science. An important opportunity is lost if we focus on the other side of language while overlooking the disciplinary history that gives way to these very same, overdetermined distinctions between sanctioned speech and its contraries. In fact, when a psychoanalytic framework is ultimately subsumed—contra Foucault—into a broader history of the human sciences where rhetoric as the art of *being moved* takes its proper place, many of these phenomena, including the ear of democracy, do not appear so strange after all.[19]

The 1920s provide a turning point in this genealogy of rhetorical citizenship, first because it poses a basic question of our age. Does the Weimar critique of liberalism entail demagoguery as a likely alternative? Important postwar political theorists like Jürgen Habermas suspected as much, and therefore a range of projects were launched that would generate more ideal conditions for public debate without demagoguery or unduly emotional rhetoric. In Kantian terms free speech has always implied a critical ear that might differentiate special interests from principles that could be universal such as human rights. Kant's *Critique of Judgment* formulates the queasiness of liberal democracy: "I must confess that a beautiful poem has always given me pure delight, whereas reading the best speech of a Roman public orator, or of a contemporary parliamentary speaker or preacher, has always been mingled with the disagreeable feeling of disapproval of an insidious art, an art that knows how, in important matters, to move people like machines to a judgment that must lose all its weight with them when they meditate about it calmly."[20] Along these Kantian lines sharpened in the 1920s, a persistent question of liberal democracy has become: Which media or modalities, which situations or circumstances, which social dispositions mitigate sophistry? How can the irrational be sidelined systematically? However, at the same time, models of practical reason have come under increasing pressure as interested in their own right and practically unhelpful, as they prove to be, for instance, highly fallible predictors of economic and political behavior.[21]

As recent research has reinserted the rational actor in an emotional scene, Weimar reemerges as a gothic laboratory where human being itself was subject to a range of happy and very unhappy experiments. Is our choice the impossible enlightenment or demagoguery? It turns out that Martin Heidegger and his contemporaries across the political spectrum loosened the hold of this binary when they considered ways of being in the world beyond rationality conceived as a universal standard instead of historically circumscribed, and occasionally useful, sets of procedures. Opposed to Heidegger on the left, for instance, witness an alternative in André Breton's *First Surrealist Manifesto*, also from that auspicious year 1924:

> We are still living under the reign of logic, but the logical processes of our time apply only to the solution of problems of secondary interest. The absolute rationalism which remains in fashion allows for the consideration of only those facts narrowly relevant to our experience. Logical conclusions, on the other hand, escape us. Needless to say, boundaries have been assigned even to experience. It revolves in a cage from which release is becoming increasingly difficult. It too depends upon immediate utility and is guarded by common sense. In the guise of civilization, under the pretext of progress, we have succeeded in dismissing from our minds anything that, rightly or wrongly, could be regarded as superstition or myth; and we have proscribed every way of seeking the truth which does not conform to convention. It would appear that it is by sheer chance that an aspect of intellectual life—and by far the most important in my opinion—about which no one was supposed to be concerned any longer has, recently, been brought back to light. Credit for this must go to Freud.[22]

Emphasizing sacred rhetoric instead, I hope to demonstrate that Breton's reliance on the Freudian irrational is warranted but insufficient; indeed, our much heralded "re-enchantment of the world" after

Nietzsche and Weber can be misleading, as I will elaborate in chapter 3.[23] Orphaned materials of modernity often turn out to be vital strains of a different genealogy altogether.

Like Walter Benjamin, I do foreground in chapter 3 both failed and extrapersonal communication—including collectivities, machines, institutions, nonhumans, unconscious language, and spiritual entities as well as material objects—to critique our rhetoric of the subject that implies a certain configuration of the sensorium (speech over audition) and then lends itself to a political system I call the voice of democracy. I am interested, like Benjamin, in the concrete historicity of our subject-object regime in its rhetorical dimension, and not just in the positive dimensions of social science. Unlike Benjamin's re-enchantment of the modern world, however, I emphasize sacred rhetoric to enable a more pointed critique of pragmatic phenomena such as the operation of "voice" in the educational and political setting, or Gothic rhetoric understood as that which exceeds the pragmatics of face-to-face communication, of the sort we find foreshadowed in this passage from the pseudo-Ciceronian rhetorical handbook *Rhetorica ad Herennium*, where a speechmaker is advised how to manipulate auditors: "The direct opening should be such that by the straightforward methods I have prescribed we immediately make the hearer well-disposed or attentive or receptive; whereas the subtle approach should be such that we effect all these results covertly, through dissimulation, and so can arrive at the same vantage point in the task of speaking."[24] In the context of our contemporary communication sciences "extrapersonal communication" is a rogue category that challenges this fantasy of manipulation by focusing on mysteries subsumed in this passage under the sign of being well disposed (*benivolus*), being attentive (*adtentus*), and being receptive or teachable (*docilis*). What is the phenomenology of such familiar advice, after all? Who is the agent and who is the patient when we are told, paradoxically, how to manipulate someone else?

Tracking the modern fate of sacred rhetoric helps us bracket, more importantly, Foucault's history of the human sciences so we better grasp not just how people are organized but also how they are *moved*: hence emotions in a previous book of mine, and the art of listening in this one. At this point, the core of my argument (chapter 2) is that crucial rhetorical phenomena, most of which can be subsumed under the sign of vocal agency, are misunderstood because we bring to bear an inappropriate framework articulated most clearly by Foucault.

In fact the social sciences have an altogether different genealogy discernible by way of sacred rhetoric, and here once again Martin Heidegger unwittingly provides a clue in his SS 1924 lecture course, which was first scheduled as a course on Augustine before Heidegger changed the topic in the effort to accelerate his planned book on Aristotle (which never appeared but instead morphed into the masterwork *Being and Time*). As Heidegger tries systematically to provide "the [ontological] concepts for things which are usually treated in a nebulous way ... in theology,"[25] Augustine provides crucial material for Heidegger's Aristotle interpretation, which, as we will see, rediscovers *rhetoric as a life science*. Consider, for instance, Augustine in *The City of God*: "By 'they that hear' [shall live, comments Augustine on John 5.25] he means those who obey and believe, and who persevere even to the end" (*qui audierint* dixit qui oboedierint, qui crediderint et usque in finem perseveraverint, 20.6). But what Augustine describes is by no means instrumental rhetoric: it would be a mistake to conclude one must simply listen to and obey God, devote oneself to following God's commandments. His point is that one's very capacity to hear depends upon how one lives. So with respect to the second resurrection, notes Augustine, "He does not say, as in the first resurrection, 'and they that hear shall live' [but rather "when all who are in their graves shall hear his voice and shall come forth"; quando omnes, qui in monumentis sunt, audient vocem eius et procedent; John 5.28–29]. For all shall not live." What this means, Augustine explains, is that "not all will have that life which, because it is a life of blessedness, is the only life worthy to be so called. For, clearly, if they were without any kind of life at all, they would not be able to hear and come forth from the tombs in their rising bodies" (non enim omnes vivent, ea vita scilicet, quae, quoniam beata est, sola vita dicenda est. Nam utique non sine qualicumque vita possent audire et de monumentis resurgente carne procedere). For Augustine, like Aristotle before him and like Heidegger much after him in 1924, rhetoric is not a skill but rather a way of life dependent upon what kind of life one lives, which might be, for instance, blessed or ungodly in religious terms, praise- or blameworthy in ethical terms, friendly or unfriendly in political terms.

In short, the history of the human sciences cannot be understood solely by way of bare-life technologies after Foucault; instead they must be understood by way of the life that can be lived one way or another, which means that persuasive technologies like rhetoric are central even if they are no longer definitive. Rhetoric moves souls. Chapter 2 shows how psychology, politics, and pedagogy are not originally descriptive disciplines à la Foucault in *The Order of Things*; they are the *prescriptive* arts of moving souls both personal and collective, drawing as they do from the first such art, rhetoric. Indeed, that is one important way that disciplines form in the first place—disciplines chase expertise. No doubt the early modern need for institutionalized disciplines of psychology, politics, and pedagogy requires explanation that goes to the heart of state reason. But by definition these new academic formations in sixteenth-century Germany and beyond hadn't yet fully developed their own expertise adequate to meet these new demands. So, like any other academic discipline in its early stages developing first principles, basic assumptions, key terms, research domains, methods of inquiry, habits of mind, and sanctioned authority, these early modern human sciences frequently had to look elsewhere, beyond their initially scant disciplinary resources. In this case, when it came to human science as the art of moving souls, rhetoric was the obvious expert domain tapped at every turn. And now, after this originating episode has been largely forgotten and subsumed into Foucault's biopolitical narrative around the human sciences, it becomes particularly helpful to revisit original disciplinary logics and practices so that their quiet persistence becomes legible once again.

Finally it is worth describing in what way my approach to sense perception—now a rich topic across the disciplines—is phenomenological and not grounded most immediately in the growing field of sound studies.[26] Following sound studies, I consider how a sensorium is not necessarily the world of sense data and its organs of reception, while recognizing how this scientific model has certainly dominated earlier periods and to a certain extent our common sense today. And though this scientific model will at times serve as a necessary object of criticism, I will instead foreground a critical ecology of the senses where (sensory) experience is purposive, emerging from a historically situated being-world nexus.[27] Thus my approach learns from sound studies where a history of the senses after Marx has been pursued in detail over the last couple of decades, focusing frequently on sound technology as history: see for instance another book by Jonathan Sterne, *MP3: The Meaning of a Format (Sign, Storage, Transmission)*. At the same time, my approach maintains a very different focal point in the ancient discipline of rhetoric because it explains how listening per se has been disciplined, and what this means for the subject of the modern human sciences. Or even more basically in a complementary formula: The object of sound studies is sound, with a paradigm example in "noise"— what it is, and how it appears historically only by way of a scene, for example noise pollution and noise abatement campaigns.[28] The art of listening finds its object of study in ontology—being moved and its disciplines—where auditing God is the paradigm example. History of the senses is where the two modes of inquiry meet.

The earliest point in the chronology where I spend significant time (chapter 2) is Melanchthon's sixteenth-century Europe, because that is where we see in detail how the modern human sciences, notably psychology, politics, and pedagogy, drew techniques from rhetoric as the art of moving souls. My historical methodology, however, is more genealogy than chronology. Thus my *narrative* starting point (chapter 1) is in fact Martin Heidegger's SS 1924 lecture course on Aristotle's *Rhetoric* because it launched this project when I was a graduate student in rhetoric puzzling over his strange understanding of the field then available only in manuscript, and because it remains either a resource for, or counterpoint to, most of what follows. Indeed, this book can be understood as a careful and often contrary conversation with Heidegger, each subsequent chapter unfolding in response to a basic question he poses explicitly, or conspicuously avoids. Thus, chapter 2: Why does Heidegger's characterization of rhetoric as the art of listening appear so odd and compelling?[29] Answering this question, ultimately, requires a new genealogy of the human sciences that takes seriously early modern sacred rhetoric, especially in the German and English Reformation and post-Reformation contexts. Chapter 3: How does Heidegger's lecture course participate in a broader sociopolitical crisis where the voice of democracy is at issue? This question, addressed as 1920s "communication," including mass communication, implicates a particular sort of human being who speaks only incidentally. Listening becomes the dominant modality when the good man speaking well, *vir bonus dicendi peritus*, no longer serves plausibly as the paradigm for rhetorical training and analysis. In a formula: authorities speak, individuals communicate, human being listens to and is affected by—is persuaded by—all sorts of things that are not located most accurately in the persuasive efforts of another human being. Hence this chapter on "extrapersonal communication" in the broadly Weimar context, where face-to-face communication is fundamentally disfigured, giving way to what Freud called persuasive adjuncts or contrivances, *Veranstaltungen*. Finally, chapter 4: What does SS 1924 mean for subsequent rhetorical theories and practices? "Voice" and "ear" in postwar pedagogy illustrate pressing contemporary problems that can be reconsidered in the classroom by way of the encounter with Heidegger's work on the art of listening.

This final point about the classroom is worth some explanation and illustration because it is also, ultimately, about my methodology, which is unconventional when it comes to historical work.

In a way I started writing this book around 1996, when seemingly separate research and teaching activities collided. At the same time that I was pouring over Martin Heidegger's then-unpublished 1924 lectures on Aristotle's *Rhetoric*—including his strange reversal of rhetorical listening over speech—I was expected to teach as a graduate student in the UC Berkeley Rhetoric Department. And only at that exact intersection could it dawn on me that a key paradox of teaching has deep historical roots worthy of patient exploration. Especially compelling was my experience of that magical transformation from learner to teacher, not by way of a slow progression over the years from ignorance to wisdom or from novice to authority, but literally from hour to hour as I learned about rhetoric in the morning then taught rhetoric in the afternoon—or sometimes the other way around. Indeed, the very progression that might run from my "listening" belatedly to Heidegger's lectures, then on to lecturing myself, appeared especially puzzling as a progression, as did the whole host of related binaries that pit listening against speaking, learning against teaching, passivity against activity. Only now the puzzle seemed solvable.

But solving the problem on paper proved difficult. As I started and finished other academic projects, this book on the art of listening simmered—sometimes languished—in the background because I could not figure out whether it should be about one half of the topic, which is historical, or about the other half, which is practical. Following certain conventions in history writing, I assumed that the two would have to be separated for publication purposes, and for the longest time I could not figure out how to accomplish that separation without undue sacrifice to the basic project, which developed as one. It took a long time researching and teaching the material before I decided that this tension might in fact be foregrounded productively.

Scholarly commitments notwithstanding, I knew at least through casual conversation that readers might rightfully expect a book on the art of listening to feel familiar. Like books on the art of speaking, a book on the art of listening should offer practical advice and have some classroom application. It should not just be about the idea; the art of listening should *feel like something*, while training us some way or another.

Shouldn't it? Below I describe how I teach related works at the intersection of self-help and textbook genres including Madelyn Burley-Allen, *Listening: The Forgotten Skill* or Michael P. Nichols, *The Lost Art of Listening: How Learning to Listen Can Improve Relationships*. Also worth mentioning in this context is the set of popular trade books including most famously Deborah Tannen, *You Just Don't Understand: Women and Men in Conversation*, including the chapter "'I'll Explain It to You': Lecturing and Listening." Perhaps especially because arts of listening have become for us so *un*familiar, the first steps seem to require intimate guidance: this part of the body not that, pay attention and orient yourself differently so that this strange thing called the art of listening might appear as such. A book about speech, by way of contrast, can better rely upon familiarity to the point where actual speaking isn't expected—there are plenty of books that are about speech on the metalevel à la John Peters, *Speaking into the Air: A History of the Idea of Communication*, which is close to mine in spirit. Or again by way of contrast, a book about education certainly doesn't have to be educational, if by that one expects some kind of classroom instruction reported or delivered.

"So have you become a better listener?" friends ask. "And what would Carla say about that?" (You can guess who she is.) Indeed, some of the most engaging material I found during my historical research did indeed offer advice about how to listen better. Don't just read Scripture at home but come to church as the "public ear"! Arrive with something in your stomach but not too much, otherwise you'll doze off; remember to jostle your slumbering neighbors, and don't just sit there leafing helplessly through your Bible as passages are cited—just listen! Meanwhile classroom exercises on the topic were essential guides to research: Is there such a thing as pure hearing? Let's see what happens if you listen quietly in your bedroom. Does that count? What about a visit to the anechoic chamber in the University of Iowa Speech Pathology and Audiology Department? Then if the exercise seems difficult—why so? And in what ways? The "why so" question demanded historical research, while the "what ways" question demanded the careful analysis of phenomenology, where Martin Heidegger proved indispensable. Eventually I realized that the classroom and the scholarship could only be separated artificially, and at the expense of the topic ultimately.

This book offers a history of rhetoric as the art of listening. Meanwhile it is constantly attentive to feelings both familiar and unfamiliar, which wind up in sections that become increasingly pedagogical, as chapter 4 gets down to the grammar of passive voice in student writing. No doubt academics often say that historical material comes alive in the classroom, while good teaching depends on historical understanding even when the topic, like rhetoric, seems practical enough. Less common in the publishing world are the traces I've left around these two activities, instead of separating them cleanly into history and theory on one side, textbook or instruction manual on the other. In doing so I take some inspiration from another book that is close to mine, Krista Ratcliffe's *Rhetorical Listening: Identification, Gender, Whiteness*, which moves comfortably between history and classroom practice like much scholarship in the subfield of rhetoric and composition. Among other things, I hope to demonstrate a type of academic work that makes good use of its motivations, while confounding in practice the expectation that classrooms benefit unilaterally from scholarship.

Ultimately, I could not do this work without my students. There is no way to work on the art of listening without students, just as there is no way to work on rhetoric writ large without the students who compose its history. In terms of argument and structure, this book is designed to demonstrate how so.

II. THE ART OF LISTENING: A COURSE IN COMMUNICATION STUDIES WRIT LARGE

Dismissed as a passive behavior that comes naturally, listening is in fact a complex and learned activity that can be practiced. Like reading, writing, and speaking, listening as a practical activity is critical for college life and beyond. But while rhetoric as the art of speaking has been a basic course in higher education for millennia, rarely does a course in the humanities focus on the art of listening. That's what we did in my spring 2005 upper-division undergraduate course "Issues in Rhetoric and Culture: The Art of Listening," which was cross-listed in departments of Rhetoric, Communication Studies, English, and the University of Iowa's Project on Rhetoric of Inquiry (POROI). The goal of this course, which I have taught subsequently at a couple different levels including graduate, is to build some practical skills in the art of listening within a humanities context that gives these skills meaning beyond function—for example, better grades, better job performance, better personal relationships—although these practical goals that so concern undergraduates are honored as well. Ultimately, however, students are expected to gain some critical perspective on the practicalities of listening by way of history and theory.

We began by reading the July 31, 2004, "Letter to the Bishops of the Catholic Church on the Collaboration of Men and Women in the Church and in the World"—a controversial document pitched against feminist theories of gender and sexuality construction. The document, coauthored by then Cardinal Ratzinger who later became Pope Benedict XVI, argues ultimately that women are particularly disposed to the virtues of "listening, welcoming, humility, faithfulness, praise and waiting." This Church document was a convenient place to start because it immediately introduced the notion that listening goes beyond its mere physiological function and must be considered a function of a social category like gender. Students were curious to know why listening is often associated with women. Such curiosity, in turn, could serve my pedagogical goals of introducing what Michel Foucault calls, after Nietzsche, a genealogical approach to the history of listening. Whence our assumptions about listening? Why, for instance, might we consider women better listeners, and when did this assumption take hold? And what do we do about that? Generally speaking, readings were selected and organized to denaturalize listening.

Our reading list included in order:

Exodus 1–21, Psalm 5, Matthew 13 "Parable of the Sower"
Murray Schafer, "Open Ears" (available in *The Auditory Culture Reader*, eds. Michael Bull and Les Back, Berg 2004)
Aristotle, *Rhetoric* (selections)
Plutarch, "On Listening"
Alain Corbin, "The Auditory Markers of the Village" (*The Auditory Culture Reader*)
Mark M. Smith, "Listening to the Heard Worlds of Antebellum America" (*The Auditory Culture Reader*)
Allen Brown, David Taylor, eds., *Gabr'l Blow Sof: Sumter County, Alabama, Slave Narratives*
Jonathan Sterne, "Medicine's Acoustic Culture: Mediate Auscultation, the Stethoscope and the 'Autopsy of the Living'" (*The Auditory Culture Reader*)
Sigmund Freud, "Recommendations to Physicians Practicing Psycho-Analysis"
Sigmund Freud, *Dora: An Analysis of a Case of Hysteria*
Hans-Georg Gadamer, *Truth and Method* (selections)
Nicholson Baker, *Vox*
Madelyn Burley-Allen, *Listening: The Forgotten Skill, A Self-Teaching Guide*

Fascinating issues appeared at every turn. Inspired by one student's journal entry, we thought in class about how we configure our listening differently depending upon the public space we occupy: in church we listen with the traditional purpose of hearing the Word of God; at the coffee house we "overhear," but without the paranoia that accompanies aural surveillance under a totalitarian regime; on the internet we didn't listen at all back then. We used Exodus to work on the ways in which the communicative situation exceeds the presentism of speaker/message/audience—a basic "transactional" communication studies model—extending, rather, over time. How, then, are we disposed to listen to the past? And what gives certain communicative nodes like the story of Exodus duration: trauma, narrative arc, transcendent principles, ritual storytelling in the Passover Seder and so on? Also, we read slave narratives with the question of power in mind: how are different social roles configured differently around listening? As a matter of survival, the slave has to listen acutely to the master, while survival and escape depend upon awarenesses of the immediate soundscape. Meanwhile the master must be relatively deaf to the needs of the slave, while remaining tuned in to any sounds of resistance. Listening is not the same thing as hearing, understood as a physical process. It is a differentiated and deeply social phenomenon that requires rhetorical analysis.

To summarize our reading, students composed a table (see below) that analyzed five different listening models—biblical, classical, historical, psychoanalytic, and business—according to four questions: (1) what is the purpose for the focus on listening in each case? (2) what is the scope of listening? (3) who is the subject of listening? (4) what are some of the key assumptions and premises of each model?

This analytic exercise encouraged students to think about the ways in which each listening model has its appropriate domain, while the most "modern" isn't necessarily the richest. Students expressed a sense of regret when they realized that only in the biblical/religious model does voice extend beyond the human, in this case to the spiritual world. Meanwhile comparative analysis allowed them to see how their favorite, user-friendly text (Burley-Allen) could not have all the answers because it worked exclusively "within the box" of a corporate model facilitating relationships between coworkers and between middle management and their employees. Comparing this corporate model to the historical models where listening is more obviously hierarchical (i.e., the biblical and classical models) gave students the tools to work out their own critique of power. "What about the CEO?" one student asked. "Does empathic listening apply equally to the CEO and the staff?"

	Biblical	Classical (Aristotle)	Historical (Smith)	Psychoanalytic (Freud)	Business (Burley-Allen)
Purpose for the focus on listening	listening is a vehicle for: -Word -authority -grace -redemption	-to master the art of persuasion -constitute audience -access truth, power	to access a different social reality (vs. sight)	-to develop the psychoanalytic method -cure patient	-to increase productivity -self-esteem -facilitate hierarchy
Scope of listening	-commands -confessions -prophecies -appeals -messages -divine truth	formal speeches: -judicial -deliberative -epideictic	-soundscapes -human voice -silence	unconscious "noise": slips, contradictions, jokes, heated language, denials, dreams	-interpersonal communication -cooperative efforts -teamwork, etc.
Subject of listening	-the faithful -the faithless -God	citizens constructed in set public situations	regular people, not just the high and mighty	-patients -ourselves as analysts or interpreters	-boss -coworker -employee
Assumptions and premises relevant to our course concerns	-the spiritual world has a voice -interpersonal communication is irrelevant -time is extended -confessor is vehicle -truth is deciphered	-private sphere uninteresting -personal irrelevant -psychology, emotion is social not individual -truth is convincing	-"noise" is a social construction that reveals history -sounds can tell truths	-listening is a matter of authority -truth is screened, covered in white noise	-"in the box" -self-help genre -personal responsibility -no historical context -no noise, soundscape, etc. -truth irrelevant

Practical activities included in-class exercises such as playing the game "Mad Gabs" and maintaining a listening journal, which helped students hone their listening skills. These journal entries were typically inspired by reading discussions and were posted before class so that I could quickly review them and pick a few to be read out loud and discussed. Here are a couple of sample journal assignments:

> (1) Choose and specify a place which can be exotic or utterly mundane (e.g., the circus or your bedroom). Spend five minutes listening to everything you can while jotting impressionistic notes that record with maximum accuracy what you hear. Then spend about 20 minutes reflecting upon your notes and the experience. Consider things like foreground/background, noise/sound/listening, conscious vs. unconscious listening, sound associations, listening strategies, whatever. Include both impressionistic notes and reflection in your journal entry.
>
> (2) Reading Exodus reminded us that listening is not just about what's directly in front of you; it happens across generations and across time. Your job is to recount a family story that has crossed generations or has at least endured over some time. It can be something silly or something grand. Then reflect upon why this story "has legs," so to speak. Spend at least half an hour on this assignment.

Finally at the end of the semester we got a chance to test our acquired knowledge with a visit to the famous Speech Pathology and Audiology Department at the University of Iowa, where the pathology of listening—more precisely hearing—thrives as a scientific discipline. Among other things, chair of the department Richard Hurtig talked about how listening works on a principle of efficiency: one of his experiments showed how we will automatically try to make sense out of spoken discourse, even if somebody inserts nonsensical words into an otherwise grammatical sentence. My students quickly realized that this principle of efficiency mitigates against the "open" and "empathic" listening encouraged by practitioners such as Burley-Allen. Despite our class critique of reductive scientific models of listening, I wanted to show students that in some ways a scientific approach to listening complements the humanistic.

The course built toward a final research paper, which each student chose based upon journal entries that resonated with readings and our class discussions. Here is the list of possible topics designed to get students thinking before working out their paper topic with me in detail:

- the devaluation of listening compared to reading, writing, and/or speaking
- the feminization of listening
- listening to God
- comparative analysis: noise, sound, listening
- listening to yourself: sound fantasies, voices, etc.
- city soundscape, suburb soundscape, country soundscape
- overhearing
- rituals of listening
- listening dynamics in two different public spaces
- listening over time, generations; stories with legs
- on frame of mind, disposition, attitude, prejudice, preference (Aristotle)
- when does "prejudice" exceed the individual and become an institution?
- listening and social status (Aristotle)
- metaphors of listening: empty vessel, blank slate, wood ignited ... (Plutarch)
- mass suffering and technologies of deafness, e.g., Sudan
- noise pollution and noise abatement campaigns
- acoustic surveillance
- the culture of confession
- listening to music (must have a strong analytic component, research, etc.)
- group hearing: e.g., the comedy club
- listening for subtext

- the soundscape of slavery
- fireworks
- national anthems
- cell phones
- sound or listening experiment (with a written analytic component)
- the "spinach in your teeth" effect: listening through distortions in the normal perceptual field

The key insight motivating my course is that listening has been neglected as a rhetorical art. Which isn't to say that listening and its cognate terms have never been studied. Comparative analysis of the five senses has been a Western philosophical preoccupation since at least Aristotle, typically followed by the conclusion that sight is the most noble of the senses with hearing a distant second (and here Martin Jay's 1993 *Downcast Eyes* is the authoritative history). Since emergence of the Annals school of social history and especially in the decades of cultural studies, listening has indeed become a hot topic, and we have seen the publication of important books that include titles like *The Acoustic World of Early Modern England: Attending to the O-Factor* (Smith 1999), *Hearing Things: Religion, Illusion, and the American Enlightenment* (Gould 2000), *Listening to Nineteenth-Century America* (Smith 2001), *Victorian Soundscapes* (Picker 2003), *The Sonic Color Line: Race and the Cultural Politics of Listening* (Stoever 2016). Social and cultural history dominates, with literary concerns running a distant third when scholars ask, for instance, "What would listeners have heard within the wooded 'O' of the Globe Theater in 1599? What sounds would have filled the air in early modern England, and what would the sounds have meant to people in that largely oral culture?" Meanwhile we have some excellent cultural histories, including Jonathan Sterne's *The Audible Past* that examines how technologies of listening such as the stethoscope shifted the boundaries of what we consider "sound" and "not sound," transforming at the same time what we consider the distinction between ourselves and our environment. As a social science, moreover, listening is a common topic in the interpersonal branch of communication studies, and one trend in pop psychology has latched onto listening as a "forgotten skill" that can increase self-esteem and professional success if mastered. Aside from the composition studies monograph by Krista Ratcliffe plus her follow-up collection with Cheryl Glenn *Silence and Listening as Rhetorical Arts* (2011), little on listening has come from the rhetorical perspective, which means that crucial angles on the topic have been neglected by scholars among others.

Rhetoric encourages one to consider listening as an essentially social phenomenon constituted in specific situations inflected by occasion, social distinction, and history. Listening from the rhetorical perspective is not hearing in the scientific sense, nor should it be understood first as a material condition in the mode of social history and cultural studies. None of these three approaches adequately explains issues that came up in my class, for instance: how do we configure our listening differently depending upon the public space we occupy, or how are we culturally configured to listen to the past, or how are different social roles such as master and slave differently configured around listening? To explain these phenomena, rhetoric is essential because that is where the terms of address take shape historically, and in our everyday life, including the classroom. In what follows I demonstrate how so.

CHAPTER ONE

Martin Heidegger on Listening
c. 1924

I. AGAINST TRIUMPHAL RHETORIC

A debilitating commonplace has the history and theory of rhetoric honoring a communicative agent, namely the speaker, at the expense of the listener. In *The Emperor of Men's Minds*, for instance, Wayne Rebhorn builds upon the rhetoric emblem Hercules Gallicus to portray the Renaissance orator, like his classical counterparts, as a fighter who triumphs over his listeners.

In their introduction to Adam Müller's *Twelve Lectures on Rhetoric* (a German work of political romanticism I will revisit in my discussion of Carl Schmitt), Dennis Bormann and Elisabeth Leinfellner explain, "Because he devotes an entire lecture to listening, Müller deserves special attention for considering a topic almost entirely neglected by earlier writers on rhetoric." To be sure, they continue, "the classical writers and... all theorists up till Müller's time considered the audience.... But listening *per se*, as an important element in communication, was usually slighted."[1] Then, landing squarely on my topic, Theodore Kisiel, in *The Genesis of Heidegger's "Being and Time,"* frames his groundbreaking commentary on the Summer Semester 1924 lecture course by way of Heidegger's aural perversity. "Rhetoric [according to Hei-

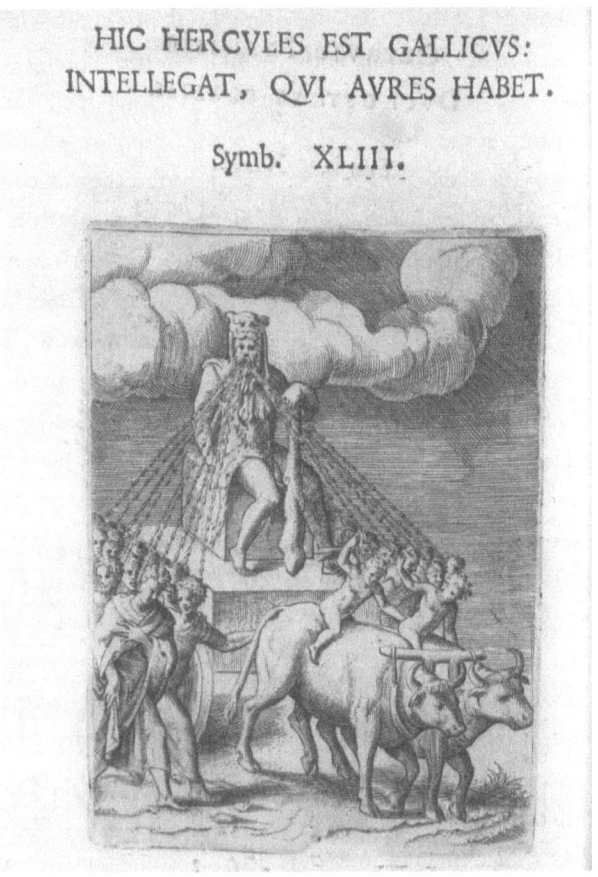

Figure 1. "Here is Hercules Gallicus: Let him understand who has ears." Achillis Bocchi, *Symbolicarum quaestionum, de vniuerso genere, quas serio ludebat, libri quinque* (Bologna: Societatem Typographiae Bononiensis, 1574), Book 2, Symbol 43.

degger's reading of Aristotle] is ... concerned with the convergence of at least three different human powers: being able to speak, to see what speaks for the matter under discussion, and to hear. Almost perversely, Heidegger's interest in rhetoric gravitates toward the latter power, in which speaking has its end."[2]

In this chapter I initiate the core of my book project in Martin Heidegger's vexed material on listening, which has both an academic and an everyday valence. When it comes to everyday experience, this means spending some time in the historical moment when listening reopened onto the scene, partially as a response to the voice of democracy that had become louder via mass media, and newly controversial both in Weimar Germany and beyond. With Heidegger's phenomenological account of listening, we become more sensitive, in other words, to everyday experiences that helped shape that moment, including most importantly passive- or middle-voiced changes of mind (tied to a critique of liberal democracy), reorientation (tied to Heidegger's disastrous political philosophy), and obedience (tied in this case to the voice of authority), the latter now broadcasting louder than ever, though not just perniciously, as theologians like Rudolf Bultmann were quick to point out. This chapter at its most fundamental level, then, is about what Heidegger called *being-moved*—a key term translating Aristotle's *pathos* into the German *Bewegtsein* or *Sein-in-Bewegung*. And, accordingly, the material in this chapter should seem and feel a certain way, not just appear as a set of abstract considerations linked systematically. Writing *about* what is unsettling when it comes to the senses and their composition should *be* in some ways unsettling if the object of study is to appear as such. But methodologically, it's important to understand how being unsettled in this way, or disoriented, depends upon the world where we find ourselves one way or another. It is not just about biology and some kind of homeostasis at the level of the organism I am. It is not about my passionate hydraulics, or any other type of equilibrium defined by a stable system whether physically mine or psychologically mine. In this case, being unsettled is a worldly affair, including what might appear to be rarefied scholarly considerations, as I hope to demonstrate. Ultimately, scholarship on listening and everyday life, including classroom experience, is all part of the same world, as we like to say, even though it can be increasingly difficult to grasp exactly how so. Here Heidegger helps.

In terms of scholarship, I argue that we reinvigorate the history and theory of rhetoric insofar as we normalize Heidegger's care for listening. That is, when we can plausibly frame Heidegger's art of listening in terms of what might broadly be considered the political theology of his moment including the work of Carl Schmitt, Weimar rhetoric transforms our historical horizon. That is where "nonacademic" experience is most obviously brought to bear, as our ways of being (or not) transform. For instance, how does Weimar alter our relationship to the rhetoric of obedience, a word of "non-freedom" that contributes to the German language cluster derived from the word *hören*, "to hear"—*gehorchen, hörig, gehören*—as Hannah Arendt reminds us? This is a question that ties together historical considerations that are strictly academic, including the nuances of philology, with everyday life. Listening obediently is something that each of us can do, at the same time that it appears distinctly in our world after authoritarian disasters of the middle twentieth century and in the midst of religious revivals after 1945 that must also contend with state reason. That is to say, inseparable are the scholarship—sanctioned words and interpretation that give us things like post-1945 "history" and "religion"— and the experiences available to me and to others in and beyond this Anglo-European scene, right now.

Or another example. What does the fateful critique of modern, deliberative democracy from both the left and the right force us to reconsider from our own late-modern vantage point, where the appeal to reason cannot be innocent? How does the emergent mass media and its famous Weimar critique reveal how the traditional rhetorical subject and (his) powers can be characterized historically? When we focus on the troubled listener in Weimar Germany, we diagnose the listener's vanishing point in the history of rhetoric, which traditionally encourages identification with a good man speaking well, and we thereby learn something basic about what binds political constitution and communicative being.

Methodologically following Heidegger, an argument that speaks directly to scholars cannot be distinguished, ultimately, from everyday life. Though the approach to listening varies, these two regions cannot be separated out completely while we imagine, for instance, some detached intellectual history, on the one hand, and my child's inattentiveness or scientific audiology, on the other. Listening is a phenomenon shared across regions of being; hence, it must be approached carefully as such. In this way, my project is an extension of Heidegger's work running up to *Being and Time* (1927) that pursues historical "destruction" on the way to his fundamental ontology, and which turns out to be, in fact, rooted in his work on rhetoric.[3] And I offer this methodological fact is no accident, since rhetoric has been defined since its inception as a reorientation in everyday practice, which means in this instance practicing that much better after studying rhetoric; or defined alternatively, as a theoretical reflection, which means understanding better when everyday speaking and listening take shape as the *discipline* rhetoric, which Heidegger studied so closely and taught so carefully around 1924.

. . .

I begin by unfolding sentence by sentence the key passage from Heidegger's 1924 Marburg lecture course *Basic Concepts of Aristotelian Philosophy*.[4] It is referred to in Karl Löwith's transcript as "Aristoteles, Rhetorik II"—namely the second book of Aristotle's *Rhetoric*, focusing on the emotions. Published in 2002 in the *Gesamtausgabe* and translated into English only recently, SS 1924 demands our attention for at least three reasons. First, this Marburg course profoundly shaped a generation of German intellectuals, including Herbert Marcuse and Hannah Arendt (who arrived at Marburg the following semester), and seminar attendees Helene Weiss, Jacob Klein, Siegfried Landshut, Hans Jonas, Karl Löwith, Hans-Georg Gadamer, and Leo Strauss, who spoke about a seminar "on Aristotle's *Rhetoric* that contained an ontology of the human passions," where affectability in general and listening in particular was at issue in ways that hit students right where they lived.[5] Second, as Kisiel has demonstrated and as I have just mentioned, this lecture course was centrally important for the genesis of that landmark in twentieth-century philosophy *Being and Time*, which means, thirdly, it represents a significant intervention in the history and theory of rhetoric broadly conceived.

Here is the key passage as it appears on the page translated into English. It is followed by a brief line-by-line elaboration, which outlines most of my key topics going forward through the rest of the chapter.

> The being-there [Dasein] of human beings, characterized as λογον ἔχον [logon echon, "having speech"], is more precisely determined by Aristotle in such a way that in the human being itself, its speaking-being still plays a fundamental role. In being-with-one-another, one can be the one speaking and the other the one *hearing*. Ἀκούειν [akouein, "hearing"] is genuine αἴσθησις [aísthēsis, "perception"]. Whether or not seeing in connection with θεωρεῖν [theōrein, "theorizing"] reveals the world in a genuine sense, it is still *hearing* because it is the *perceiving of speaking*, because it is the *possibility of being-with-one-another* [Miteinandersein]. The human being is not only a speaker and a hearer, but is for itself such a being that *hears itself*. Speaking, as self-expression-about-something, is at the same time a speaking-to-oneself. Therefore, the definition of λόγον ἔχον further contains in itself that the human being also has λόγος [logos] in the mode of *hearing this, its own speaking*. In human beings, there is a being-possibility that is to be characterized as ὑπακούειν [hupakouein, "hearken, be obedient to, obey"]. Aristotle exhibits this basic phenomenon through concrete contexts of being-there themselves, through peculiar phenomena that are touched upon in Book 1, Chapter 13 of the *Nicomachean Ethics*, and that Aristotle designates as παράκλησις [paraklēsis, "incitement"], νουθέτησις [nouthetēsis, "admonition"], ἐπιτίμησις [epitimēsis, "reproach"] (1103a1). All of these modes of natural speaking-with-one-another carry in themselves the claim that the other does not merely take notice of something, but *takes* something *up*, *follows* something [etwas *befolgt*], *reflects* on something. The other *repeats* that which is spoken in such a way that in repeating he *listens* to it, such that the following results: *in the being of the human being as concernful lies the possibility of listening to its speaking.* (72)

(1) To start with, not λογον ἔχον as a rational creature, but rather a speaking-being. In Marburg's Neo-Kantianism, recalls Gadamer in his

interview for my coedited book *Heidegger and Rhetoric*, logos was just "reason," but through Heidegger's reading of Aristotle, Gadamer grasped, to his great surprise, "that *logos* has something to do with speaking" and thus the way was opened for a serious consideration of rhetoric. As Gadamer describes it, this moment was a basic reorientation of the sort that drew students in droves to the lectures of the "hidden King" who was rescuing Aristotle from historical obscurity on the way to a complete reorientation of philosophy, including what it meant to sit in that very lecture hall listening to one's world transform by way of philosophical exegesis, of all things.

(2) That said, speaking is not primarily a matter of ποίησις (poiēsis, "personal mastery, creative autonomy"), or willful imposition on an audience (Wittgenstein would similarly argue there is no such thing as a private language). Instead, speech is a function of *Miteinandersein* ("being-with-one-another") and hence it must be conceived more fundamentally as a human capacity in its "passive" or "pathetic" dimension. Rhetoric, in other words, should be considered δύναμις (dunamis, "capacity") primarily and then secondarily a τέχνη (technē, "art" or "technology").

(3) As opposed to detached seeing in a certain mode of theory (θεωρία), "hearing" therefore designates a more basic aesthetics of our shared world.[6] But in 1924 and a bit later in *Being and Time*, Heidegger will take pains to point out this doesn't mean physiological hearing as one of the five senses that lends itself to empirical measurement. "What we 'first' hear is never noises or complexes of sounds, but the creaking wagon, the motor-cycle" (§164), the voice of the friend or enemy. In 1927 Heidegger gives us this formulation: "hearing constitutes the primary and authentic way in which Dasein is open for its ownmost potentiality-for-Being—as in hearing the voice of the friend whom every Dasein carries with it.... Being-with develops in listening to one another [Aufeinander-hören], which can be done in several possible ways: following, going along with, and the privative modes of not-hearing, resisting, defying, and turning away" (§163).

(4) Crucial for Heidegger's return to a technical rhetoric is the critique of the tradition cited at the opening of this chapter where ethical weight is placed squarely on the speaker, who stands in for us as the active subject of rhetoric, while the abject audience stands in for our vulnerabilities, which include listening, learning, feeling, absorbing, obeying, and so on. Heidegger would have none of the school discipline that supposedly dominated the Hellenistic and early Middle Ages, returning instead to rhetoric as a concrete guide for the interpretation of Dasein: "The human being is not only a speaker and a hearer, but is for itself such a being that *hears itself*," and in 1927 this would mean the call of conscience.[7]

(5) Not solipsism but exactly the opposite—namely, being-open in the listening modes carefully distinguished across Aristotle's practical treatises, which include the *Rhetoric, Politics,* and *Ethics,* through the transitional text *de Anima* into what we normally bracket off as the natural scientific treatises on *Physics* and *The Motion of Animals,* which situate being-open humanly in the context of being-moved generally. Hence, "Grundbegriffe Der aristotelischen Philosophie," not in the end "Aristoteles, Rhetorik II." The passion-action nexus situates specifically human modes of engaged listening: "In human beings, there is a being-possibility that is to be characterized as ὑπακούειν."[8]

(6) Typically, in 1924 Heidegger situates Aristotle's *Rhetoric* in a continuum of life processes whereby epideictic, or ἐπαινός (epainos, "praise") and ψόγος (psogos, "blame") rhetoric, appears not as persuasive technique we learn in school, but rather as an inherent psychic capacity touched upon in the *Nicomachean Ethics*. The alternative formula ἐπιτίμησις / παράκλησις (translated by Barnes as "reproof" and "exhortation") are "modes of natural speaking-with-one-another" carrying in themselves the claim that the other "does not merely take notice of something, but *takes* something *up, follows* something [etwas *befolgt*]."[9]

Before elaborating any further on these key themes in Heidegger's work on Aristotle's *Rhetoric*, we should pause to witness how they appear as controversial in the first place. It turns out that Heidegger must talk back to scholars on their own terms, if rhetoric as the everyday art of listening is to appear as such.

II. HEIDEGGER'S COMMENTARY ON ARISTOTLE'S *RHETORIC*, AND THE DESTRUCTION OF THE CORPUS ARISTOTELICUM

The most important scholarly element of Heidegger's 1924 commentary is his radical repositioning of the *Rhetoric* in Aristotle's corpus, with all of the attendant consequences for philosophy, as Heidegger works out his critique of metaphysics. This scholarly argument also winds up being consequential for rhetoric per se, which winds up looking very different after Heidegger destroys the Aristotelianisms that imposed themselves historically. In a word, Heidegger completely reorients scholarly inquiry around the controversial type of rhetoric we now call *motivistic*.

First of all, rhetoric after Heidegger's engagement lends itself better to research on rhetoric as the art of, and capacity for, listening: being-moved. To that end Heidegger says in these 1924 lectures, "The *Rhetoric*'s analysis of the πάθη [pathē, "passion"] has this intention: to analyze the various possibilities of the hearer's finding himself, in order to provide guides as to what must be cultivated on the part of the hearer himself" (this is the Metcalf and Tanzer translation, including the gender specificity mitigated in the German; *Basic Concepts*, 115). Moreover, this interpretation goes beyond a slogan, building out substantially and historically, while contradicting what is for us a more familiar rhetoric emblem, Hercules Gallicus, who triumphs over his listeners—rhetoric as the fantasy of unilateral psychagogy.[10] Substantially Heidegger works out via Aristotle the hearer's task: to take a position, first toward the world in some political sense where a threat might be characterized in the deliberative context. "I am, at a definite moment, in a dangerous situation, in a moment of terror, in the state of composure. I can relate the disposition characterized by terror to a possible being-composed with regard to it" (116). But also in terms of epideictic rhetoric where the listener "does not merely take notice of something, but *takes* something *up*, *follows* something [etwas *befolgt*], *reflects* on something" (72). Later and independently, Jeffrey Walker will give us something similar when he explains how epideictic "shapes the fundamental grounds, the 'deep' commitments and presuppositions, that will underlie and ultimately determine decision and debate in particular pragmatic forums."[11]

And with this turn to a certain kind of rhetorical obedience we must now ask in what regard does the listener obey if not just politically, which points us toward the following day's lecture when Heidegger details how the Aristotelian doctrine of the πάθη had "quite an effect on subsequent philosophers and theologians," while he provides an intriguing bibliography including Augustine, Johannes Damascenus, Gregory of Nyssa/Nemesius, Dionysius the Areopagite, and Martin Luther (a close colleague of Philip Melanchthon, who plays a key role in the next chapter). But essentially since Luther, Heidegger qualifies, "The whole development of the doctrine of the affects, up to the present, has not been analyzed philosophically," lapsing instead into what came to be called psychology, where the passions showed up as psychological states tied primarily to the human organism, instead of appearing as they do in the world, where psychological states find their meaning. Indeed, when it comes to more recent work, according to Heidegger, "Only *Dilthey*, in his 'The Worldview and Analysis of Human Beings since Renaissance and Reformation,' has given thorough treatment to the πάθη and characterized their *significance* for psychological states" (120, latter italics mine). Hence, in Heidegger's time, motivistic rhetoric, as we now call it, had become untenable because it had been broken down into states that are merely psychological, while the motivating techniques of rhetoric had splintered into practical recommendations in the handbooks and grade school primers. Revisiting Aristotle and those earlier traditions, Heidegger could demonstrate, had the capacity to destroy centuries of reading Aristotle poorly, while rediscovering motivistic rhetoric in the world.

That said, a return to motivistic rhetoric now, after Heidegger, seems deeply suspicious in ways that condition how we view the field fundamentally. This contrary attitude is well represented by Thomas Conley, who gives it due attention in his rich history of *Rhetoric in the European Tradition*. Indeed, Conley treats motivistic rhetoric according to late twentieth-century convention, against which I will make my final point about rhetoric after Heidegger's 1924 lectures. We are now revisiting the rhetoric of passions beyond the threat of bad government: demagoguery, absolutism. This point can be set up with Conley's unwilling assistance—he really loathes Heidegger for plenty of good reasons—as Conley concludes his chapter on rhetoric in seventeenth-century Europe with the following critique of motivistic rhetoric, including (1) the divorce of persuasion from argumentation, (2) the focus on psychophysiology, and (3) the interest in will manipulation—all qualities of motivistic rhetoric that Heidegger did indeed find compelling. "Finally," Conley remarks,

> if we view these transformations in an even wider perspective, that of social and political developments, we can see that it is not a mere coincidence that such transformations occurred when and where they did: in France, during the reigns of Louis XIV... and in England... about the time of the Glorious Revolution of 1688, which brought about the last of a series of restorations of monarchy.... The sort of rhetoric we see suggested by Hobbes and by Lamy, and even before them in the affective rhetorics articulated earlier in the century, seems particularly well suited to an atmosphere in which absolutism came to be seen as the only practical solution to social and political disorder.[12]

In fact, suspicion of motivistic rhetoric includes a majority of postwar scholars defending rhetoric from its detractors—notably Brian Vickers, who offers all sorts of wonderful observations about the figurative life of emotions while at the same time clinging to the Ciceronian formula revived in the Renaissance: *ratio atque oratio* ("reason and speech"), or as his Trebizond put it: "reason does not do any good unless bodied forth in speech" that moves.[13] This is another reason why Heidegger's recently rediscovered interest in Aristotle's *Rhetoric* is important: because it productively flies in the face of postwar rationalism—a mindset that sends us back to the rhetorical tradition awkwardly. At the same time, Heidegger's plea is not just for passionate rhetoric, but rather for careful analysis of factical life in the mode established by Aristotle.

Ratio atque oratio is an ethical compromise contradicted by Heidegger in the 1924 lectures, where his historical introduction to the concept pathos scrupulously avoids the secular humanist tradition along with the manipulative psychology that ties emotions to the untrained mind—a mind that appears better off with no passion at all. Instead, for Heidegger pathos runs from Aristotle to Luther, where a basic emotion such as fear makes our being with one another—hence our being in the world—concrete, moving us in our fundamental beliefs. So Heidegger remarks in the Bultmann seminar: "Luther does not see sin as the accumulation of errors but rather draws attention to *affectus*, that is, to the mode of man's being-placed in relation to things, to the being-displaced and being-horrified [*Entsetztsein*] by them that arises from his clinging to them."[14] Dilthey offers positive examples, including the passion of Christ, which orients being factically, as Heidegger would say at the time.

Though according to Heidegger, tradition lost an understanding of rhetoric as it became in Hellenism and in the early Middle Ages "merely a school discipline," he is in these lectures and elsewhere during the 1920s—from his course on the phenomenology of religion through his course on Plato's *Sophist*—committed to making the discipline "transparent" by asking about the concrete function of Aristotelian rhetoric in its historicity, and with some scholarly daring, by resituating Aristotle's *Rhetoric* in the corpus understood very differently: not as the victim of academic bifurcation with natural sciences on one side and human sciences on the other. Rather, Heidegger treats Aristotle's *Rhetoric* in its continuity with Aristotle's *Physics*, which offers basic concepts rooted in the Greek way of life. Or as Heidegger put it in his 1922 introduction to the Aristotle book that never appeared but rather morphed into *Being and Time*, "Beings in the how of their being-moved became the central phenomenon for Aristotle, and the explication of this phenomenon was the main topic of his physics."[15] It is in this scholarly context where rhetoric is rediscovered by Heidegger—*beings in the how of their being-moved*—contra the schoolmen and schoolteachers who would make it instrumental, contra classicists who would make it a superadded aesthetic, and contra the neo-Kantians like Paul Natorp who dominated Marburg at that time, producing what Heidegger considered an over-hasty and epistemologically driven condemnation of Aristotle's sloppy psychologism in the *Rhetoric*. To this day one might invoke a host of similar dismissals from the perspective of philosophy, including David Ross, who called the *Rhetoric* "a curious jumble of literary criticism with second-rate logic, ethics, politics, and jurisprudence, mixed with the cunning of one who knows well how the weaknesses of the human heart are to be played upon."[16]

In fact, rhetoric, Heidegger could proclaim a couple of years later in 1924, is no less than the elaboration of Dasein in its concreteness, *the hermeneutic of Dasein itself*:

> At the time of Plato and Aristotle, being-there was so burdened with babble that it required the total efforts of them both to be serious about the possibility of science. What is decisive is that they did not take up a new possibility of existence from just anywhere, such as from India and thus from the outside, but rather *from out of Greek living itself. They were serious about the possibility of speaking.* That is the *origin of logic*, the doctrine of λόγος. The current interpretation is unsuitable for gaining an understanding of logic. The current way of considering rhetoric is equally a hindrance to the understanding of the Aristotelian *Rhetoric*. In the Berlin Academy edition, the *Rhetoric* has been put at the end. They did not know what to do with it, so they put it at the end! It is a sign of complete helplessness. The tradition lost any understanding of rhetoric long ago, since it has become simply a school discipline even in the time of Hellenism and in the early Middle Ages. The original sense of rhetoric has long disappeared. Insofar as one forgot to inquire into the concrete function of Aristotelian logic, one gave up the basic possibility of interpreting this so that it would

thereby become clear that rhetoric is nothing other than the discipline in which the self-interpretation of being-there is explicitly fulfilled. *Rhetoric is nothing other than the interpretation of concrete being-there, the hermeneutic of being-there itself.* That is the intended sense of Aristotle's rhetoric. (*Basic Concepts*, 75)

For Heidegger, Aristotle's *Rhetoric* winds up playing a doubly important role in his famous and consequential destruction of Western metaphysics. The first role is negative, as it is marked by rhetoric's marginal status in the traditional Corpus Aristotelicum, and the purported helplessness of its most famous scholars, including August Immanuel Bekker.

The fact of the matter is that the landmark Berlin Academy edition that we still use today for its careful scholarship back to manuscripts and its organizational page/column/line numbering system also helps solidify for modern scholars an organizational system that cannot be attributed to Aristotle himself, and can thus lead to unwarranted intellectual assumptions, as Heidegger so churlishly said in his lecture. After Aristotle's death in 322 BCE, he (unlike Plato) left in the hands of his disciples a collection of texts that were unedited and without purposeful classification; indeed copies of Aristotle's writings were rare and no corpus existed until after Andronicus (see below).[17] As the great classical philologist Ingemar Düring put it in 1957, all attempts to reconstruct his biography must be highly conjectural, and in particular "we know nothing about the disposition of his work."[18] It was in fact the first-century BCE Aristotle edition and catalog of peripatetic Andronicus of Rhodes—no longer extant but referenced reliably in subsequent sources—that initiated organizational projects tied to later perspectives as much as to Aristotle's own efforts. Likewise the earliest catalog of Aristotle's writings, thought to be an inventory of the manuscripts acquired fairly soon after the Alexandrian library was established, seems arranged in a manner that is purely "matter-of-fact," not based on principles inherent in Aristotle's work.[19] Since, as Düring points out, systematic distinctions reliably attributable to Aristotle are few, they serve primarily the purposes of later interpretation.

So Heidegger is not just grasping at straws when he criticizes Bekker for placing Aristotle's *Rhetoric* at the end of his Berlin Academy edition. Indeed, Bekker's entire organizational scheme had more to do with bibliographical tradition as it made sense to modern scholars working between 1831 and 1870. Bekker's edition is divided into five subject areas: (1) logic and argumentation theory, (2) natural science, (3) first philosophy = metaphysics, (4) ethics and politics, and (5) rhetoric and poetics. And this arrangement most immediately referenced the *editio princeps* of Aldus Manutius (Aldo Manuzio; printed 1495–1498) that actually left out the rhetoric and the poetics altogether; these two works were first printed by Manutius in the *Rhetores Graeci* of 1508.

This marginality of Aristotle's *Rhetoric* is for Heidegger an important indication that a set of scholarly and interpretive traditions first need to be "destroyed" ("Destruktion," *Being and Time*, 44). This means at the very least removing Hellenism, where Aristotle's works were first organized according to extraneous principles,[20] exceeding school rhetoric that would reduce it to a mere skill, and circumventing the speculative and more specifically Latinate uptake of Aristotle's work—whether in philosophy or Christian theology—which "speak in borrowed categories that are foreign to their own domains of being."[21]

For Heidegger, the second important role played by Aristotle's *Rhetoric* is positive, as it embodies the Greek way of life, which puts it at the very heart of Aristotle's corpus next to the *Physics*, with κίνησις (kinēsis, "motion") at the key point of intersection. Again, "beings in the how of their being-moved"[22] vs. the traditional metaphysical distinction between being and becoming.

That is why the second book of Aristotle's *Rhetoric* plays such an important role for Heidegger as it reorients the entire Aristotelian corpus and hence the traditions of its interpretation, which would include our own post-Enlightenment interpretation of passionate rhetoric that separates it from reason, or makes it a matter of human experience, not physical nature: *Geisteswissenschaft* as distinct from *Naturwissenschaft*.

Here in Heidegger's story circa 1924, Werner Jaeger becomes important, as Jaeger's monumental work *Aristoteles: Grundlegung einer Geschichte seiner Entwicklung* had just appeared in 1923 after more than a decade of noteworthy scholarship. In 1924 Heidegger acknowledges this text—as he had to—by way of the lecture's introduction, enlisting Jaeger as an ally in the scholarly project of curtailing the apparent unity of an Aristotelian system (*Basic Concepts*, 4) while sanctioning new inflections of Aristotle's basic concepts including pathos and kinēsis most importantly; Jaeger definitively included *De motu animalium* in the Aristotelian corpus, as it had been considered spurious by previous scholars, including Bekker. Thanks in part to Jaeger, *De motu animalium* and *De partibus animalium* could play an important role in the analysis of being-moved rhetorically, as this human phenomenon is situated by Heidegger with respect to other types of movement across animals, plants, and inanimate objects (*Basic Concepts*, 159–160: "Proof from the Character of Being-Moved Itself").

Heidegger is uncharacteristically coy about naming Jaeger, however, when it comes to his devastating critique of the *Geisteswissenschaft/Naturwissenschaft* distinction that Jaeger reinforced. For Jaeger, the traditional problem of the scholastic interpretation of Aristotle was its one-sided spiritualism and attendant focus on Aristotelian abstraction, while neglecting the relationship Aristotle continually forged between experience and concept development, described by Jaeger as a progressive relationship between *Geisteswissenschaft* and *Naturwissenschaft*. "There was no steady advance of natural and mental science to serve as breeding-ground, and therefore none of that fruitful interaction between experience and conception from which Aristotle's speculative notions had drawn their flexibility and their adaptive power. Since then there has been no break in the continuity of our idea of Aristotle."[23] Thus Jaeger, not surprisingly, has little to say about the *Rhetoric*, which is mentioned only in the context of systematics and style. Heidegger takes the destruction of Aristotelianism in a different direction altogether.

Heidegger treats Aristotle's practical and naturo-theoretical writings holistically, and by doing so he relocates the long-misplaced discipline of rhetoric along a continuum of being that includes the nonliving.[24] Or as Gadamer told us in a fascinating interview for the collection *Heidegger and Rhetoric*, Heidegger used the *Rhetoric* to make Aristotle a phenomenologist: "That Aristotle suddenly became a phenomenologist was exactly what Heidegger accomplished and was quite the exception. He worked so long on Husserl, until Husserl believed him about Aristotle. And it is remarkable how correct Heidegger was, wouldn't you agree? The way Hartmann and all the others, even the philologists, treated Aristotle certainly did not present him as a contemporary opponent! It was pure history. But with Heidegger, Aristotle suddenly came alive."[25] And in fact we find the following example in SS 1924: "One would like to say that the way Aristotle primarily sees the genuine being-moved of plants is almost phenomenological, as is shown by *De anima* 413a26 sqq. Plants, which he speaks of here, have this distinctive being-possibility of being-in-the-world—that they grow 'out toward opposed places, directions'" (*Basic Concepts*, 159).

According to Heidegger's reading of Aristotle, Being-with-one-another turns out to be only one way of being among many—living and nonliving, human and nonhuman. The shared ontology of all Being, claims Heidegger, is grounded in the categories of Aristotle's *Physics* ("Die Forschung, die über die φύσις handelt, ist nichts anderes als die Gewinnung der primären Kategorien, die Aristoteles nachher in seiner Ontologie ansetzt" [*Grundbegriffe*, 284] = "the research that treats φύσις is nothing other than the *obtaining of the primary categories* that Aristotle subsequently develops in his ontology" [*Basic Concepts*, 193]). The pathos of a stone allows it to become part of a wall, the pathos of a plant to grow, the pathos of an animal to perceive imminent danger and to shriek a warning to others. So why, ultimately, should there be any philosophy beside this science—the φυσική—asks Heidegger in completing an indirect proof he finds in *De partibus animalium*? "But there are also beings-in-movement that are not in the mode of living, insofar as νοῦς [nous, "mind"] is the decisive possibility" (*Basic Concepts*, 157). Unique to human pathos is a dependence on νοῦς ποιητικός: the human capacity that allows us to extend into every domain of being and be moved even by things that are *not* there in body. Thinking allows us to be with others in a manner unattainable for other animals ("in diesem Denken-daran bin ich mit ihm" [*Grundbegriffe*, 326]). Though only human being is moved to discourse, or logos, Being-moved is essential to all (*Sein-in-Bewegung*). What we share with things of all sorts is body-in-movement, a movement characterized by pathos. Heidegger sees this as one of Aristotle's most profound insights into the nature of rhetoric: Being-moved—the heart of rhetoric—necessarily exceeds the rational psyche because people have bodies of a certain sort. We are there, we grow and decompose, we can be damaged or excited, mobilized or dispersed. "Wenn zum Lebenden mitgehört das Sein in einem σῶμα [sōma, "body"], dann gehört auch zur rechten Erfassung des Grundphänomens der πάθη das σῶμα, und der φυσικῶς ist mitbeteiligt an dieser Herausstellung" (*Grundbegriffe*, 226). Being-moved in a human way is thus a continuous function of physiology and shared minds, as this central example of φόβος [phobos, "fear"] demonstrates:

> In what follows we will come to understand how fear and the πάθη stand in relation to logos, insofar as logos is taken as speaking-with-one-another, as that which effects the elaboration of Dasein in its everydayness. Insofar as the πάθη are not the annex of psychological events, but compose instead *the ground upon which language grows and to which expressions return*; the πάθη provide *the fundamental possibilities in which Dasein finds itself and orients itself.* This basic Being-oriented, the lighting of Being's being in the world, is no *knowledge*, but is instead a *finding-oneself* variously determined, depending upon the ways Being can be there. (*Grundbegriffe der aristotelischen Philosophie*, 262; my translation)

So with Heidegger we might say that *ratio atque oratio*—or any related rhetoric that considers emotion the annex to psychological events—must work around the vast reach of Aristotle and the sacred rhetorics that orient Dasein: in 1922 Heidegger pursues this so-called *Greco-Christian interpretation of life* (125). If instead, with Heidegger, we avoid this awkward detour, then the history of rhetoric does indeed open up differently as we ask about Being: Oriented how? Toward what, and to whom?[26] But inquiry driven by these questions will not be guided by some kind of mystical theology, as Heidegger's Christianity might imply, nor will it be guided by some kind of modern natural science, as "life" implied during a moment in the 1920s when such inquiry prevailed next to the various life-philosophies of Dilthey, Bergson, Simmel, von Uexküll, and others (162). If the human being is determined as ζῷον λόγον ἔχον, a living being of a certain sort, "life" will not be understood through the modern biological concept, nor should it be considered something "wild, profound, and mystical," Heidegger quips (16). Instead the being-orientations of human being—λόγον ἔχων—will best be understood through the analysis of our being-with-one-another in speech, though Heidegger finds the efforts of his contemporaries disappointing: "Today we have a primitive notion of language or none at all." So, according to Heidegger, if we want to know why speaking is speaking-with-others, we would do better returning to the Greeks and one text in particular: "The concrete document for the originality of the Greek view is the entire *Rhetoric*" (43). There we find the specific determinations of speech and thus human being *per se*, which does overlap with other types of animal being in so far as we indicate, entice, and warn (39). But unlike other animals, the human animal is *not* necessarily tied to its immediate surroundings in the modalities of babbling (74), speaking about, counseling, talking through (43), encouraging, persuading, exhorting, letting something be said (i.e., hearing) (76), deliberating, judging, exhibiting (85), proposing (88), supposing (139), and of course refuting and confronting (33).

So, finally refuting and confronting: Though I think Conley's treatment of motivistic rhetoric is misleading in many ways, he is perfectly justified as he questions how Heidegger's own rhetoric is oriented politically, and this is where I will conclude by explaining when and why Aristotle's *Rhetoric* dropped out after 1924.

III. LISTENING OBEDIENTLY

If we compare Heidegger's work on Aristotle's *Rhetoric* II to his later 1930s reading of Nietzsche on "Will as Affect, Passion, and Feeling," one sees the internal logic that drives Heidegger's disastrous political philosophy.

> Affect: the seizure that blindly agitates us. Passion: the lucidly gathering grip on beings. We talk and understand only extrinsically when we say that anger flares and then dissipates, lasting but a short time, while hate lasts longer. No, hate and love not only last longer, they bring perdurance and permanence for the first time to our existence. An affect, in contrast, cannot do that. Because passion restores our essential being, because it loosens and liberates in its very grounds, and because passion at the same time reaches out into the expanse of beings, for these reasons passion—and we mean great passion—possesses extravagance and resourcefulness, not only the ability but the necessity to submit, without bothering about what its extravagance entails. It displays the self-composed superiority characteristic of great will.[27]

Though merely a gloss on Nietzsche, not exactly Heidegger's political manifesto, this scenario does voice fatefully for Heidegger how the body politic is subordinated to the "great will" unreflectively, including as it would happen in his earlier 1933–34 political speeches, to Hitler's "one great will of the state"—just as someone like Conley would have suspected.[28] Rhetoric gives way to demagoguery just as the passions rise up against modern life that had become, according to Heidegger, profoundly inauthentic. After the middle 1920s, Aristotle's *Rhetoric* recedes from Heidegger's work because factical life itself would have to be torn violently out of its modern trappings—the great passions of love and hate speaking to auditors more extravagantly than Aristotle would ever allow. From this point on, Heidegger would return instead to the pre-Socratics Heraclitus and Parmenides; the poets, including Hölderlin most importantly; and, as we have just seen, Nietzsche, whose nihilism rubs off more than Heidegger would admit.

Thus it matters crucially who is talking and who is listening. For instance εὐδαιμονία [eudaimonia, "human flourishing"], qualifies Heidegger, is determined in being with others—for example family, friends, and fellow citizens—but not *all* others (66); Aristotle warns "we are in for an infinite series" if we try to extend the social nature of man to ancestors and descendants and friends' friends (*Nic. Eth.* 1097b 8–14). In short, the ways we are in the world, the ways we speak and listen, depend upon our cares and their limitations; Heidegger says: "*in the being of the human being as concernful lies the possibility of listening to its speaking.*" Therefore also the appropriate nickname for the course: "Aristoteles, Rhetorik II." If a rhetoric is to properly outline the practical contours of our speaking-being, properly situated in the reasoned outcomes of judicial and deliberative rhetoric, for instance, it will first require a nuanced account of the emotional ties and antipathies that define community and establish relationships within and without community. Though at points in the 1924 lecture course he blames the sophists for the alienation of Greek Dasein against which Aristotle reacts (75), Heidegger in fact reads Aristotle like a sophist insofar as the reasoned outcomes of judicial and deliberative rhetoric are grounded in more basic rhetorical commitments shaping community (*Mitsein*), such as the cleavage of friend and enemy.[29] For our contemporary sophist Jeffrey Walker, epideictic grounds practical debate by shaping the imaginaries through which individual members of a community identify themselves.[30] Heidegger, however, grounds logos in pathos ("der *logos* in den *pathe* selbst seinen Boden hat" ["logos has itself a ground in pathos"] 177), spending a good deal of time on the example of fear as a motivation for political deliberation that always includes the possibility of speaking-against-one-another (*Gegeneinandersprechens*) and being-against-one-another (*Gegeneinandersein*, 138).[31] Finally, to anticipate the conclusion of this chapter, we should remember Carl Schmitt's qualification of emotion in *The Concept of the Political*, a work that Schmitt sent Heidegger around the time they both joined the Nazi party in 1933 and to which Heidegger responded warmly indicating he hoped Schmitt would help him reconstitute the Law faculty at Freiburg where he had just been appointed Rector: "The enemy in the political sense need not be hated personally, and in the private sphere only does it make sense to love one's enemy, i.e., one's adversary" (29). Similarly, for Heidegger in 1924 it would not be inaccurate to say institutions are rhetorically constituted precisely by impersonal emotions where, for instance, warfare is the defense of a way of life, not the expression of personal fears; law is the codification of justice, not the desire for personal revenge; ceremony is the instantiation of honor, not the occasion for personal hubris.

If rhetoric is a matter of our basic ways of life and their limitations, what are the relevant contours of life in 1924 that shape Heidegger's focal concepts for rhetoric including listening-as-obedience? For instance, obedience to what and to whom? First, we should remember that Heidegger's previous religion courses in Freiburg were about receiving the Word of God in Paul's letters, while at Marburg, Heidegger worked closely with New Testament theologian Rudolph Bultmann, who regularly characterized the relationship between God and man as *Deus loquens/homo audiens* ["God speaks/mankind listens"].[32] In his essay "The Concept of the Word of God and the New Testament" Bultmann writes, for instance, "Everything depends on hearing this Word. He who has ears to hear, let him hear! Take care what you hear! Hear and hold it fast! [Mark 4.9, Luke 4.24, Mark 7.14]. The hearing, therefore, is not a mere physical act; it is obedience which entails action."[33] Or as Heidegger himself put it when visiting Bultmann's seminar in 1924 to talk about "The Problem of Sin in Luther," humankind does not remain silent after the Fall but speaks gracefully, *loquitur*. At the same time, we should remember, according to Heidegger, "how the being of God is always conceived of as *verbum* ["word"], and the fundamental relation of man to him as *audire* ["to hear"]."[34] No doubt Heidegger's rhetoric in 1924 should account for this religious and theological trajectory as well as Aristotle; indeed we would all do well to keep religion in mind when theorizing rhetoric so as to immediately qualify some of our more simplistic speaker → message → receiver models of communication that exclude what might broadly be called the extrapersonal (chapter 3).

Listening-as-obedience is a more ominous rhetorical disposition when situated in a way of life that includes on one side Carl Schmitt's 1922 account of the fundamental obedience that defines politics, and on the other side Adolf Hitler's reversion to the irrational appeal of speech in the second volume of *Mein Kampf* (1927), where he devotes an entire chapter to the significance of the spoken word [*Rede*]: "All great, world-shaking events have been brought about not by written matter but by the spoken word.... [I]t is often a question of overcoming prejudices that are not based on reason, but, for the most part unconsciously, are supported only by sentiment [*Gefühl*]."[35] After all, who likes to consider him or herself a follower led by the nose, or by the ear as the case may be, especially when the leader is someone like Adolf Hitler? It would be an understatement to say the Nazis, who famously included both Heidegger and Schmitt in 1933, gave the *Führung/Gefolgschaft* formula a bitter taste from which we have never recovered, to the detriment of our rhetorical theory that finds false refuge in the good man speaking well, or in the antipathetic disposition called "active listening" where the honor lies only in judging.[36] Heidegger's rhetoric in 1924 accounts for a religious and theological orientation that achieves a certain kind of historicity by way of Aristotle. Meanwhile a more sinister version of this rhetorical relationship appears ten years later in a political context when it is no longer God who commands obedience, but rather a great leader, or in German, *Führer*.

To reiterate my methodological argument: when our rhetorical theory and our histories of rhetoric are oriented toward certain virtues of deliberative democracy—such as the free speech–active listening dyad—as antidotes to Nazi or other forms of demagoguery, we can lose our ability to grasp adequately a wide range of unavoidable rhetorical activities, including things like passive listening, obeying, following, feeling, and so on. The trick in my opinion is not to systematically detach rhetorical terms like these for the sake of a political ideal but rather to grasp rhetoric as it forms particular ways of life, which compels us to ask: Obedience to what end, to whom, for instance; listen to what and to whom; feel what and for whom? In this regard I follow Heidegger. I depart from Heidegger insofar as the ways of life and limitations in 1924 Weimar offered rhetorical possibilities characterized most importantly by the rise of mass media and a distinct crisis of deliberative democracy. Not to be glib, but his friends and enemies are for the most part not mine. I now conclude this chapter by briefly outlining what this friend/enemy distinction might mean for the art of listening in Heidegger's 1924 lecture course.

Two years earlier in 1922, Carl Schmitt offered in *Political Theology* this critique of the bourgeoisie as a "discussing class," or in the words of Schmitt's reactionary harbinger Donoso Cortés,[37] *una clasa discutidora*.

> I do not consider this to be the last word on Continental liberalism in its entirety, but it is certainly a most striking observation. In view of the system of a Condorcet, for example ... one must truly believe that the ideal of political life consists in discussing, not only in the legislative body but also among the entire population, if human society will transform itself into a monstrous club, and if truth will emerge automatically through voting. Donoso Cortés considered continuous discussion a method of circumventing responsibility and of ascribing to freedom of speech and of the press an excessive importance that in the final analysis permits the decision to be evaded. (62)[38]

What does Schmitt consider the disciplinary mode for this discussing class? His 1919 book on *Political Romanticism* proposed rhetoric-as-sophistry with especially harsh words for the art of listening according to Adam Müller, whom we met at the beginning of this chapter.[39] Quintessential liberal romantic and author of *Die Elemente der Staatskunst* and *Twelve Lectures on Rhetoric*, which includes an entire lecture on the art of listening, Müller's discourse is repeatedly built around a major figure of speech, antithesis, and according to Schmitt, Müller cannot think at all unless in conversation that swerves aimlessly between subject and object, positive and negative, speaker and listener (38). Thus Schmitt delights in telling the story of this "sophist" Müller in Berlin who convinced the liberal Hardenberg to finance two newspapers under his editorship, one a venue for government propaganda, the other oppositional.

Martin Heidegger's *Being and Time* critique of "idle talk" [*Gerede*] is well known, but in the context of this inquiry it is interesting to note how in 1924 that critique is similarly framed in terms of the slide from rhetoric to sophistry when he provides what he admits to his students is a strange definition of ζῷον λογον ἔχον: "the human being is a living thing that reads the newspapers." "One must take fully into account that the Greeks lived in discourse," continues Heidegger,

> and one must note that if discourse is the genuine possibility of being-there [Dasein], in which it plays itself out, that is, concretely and for the most part, then precisely this speaking is also the possibility in which being-there is *ensnared* [verfängt]. It is the possibility that being-there allow itself to be taken in a particular direction and become absorbed in the immediate, in fashions, in babble. For the Greeks themselves, this process of living in the world, *to be absorbed* in what is ordinary, *to fall* into the world in which it lives, became, through language, the *basic danger of their being-there* [Dasein]. The proof of this fact is the existence of *sophistry*. (74)

For both Heidegger and for Schmitt it would seem "genuine discussion" is possible but not under the conditions of Weimar liberalism, where the abstract ideals of *Vernunftrepublikaner* [reason-republicans] like Thomas Mann merely obfuscate the realities of inauthentic discourse including propaganda. In *The Crisis of Parliamentary Democracy* (1926) Schmitt writes, "The situation of parliamentarism is critical today because the development of modern mass democracy has made argumentative public discussion an empty formality.... The masses are won over through a propaganda apparatus whose maximum effect relies on an appeal to immediate interests and passions. Argument in the real sense that is characteristic for genuine discussion ceases."[40]

Indeed by 1935 Heidegger with the help of Heraclitus had managed to tie this expressly rhetorical critique of liberalism directly to the Nazi regime, which *could have* responded with greatness, Heidegger mused. In the quickly famous Freiburg lectures collected in English as *An Introduction to Metaphysics*, Heidegger begins by interpreting the logos of Heraclitus in terms of true hearing, *Hörig-sein*—which is a following— as opposed to "mere hearing" that "scatters and diffuses itself in what is commonly believed and said, in hearsay" (129). Because people are always dealing with essents they turn away from being, thrashing about in what is most tangible. "The one holds to this, the other to that, each man's opinion hinges on his own; it is opinionatedness" or obstinacy that makes it impossible to be a follower (*hörig*) and to hear (*hören*) accordingly (130). As Schmitt disparages a neo-sophistic swerve from one side of an argument to another, Heidegger mocks this-and-that with Heraclitus—unhinged opinions that attach themselves "only to the one or the other side and supposes that it has captured the truth" (131). Moreover, by this time in 1935, rhetoric as the "hermeneutic of Dasein itself" had lost its grip completely because such an understanding remained only within the realm of everyday speech: because "the Greeks also knew of the phonetic character of language, the *phōnē* ["sound"]. They established rhetoric and poetics. (But all this did not in itself lead to an appropriate definition of the essence of language)" (64). No doubt logos-as-true-hearing had always been fragile, but modernity had rendered practically everything, including language, subject to mere manipulation. In a key passage Heidegger contrasts *polemos* in the sense of Heraclitus with modern polemics:

> *Polemos* and *logos* are the same. The struggle meant here is the original struggle, for it gives rise to the contenders as such; it is not a mere assault on something already there. It is this conflict that first projects and develops what had hitherto been unheard of, unsaid and unthought. The battle is then sustained by the creators, poets, thinkers, statesmen. Against the overwhelming chaos they set the barrier of their work, and in their work they capture the world thus opened up. It is with these works that the elemental power, the *physis* first comes to stand. Only now does the essent become essent as such. This world-building is history in the authentic

sense.... Where struggle ceases, the essent does not vanish, but the world turns away. The essent is no longer asserted (i.e. preserved as such). Now it is merely found ready-made; it is datum. The end result is no longer that which is impressed into the limits (i.e. placed in its form); it is merely finished and as such available to everyone, already there, no longer embodying any world—now man does as he pleases with what is available. The essent becomes an object, either to be beheld (view, image) or to be acted upon (product and calculation). The original world-making power, *physis* degenerates into a prototype to be copied and imitated. Nature becomes a special field, differentiated from art and everything that can be fashioned according to plan.... When the creators vanish from the nation, when they are barely tolerated as an irrelevant curiosity, an ornament, as eccentrics having nothing to do with real life; when authentic conflict ceases, converted into mere polemics, into the machinations and intrigues of man within the realm of the given then the decline has set in. (62–63)

So, according to Heidegger, at this point in 1935 creators had essentially vanished—though not completely—from the nation along with the essence of language now showing up as the mere manipulation of words just like other things of "value" in a global economy where everything is fungible. Thus Heidegger's express disdain for the philosophy of National Socialism, which at that time fished about for values and totalities. However Heidegger also makes it crystal clear that the creators, poets, thinkers, and statesmen strong enough to struggle for the nation *might have* lived the "inner truth and greatness" of National Socialism if things had turned out differently, and by that he means a different "encounter between global technology and modern man" (199). Moreover, such possibilities were not qualified by Heidegger after the war when *An Introduction to Metaphysics* was republished—much to the disgust of Jürgen Habermas, for whom this evasion was decisive[41]—until perhaps at the end of his life in the famous, posthumously published *Der Spiegel* interview when even such creators have vanished completely leaving us where, Heidegger laments, "only a god can save us."[42]

Heidegger did not have a democratic bone in his body. But, of course, not even our grand postwar theorists of deliberative democracy like

Habermas and Perelman think the public sphere is innocent; in his work on audience Perelman notes, for instance, the significance of Churchill forbidding British diplomats even to listen to any peace proposals German emissaries might try to convey (*The New Rhetoric*, 17). "Inimicorum vox audienda non sit": the voice of enemies should not receive a hearing (Gratian, *Decretum* C.3.5.). From both left and right it matters who would listen to whom, and through which channels. Put differently, rhetoric may be a capacity as Heidegger argues in 1924, but it is also a technology and it matters what kind.[43]

Rather noncommittally, from 1924 to 1927 Heidegger insists practical discourse depends upon the careful contours of community where hearing must be grasped simultaneously as the possibility of being-with-one-another, *Miteinandersein*, and being-against-one-another, *Gegeneinandersein*. Later it became clear that the enemy [*Gegner, Feind*] was—in the typical mode of Weimar conservatism that included Carl Schmitt most importantly—liberal democracy and Soviet technology both reinforced by Jewish interests, as we have learned in the recently published Black Notebooks. Although he explicitly condemned the liberal rhetoric where speaking and listening is a parlor game, Schmitt like Heidegger foregrounds a rhetoric of identity, and his concrete examples are chilling. Even deliberative democracy requires "first homogeneity and second—if the need arises—elimination or eradication of heterogeneity," argues Schmitt in 1926, and his examples include not only ancient Athens but modern Turkey with its radical expulsion of the Greeks and its "reckless" nationalization, and the Australian Commonwealth that restricts immigration to the right type of settler (334–35). About twenty years later in his 1942–43 course on Parmenides, Heidegger himself would not be shy about populating his decisive moments with real people and populations, mobilizing for a critique of technology this rather unholy application of now familiar Scripture: "He who has ears to hear, i.e., to grasp the metaphysical foundations and abysses of history and to take them seriously *as* metaphysical, could already hear two decades ago the word of Lenin: Bolshevism is Soviet power + electrification."⁴⁴ Doing the math, we should assume next to the babble of liberal democracy, that's what Heidegger himself began hearing as he delivered his breathtaking 1924 lectures on *The Basic Concepts of Aristotelian Philosophy*, focusing on the *Physics* and the *Rhetoric* next to each other, of all things.

CHAPTER TWO

Being-Moved

A Disciplinary Prehistory

The art of listening is difficult to grasp because its practicalities are now less obvious than speaking, and because we have lost touch with our relevant ways of knowing: what listening is with respect to speech, how it is distinguished from hearing, and what it means for human being outside of what the human sciences explain well enough. Our modern disciplines no longer know about listening beyond a narrow bandwidth I'll describe, and ironically the great historian of the human sciences Michel Foucault is centrally responsible, though he certainly is not alone, as almost all historians make the same fundamental mistake when it comes to rhetoric and its role at the origin of the human sciences. My wager is that we learn practically everything we need to know about rhetoric as the art of listening when we can make sense of it against Foucault and others like minded.

Foucault's famous history of the human sciences focused on "the order of things," and in doing so it overwhelmed a rhetorical perspective that can track the arts of moving souls: most consequentially pedagogy, politics, and psychology. If we revisit Foucault from a rhetorical perspective we get results: (1) at the level of architectonic, where we rediscover rhetoric's role at the inception of the human sciences, and (2) at the level of thematic, where we can make better sense of rhetorical phenomena such as the sacred arts of listening in the Renaissance, which feature a "public ear." That is to say, grasping the very phenomenon requires some scholarly work in order to unravel the disciplinary history that now gives us listening in relatively narrow modern forms—often in terms of interpersonal communication where speaking and listening bounce back and forth between agents, or in terms of the hearing science audiology. At the same time that our contemporary human sciences have made all sorts of advances along these lines, they have lost adequate resources to treat listening ontologically, as I laid out in the last chapter on Heidegger's rhetoric lectures, where being-moved was at issue centrally.

The shaping of psyche. The dynamics of a body politic. No doubt these topics still mean something almost fanciful, and in some form, they remain of interest to the relevant human sciences. But they remain of interest primarily as metaphors, which, if they are to be treated analytically, must resolve into more sober scientific categories, including most obviously psychological individuals and social groups. The art of moving souls, where rhetoric offered basic expertise, now seems untenable, and with it goes our ability to grasp all sorts of phenomena that persist nevertheless. How do minds actually change? How are we moved politically? How does education shape human being beyond the progressive accumulation of knowledge? In some form, each of these questions can be addressed by way of the relevant human sciences. But in each case, something important is lost when the objects of analysis tend toward brains along with their statistical patterns, or toward categories of the psychological individual and their aggregation. One goal of this chapter is to demonstrate how a return to rhetoric and the origins of the human sciences shifts our object of analysis, where we can now rediscover things like changed minds, political movements, and tutored souls literally not metaphorically. "Listening" is the phenomenon that cuts across all three of these examples, and it remains the focal point in what follows.

It turns out that Foucault's late interest in the pastoral *does* pick up this rhetorical thread, although he never was able to revise the disciplinary and biopolitical history implicated therein. This chapter initiates just such a revision on his behalf, so to speak, paying particular attention to historiographic questions, and then finally to discussions of biopower that wind up looking very different from this perspective. From a rhetorical perspective, I argue, Foucault's history of the human sciences and his analysis of biopower actually reinforce the very positivism in the human sciences that his work was designed to dismantle. In what follows I lay out what Foucault inadvertently shares with our contemporary human sciences, and what quiet alternative persists in the history of rhetoric he nearly pursued.

I. THE PROBLEM WITH FOUCAULT'S DISCIPLINARITY

Recently scholars have reconnected Michel Foucault's philosophically inflected *parrēsia*, or frank speech, to classical rhetoric that, ultimately in Foucault's analysis, is aligned with flattery.[1] But before his final turn toward classical antiquity, Foucault spent many more years working on early modern human sciences where, again, rhetoric *could have* appeared central. It did not. Paying close attention to the role "speech" plays in Foucault's influential history of the human sciences, however, teaches us how the history of the human sciences goes wrong from a rhetorical perspective. In *The Order of Things* (1966) Foucault famously explains how speech is *clarified* in the post-Classical human sciences where "man" first appears as such:

> The modern themes of an individual who lives, speaks, and works in accordance with the laws of an economics, a philology, and a biology, but who also, by a sort of internal torsion and overlapping, has acquired the right, through the interplay of those very laws, to know them and to subject them to total clarification—all these themes so familiar to us today and linked to the existence of the "human sciences" are excluded by Classical thought: it was not possible at that time that there should arise, on the boundary of the world, the strange stature of a being whose nature (that

which determines it, contains it, and has traversed it from the beginning of time) is to know nature, and itself, in consequence, as a natural being.[2]

To summarize, although "Renaissance 'humanism' and Classical 'rationalism' were indeed able to allot human beings a privileged position in the order of the world … they were not able to conceive of man."[3] Importantly, a decade later Foucault would replace "man" in this summary with "population,"[4] but more on that anon. First it is worth understanding this rather complicated story as it is told around 1966.

Foucault's "Classical" (early Enlightenment) thought may have paid attention to human nature recognizing, for instance, in natural history and the analysis of wealth the existence of particular human needs, desires, and capacities. But according to Foucault, human nature proper was produced in the European (late) seventeenth and eighteenth centuries as a correlate to general categories of representation. Human needs were understood in terms of their satisfying object and its price; human desires were named and classified according to general taxonomic habits; human capacities such as imagination and speech were reflected in a natural order. Hence "the order of things." As they matured, the human sciences invented human nature itself by way of these orders of representation, including universal monetization, mathesis universalis and its grid-like taxonomies across the natural world, and logic or universal grammar. Earlier in the Classical age there existed no domain proper to human nature, Foucault famously argues, indeed no consciousness of man as such. Man, as the being whose nature is to know itself "as a natural being," simply did not exist until the end of the eighteenth century, when the human sciences of economics, biology, and philology consolidated this new reality, as Foucault tells the story so powerfully.

In *The Order of Things* human beings are produced as the object of sanctioned knowledge: the deep structure that determines what kind of information can be accounted for and what remains outside, the methods for organizing relevant information, the discursive regularities that address a particular form of life. Ontology, in short, is the product of epistemology; or perhaps more accurately, ontologies are for Foucault only a second order reflection upon the epistemology of an age and the sorts of life it produces. At this point Foucault's approach productively establishes a radical break with questions about "man's" role, his dignity or his nature, all of which assume that there is a man whose role, dignity, or nature can be assumed before quibbling about the details. Instead, Foucault asks critically: What are the epistemic conditions that produced man, and what is the history of these conditions? Such questions successfully circumvent the assumptions of philosophical anthropology while promoting a more radically historical inquiry into the intellectual culture of early modernity. Thanks to this work, a new sort of inquiry is possible that does not reduce conceptual history to the history of a term such as *man* or *human nature*—tracking its historical variation and reoccupation—but instead subordinates the terms to particular conditions of use, filled out with concrete subjects as they appear. By any measure a methodological step forward.

From a rhetorical perspective the problem with Foucault's approach in *The Order of Things* is that it is deterministic in terms of epistemology—ways of knowing determine ways of being. And this constraint ultimately explains why he puts the invention of human nature that marks modernity at the end of the eighteenth century. But I will locate it two centuries earlier, at the time of the Protestant Reformation, and in the exemplary work of Martin Luther's academic lieutenant, the rhetorician and theologian Philipp Melanchthon. For Foucault, human nature is first a product of the human sciences—no more, no less. Perhaps it was "directly presented to discourse" in the natural sciences of the Classical age, given a definitive status and accorded a good deal of attention, but it had no independent epistemological status before the nineteenth century, and thus also no ontological consequences. On these grounds Foucault polemicizes that the concept proper did not exist, nor the man so addressed. I, too, argue that human nature is a product of the human sciences, but I define the human sciences differently. Neither just the disciplines that take as their object man as an empirical entity (nineteenth-century economics, biology, and philology [*Order of Things*, 344]), nor just the reflexive "meta-epistemological" disciplines that try to explain what makes man capable of treating himself as an empirical entity (Foucault's psychology, sociology, the analysis of literature and mythology [367]), the human sciences are better understood, first, as *meta-practical*. They are interventionist disciplines that reflect practice in more or less systematic fashion. Hence the disciplines that regularly draw attention to practice are pedagogy, politics, and psychology broadly conceived, as well as rhetoric—the first such "human science" and key resource for those that come after. Specifically, I will suggest that tracking the modern fate of sacred rhetoric helps us bracket Michel Foucault's history of the human sciences, thereby allowing us to better grasp not just how people are managed, but also how they are moved. The core of my argument is that *movere* fits poorly into the biopolitical framework built by Foucault, which means that we should adopt Foucault's rich material with some skepticism while cultivating more appropriate disciplinary alternatives.

Foucault's characterization of the human sciences does at least mark out its domain in an intuitive and terminologically precise manner. But it also precludes the possibility of considering the human sciences as engaged reflection upon practice—which is a serious distortion if one indeed wishes to treat the human sciences archaeologically. At this stage in his early career, Foucault is left without a way to explain the history of human nature as anything other than a correlate to the history of thought. Addressing this error, I begin chronologically with the pedagogy of the German Reformation because it best demonstrates the accelerated development and integration of meta-practical disciplines during this period that produces human nature in its modern form—a human nature that emerged out of the extended battle for man's soul—from the effort to render the soul susceptible to grace, doctor it, and train it to the body politic.

It should be noted that, along with the pastoral I discuss in this chapter, Foucault does devote significant attention in his late lectures to psychagogy as the movement of souls. However this movement is contrasted explicitly with rhetoric insofar as Foucault treats psychagogy (*psuchagōgia*) as a truthful relation to being, which is to say a special kind of philosophical relation. The key passage comes at the end of the final Collège de France lectures, where Foucault focuses on Plato's *Phaedrus* in his effort to identify a specifically philosophical and political practice of truth:

> The discourse of rhetoric, the mode of being of rhetorical discourse is such that, on the one hand, indifference to the truth means that it is possible to speak for or against, for the just as for the unjust. And, on the other hand, rhetorical discourse is marked by being concerned solely with the effect to be produced on the soul of the listener. In contrast, the mode of being of philosophical discourse is characterized by the fact that, on the one hand, knowledge of truth is not just necessary to it, it is not just its precondition, but is a constant function of it. And this constant function of the relation to the truth is in discourse, which is the dialectic, is inseparable from the immediate, direct effect which is brought about not just on the soul of the person to whom the discourse is addressed, but also of the person giving the discourse. And this is psychagogy. The *tekhnē* peculiar to true discourse is characterized by knowledge of the truth and practice of the soul, the fundamental, essential, inseparable connection of dialectic and psychagogy, and it is in being both a dialectician and a psychagogue that the philosopher will really be the parrhesiast, the only parrhesiast, which the rhetorician, the man of rhetoric cannot be or function as. Rhetoric is an *atekhnia* (an absence of *tekhnē*) with regard to discourse. Philosophy is the *etumos tekhnē* (the genuine technique) of true discourse.[5]

Here Foucault's classical "movement of souls," or psychagogy, references indirectly his work on pastoral care as it appeared a few years earlier in his lectures translated as *Security, Territory, Population* (which I will pick up at the end of this chapter), and thus to his even earlier history of the human sciences. Note that the story Foucault tells is expressly *not* about "formulae employed to convince, persuade, and lead men more or less in spite of themselves," as he puts it in the 1978 lectures. It is not about such formulae as they coincide with "politics, pedagogy, or rhetoric." Instead Foucault's story is ultimately about "something entirely different. It is [about] an art of 'governing men'" (165). And the figure to be recuperated in this long project is clearly not the rhetorician, whose manipulation of souls is suspect even as it might quietly shape the human sciences Foucault studies. Recuperated instead is the *genuine philosopher*, and with that appearance the actual history of rhetoric recedes into the background.

In any case, Foucault's work stands as a scholarly monument around which we must labor. But for the sake of argument I suggest a better framework for our purposes than his "human sciences" would be the "practical arts," understood as interventionist disciplines that reflect practice in more or less systematic fashion. Or we can say that the practical arts of antiquity—ethics, psychagogy (i.e., Socratic "movement of souls"), and politics, as well as rhetoric and poetics viewed from a practical perspective—were elaborated in modernity and consolidated for new purposes, becoming what we can call in retrospect the proto- or early human sciences. Methodologically, in other words, we can learn from Foucault as we work from a different disciplinary orientation.

No doubt we still learn from the ways in which Foucault ties an important thematic—in this case "human nature"—to the historical disciplines that produce it. Consider the relevant disciplines archaeologically, in other words, and discover how human nature takes shape in the first place, and then in disciplinary detail that allows us to better understand and critique the relationship between the emergent human sciences and the consolidation of key psychological, racial, and sexual forms of human being. But methodologically we should notice that along the way we are not just learning about an important theme, but also at the very same time we are learning about historical periodization. Here's how it works: If a scholar interested in rhetoric, for instance, investigates human nature through the lens of philosophical idealism and its real-world effects, as did postwar intellectual historians in the wake of Kristeller,[6] Garin,[7] and Trinkaus,[8] then it is sensible to conclude that human nature was conceived of differently in pre-modern and modern periods with the Italian Renaissance marking the break.[9] If a scholar interested in rhetoric investigates human nature from the perspective of epistemology per se, as does early Foucault, then the very concept can readily be seen as an eighteenth-century invention. Noticeably missing is an investigation of human nature from the perspective of the history of the practical arts, and in particular from the perspective of the first practical art: rhetoric.[10]

What happens to the history of the human sciences when we take seriously the practical work of moving souls as it is treated by Foucault briefly, and as it is treated in the rhetorical tradition extensively? What if psychology, pedagogy, and politics are first considered meta-practical arts, like rhetoric, instead of soft natural sciences that exercise biopower?[11] We produce a new genealogy of the human sciences that allows us to grasp important biopolitical phenomena Foucault missed and that we have missed accordingly.

After Foucault, accounts of being—described, identified, taxonomized, administered—predominate where the natural and human sciences agree. In fact, human science is now regularly conceived of as biopower, a Foucauldian concept picked up prominently by Giorgio Agamben, Ian Hacking, and many other leading scholars. One might wonder, why this implicit non- or anti-rhetorical tendency? The historical dominance of philosophy over rhetoric offers one explanation, and here, again, Foucault provides the key. Even though he typically rejected the description of his work as philosophy per se—insofar as that meant for him a twentieth-century discipline arm's-length from history and politics—philosophy (not rhetoric) understood classically, as a political orientation toward truth shapes much of his work, including his analysis of biopower and the academic disciplines that produce it. Characteristically, in his methodological introduction to a key lecture course, *Security, Territory, Population*, Foucault explains, "in one way or another, and for simple factual reasons, what I am doing is something that concerns philosophy" understood as the politics of truth (3). In contrast, I argue that biopower and its disciplines can be better understood from the perspective of rhetoric. And once this perspective on the human sciences shifts, an important set of dyads—active/passive, agent/patient, voice/ear—appear differently, and the art of listening itself emerges as vital.

On the way toward this conclusion, however, we first must take seriously the practical work of moving souls. As noted above, psychology, pedagogy, and politics should be revisited as practical arts, like rhetoric, instead of soft natural sciences that exercise biopower. Doing so obliges a return to the origins of the human sciences not in Foucault's Classical age but, rather, two centuries earlier when the reformation of human nature became a central concern, at least in the European and colonial contexts.

II. MOVING SOULS: RHETORIC AND THE EARLY MODERN ORIGINS OF THE HUMAN SCIENCES

The German Reformation theologian and rhetorician Philipp Melanchthon can be credited for practically grounding the modern human sciences, although one would not know it from reading Georges Gusdorf, Michel Foucault, Donald Kelley, Roger Smith, Fernando Vidal or, for that matter, most of the recent scholarship in the leading journal on the topic *History of the Human Sciences*.[12] Melanchthon's innovation lies in his practical treatment of a human being forged at the intersection of two theological principles. First, since God works in and through a living human being, human nature can be studied in terms of natural philosophy and not just Scripture. Second, since human nature is wanting—*infirma natura hominum*—we are subject to the practical arts of medicine and rhetoric, the two disciplines that provide some hope of therapy: medicine addresses the pathologies of the body and rhetoric addresses the pathologies of the soul. Considering Melanchthon's influence in the schools and universities across Europe, it is worth reconsidering these humanistic origins of the modern human sciences designed to *reshape* humankind instead of describing it or subjecting it to experimental science.[13] I now briefly revisit some counterintuitive disciplinary arrangements in the early modern context in order to circumvent received assumptions about how the human sciences work, sciences that addressed the new needs of a reformation by cobbling together preexisting sources and practices.

As preparation for the traditional higher faculties of medicine, theology, and law, Melanchthon defines three arts: the art of "persuasion," which includes moral philosophy, history, and the study of literature-as-moral-example; the art of logic, which includes grammar, dialectic, and rhetoric; and the art of physics. Since all arts are means to maintain private life or guide public life, the *genos protreptikon, genos logikon,* and *genos phusikon* are ultimately taught for practical reasons.[14] At the risk of further complicating matters, it is critical to recognize that rhetoric—as either specific art or as architectonic—is central to all three of these disciplinary modalities: (1) it is a source for logical topics and for training in syllogistic thinking in the *genos logikon*; (2) it is the traditional domain in which one learns how ethos and pathos persuade and is thus a source for the *genos phusikon*; and finally (3) rhetoric orients study in physics to its proper end, namely, the partial restoration of lapsed human nature. Thus rhetoric is also a source for Melanchthon's *genos protreptikon*, or civic art of persuasion. Moreover, there is every indication that Melanchthon consciously put rhetoric to use in architectonic fashion. In an important preface to Cicero's *De officiis*, for instance, Melanchthon announces the efficacy of this Greek (or more specifically pseudo-Galenic) idea: "An art is a system of habituated definitions the end of which is to foster life." Immediately citing Quintilian's *Institutio oratoria*, rhetoric then is identified as the single and sufficient example of such an art.[15] Scientific projects that foster life, in other words, are modeled on the art of rhetoric à la Quintilian, who had carefully defined the spheres of activity where such rhetorical fostering is possible. Perhaps more importantly, from Melanchthon's perspective, those definitions had become habituated over time so that human lives were already bound up materially in the project of renewing human nature.

That is why Melanchthon gives us a strange physics of human nature, instead of a metaphysics one might readily expect from a theologian like him.

More broadly, human nature in the early European sixteenth century was the product of a science designed to master the physics of passivity. What deserved scrutiny was not our depraved natural desires and inclinations but rather the dynamics of passive susceptibility: how we listen, learn, and change. Once again, this is why rhetoric assumed an important position in both Reformation doctrine and practice. The rhetorical tradition had established in fine detail the mechanics of speech situations, pedagogy, and motions of the soul. Comparing Melanchthon's final *Rhetoric* to his *Liber de Anima* ("On the Soul"), we see in dramatic terms the transfer of techniques from the discipline of rhetoric to theology, to political science, and beyond.

Following classical design, Melanchthon divides the parts of an oration into the exordium, narration, proposition, confirmation, rebuttal, and peroration. The peroration materializes rational argument by way of the emotions, and it provides a model for the hermeneutics of reading Scripture. But it is the scientific implications of the exordium that are of particular interest. According to Melanchthon, the function of the exordium is "to prepare the souls of the auditors" (*praeparandi sunt animi audientium*) along three lines: auditors are rendered benevolent, attentive, and docile (*benevolos, attentos et dociles*). First, benevolence is achieved when the business at hand is set up in terms of quotidian niceties, whether that be appreciation for the opportunity to speak, a self-deprecating comment, or some other device one uses as an indirect invitation to listen. It also is a strategy the speaker uses to establish his honesty, credibility, and amicability before the real issue is addressed. Melanchthon offers an example from Paul because it ties rhetorical art to everyday life: Paul begins his letter to the Romans by praising their lived faith. Second, according to Melanchthon, auditors are rendered attentive when the magnitude and significance of the issue at hand is emphasized, as when Paul tells the Romans that he is not ashamed of the gospel, because it is the power of God. Finally, auditors are rendered docile, for example when Paul gets to the heart of the matter: the gospel reveals God's grace. Thus, Melanchthon offers much more than illustrations of technical rhetorical principles, as did many scholars of biblical rhetoric.[16] He expands their disciplinary scope from the classroom exercise and university disputation to everyday religious experience, as it takes rhetorical form.

Everyday rhetoric renovates the image of God that languishes in human nature. As Melanchthon remarks in his *Liber de Anima*, although humankind is fallen, nevertheless there remains in humankind a vestige of God expressed by way of common sense (a Stoic *sensus communis*). The notions thus expressed are both precepts of natural law (e.g., Thou shalt not kill) and unambiguous formulae, such as the syllogism that allows one to apply natural law in any given case (I shall not kill). The image of God that produces in human nature this *lumen naturale* ("natural light") is no doubt weak, but it can be strengthened by way of sacred rhetoric. One invokes God in daily prayer (*quotidiana invocatione*) and considers God's testimony inscribed by way of logos, the Word. What we witness, then, as we move from a treatise on good speaking to theology, is that the rhetorical techniques used to persuade remain the same, but the rhetorical situation is redoubled. The self is rendered benevolent, attentive, and docile by way of daily prayer. Only after souls are readied can the Holy Ghost act as rhetor, delivering God's message. Melanchthon's discussion of self-persuasion clearly harkens back to Quintilian. But the inner life in which it functions has been renewed. Where hope dilates and guilt convolutes, prayer is oriented toward a life worth living.

Augustine, himself a teacher of rhetoric, encouraged preachers to entreat and reprove, rebuke and exhort where reason resisted. But it was first in the Reformation that the Holy Ghost was boldly described as "rhetor," distending in resolute hope those hearts that had been brutalized by more violent passions. Witness Luther in his commentary on Psalm 121:

These words are better read in the future tense: "It will not come to pass that your foot will move, nor that he who watches over you will sleep." This verse stands in relation to the previous insofar as the prophet has set down an exhortation to the end, he does this so as to demand with promises, he urges and exhorts that faith must be retained in divine aid. It is however absolutely necessary to encourage and urge not only others, but ourselves, in response to those dangers and vexations which are visible and immediate. For the things that sadden us are present, while those that console us are absent. Wherefore it is necessary that, while those things that vex us are present, we are encouraged through the Word to patience and perseverance. Moreover, this experience should be conjoined to doctrine. For our eyes are much too weak to extend to the invisible, to see the end of present affliction. Our nature retains a way to see how it can be freed, but when this is not evident, our nature aches as if it [our way to freedom] were hidden and invisible. We therefore need exhortations so that (if I may express it so) the shallow and constricted nature of our heart is dilated, enhanced, and prolonged.... Therefore the Holy Ghost rhetorizes [*rhetoricatur*] so that the exhortation be more manifest.[17]

It is a passage stunning both in its interpretive strength and in its bold flirtation with blasphemy. Associated over the centuries with lowly arts of cooking and magic, lying and loquacity, rhetoric would seem a bitter pill to give the Holy Ghost.

Let us summarize the rhetorical formulas Luther assimilates into what we might call his religious existentialism.[18] First Luther insists that *absentia praesentia facere* ("to make absent things present") is a solipsistic principle before it is altruistic: we must persuade ourselves if we are to have any hope of persuading others. Similarly, Quintilian offered this advice about good rhetoric: "essential for moving the emotions of others is first to move oneself" (6.2.26). However, Luther expands this rhetorical principle beyond the altruistic, where one conjures emotion for the sake of another represented in court, for example, raising it to the level of an existential principle. He describes how our nature is brutalized by seeing only what is directly before the eyes, most often things dangerous and vexing. Hearts without hope of redemption are full of fear, confined to the passions that correspond to terrible memory and present threat. What one lacks in this state of nature is a visceral sense of a future that might be anything other than more of the same. Hope is what the Holy Ghost provides by way of rhetoric in a vivid future tense: it is the divine Promise that speaks through the Gospel. So just as classical rhetoricians recommended that the rhetor stir fortuitous emotions in the legal or political arena by rendering the absent present, Luther suggests that the Holy Ghost implants patience and perseverance in the heart by vividly illustrating a future full of hope. Where a jurisconsult can illustrate circumstances of a crime in detail vivid enough to make judges weep (*enargeia* in Greek and *illustratio* in Latin), the historical Passion of Christ can be illustrated, in detail vivid enough to make it felt immediately in the sinner's heart, inspiring faith. For Luther, then, faith is a calm emotion and the product of a sacred rhetoric.[19]

Against this Lutheran background we notice how Melanchthon's physics of persuasion extends from inner life into the political arena and beyond, into the entire spectrum of human activity. Analyzed in *Liber de Anima* as a subcategory of the *potentia locomotiva*, the "passive intellect" lets things happen. Melanchthon reminds the reader that

> following upon the activity of the inventive intellect, another faculty recognizes and accepts such dictates. This faculty is called the passive intellect. Aristotle sees it in all of life: in the arts, in public and private deliberation, in military strategy, in poetics and eloquence, some faculties are more acute than others and the passive intellect is stronger with the faculty of invention. As Themistocles needed forethought and the creative intellect to persuade citizens to leave the city and board ships, invention must eventually be reconciled with the deliberative capacities of an audience and find acceptance.[20]

Even if agency overpowers patience, patience is nonetheless necessary for activity to take effect, and this principle could have radical consequences across the spectrum of everyday experience. For us, a few lateral examples help illustrate. Radical reformer Sebastian Franck in his *Paradoxes* (1534) would say that only through sheer suffering, resignation, and surrender might one be impregnated by the power from on high. Later, in the English context (c. 1609), John Donne would pursue a similar passive principle in his holy sonnet "Batter My Heart, Three-Person'd God." But the principle could also have practical consequences for everyday experience, including what one learns in school. Luther would say that the Word of God finds entrée through natural and sacred languages, so one should study passively in order to become a better vehicle. Melanchthon warns that products of the inventive intellect, if they are to have any consequences, need to be heard, understood, and synthesized in sometimes pedestrian forms. Only then, and only if circumstances are appropriately disposed, might one expect life to be lived well enough. Or, to put this in terms of the disciplines available in this Reformation context, the human sciences conceived rhetorically might make life barely livable as they provide some practical opportunities for self and social improvement.

Melanchthon's insertion of rhetoric into the heart of the nascent human sciences, or what he calls the (practical) arts, is both influential in its own right and representative of a larger tendency. Perhaps most significantly Erasmus in 1526 had similarly called attention to the proper use of practical arts of the soul by translating and introducing three of Galen's treatises. No doubt Melanchthon evokes Erasmus when defining in his own work the *artes animum*, which turns out to be a key term not far from Foucault (see below).[21] However the humanist Melanchthon was in a unique position to articulate the human sciences—including rhetoric—in new and consequential fashion by adjusting breakthroughs in natural philosophy to the new demands of Lutheran theology.

The human sciences are a direct result of a theology that puts tremendous weight on humankind's fallen nature. There is indeed something to the claim of Kristeller, Garin, and Trinkaus that the view of humankind in Reformation thought was dour, at least in comparison to the expressed optimism of Renaissance philosophers. But out of a deep pessimism about the natural capacities of lapsed humankind came the opportunity to intervene systematically and radically in the human condition. If not born, at least the good person might be made. So, starting with the obscure image of God in humankind (*imago Dei*), human nature would have to be invented practically from scratch. It is thus no accident that the Reformation produced a series of fervent pedagogues, preachers, and other meddlers in human affairs, including those experts in rhetoric, the Jesuits of the Counter-Reformation. The political dimension of sacred rhetoric is expressed, for instance, in the grand style by confessor to Louis XIII and political rival of Richelieu, Nicolaus Caussin. Rhetoric could play into Jesuit strategy: the divine origin of sacred rhetoric empowered its legitimate spokespeople above kings; rhetoric's exegetical powers could save deluded Christians; and its ability to mediate distance made it possible to reach non-Christians either at home or in the most remote outposts of the expanding Christian world. Ultimately, no matter where one stood in the Christian world, one could learn from Caussin's rhetoric of power. The *Eloquentiae sacrae et humanae parallela* was read beyond French borders, and reprinted, for instance, as late as 1681 in Köln. And despite its confessional specificity, it would be canonized by Daniel Georg Morhof in his history of rhetorical pathologies.[22]

I should make it clear that this is not a faith-based argument about the origins of the human sciences, nor is it even a scholarly argument from the point of view of theology or religious studies. Instead the argument here is that secular rhetorics *worked through* a certain kind of religion to produce the early human sciences. The most salient religious fact in the context examined is that humankind sins, and sin cannot be attributed to God. Its immediate causes lie elsewhere. Sin is the wedge driven into the chain of causation that might have run unbroken from God through humankind down to the smallest atom in the universe. It violently wrenches open a gap in which human behavior is underdetermined, where urgings, threats, and the art of persuasion are all that one has, where ultimately transient institutions such as ritualized prayer and civil law provide what stability there is, where Satan and cynical social technology are constant threats. Sin makes sacred rhetoric necessary, and rhetoric dissolves in the human sciences.

But what does Melanchthon's strange science of humankind have to do with our current conception of the human sciences? Is it simply a path not taken on the way to positive human science, an inspired curiosity? Melanchthon's practical arts of the soul in fact challenge both the philosophical distinction between human and natural science, and the historiography that gives this distinction its form. Even beyond Foucault it is still difficult to find "human science" and "human nature" treated appropriately. Here are some key instances. Though common practice especially in the German context, it is nonetheless anachronistic to apply the term human sciences, or *Geisteswissenschaften*, to disciplines predating the mid-nineteenth century, when the term was established by Schiel, Helmholtz, and Droysen as a catch-all contrary to the natural sciences, or *Naturwissenschaften*.[23] J. S. Mill's "moral sciences" would be equally problematic nomenclature for the domain established by Melanchthon, because it aimed at deducing social laws and establishing causes, not transforming people and populations. Finally, Aristotle's "practical sciences" is a misnomer translated from the other side of history, as it carves out a domain "made or modified by man" contrasting with the domain of natural science.[24] So, generally, there are two ways this philosophical distinction is made. One follows the tradition of German hermeneutical philosophy in drawing a fundamental distinction between the practical human sciences and theories of "natural" things, with the former treating changeable human habits, skills, and institutions, and the latter treating physical phenomena subject to precise definition and knowledge. The "positivist" position, by contrast, draws the distinction between human and natural science not as a philosophical principle so much as a matter of degree. That is to say, the human sciences are thought to differ from the natural sciences not because they treat essentially different objects using essentially different methods, but rather because the former is a "soft," or less rigorous version of the latter. In this positivist scenario the emergence of the human sciences is usually located in the early Enlightenment and, more specifically, in the sort of desire Hume expressed in his *Treatise of Human Nature* to do for internal human nature what Newton had done for external nature. No doubt the clarity of these hermeneutic and positivist positions has been disputed and the periodizations contested, but basic contours of this division remain.

Melanchthon's Reformation project encourages us to relax our fixation upon natural scientific initiatives of the seventeenth and eighteenth century that obscure what was, and still is, broadly taken to be humanistic in the human sciences. For Melanchthon rhetoric as an architectonic discipline not only teaches, it also transposes emotions and moves the soul; it establishes functional patterns for those disciplines explicitly designed to reflect upon and systematically intervene in human activity. Although it had an irreducible descriptive moment, Melanchthon's proto-human science was essentially *prescriptive*, designed to cure and refashion humankind into more graceful creatures. With this rhetoric of the human sciences in view, then, a whole host of rhetorical phenomena start to make sense where they might not have otherwise. Most importantly, when we shift our perspective from a classical "art of speech" to sacred rhetoric as it infuses the early modern human sciences and its particular concern with human experience transformed, rhetoric reappears as the "art of listening." With this new perspective on hand it becomes possible to make sense of some historical objects of study that would otherwise remain strange or obscure, one of which is early modern listening culture and the social science that shapes this unfamiliar object of study.

III. RHETORICAL ANTHROPOLOGY

Taking a step back, is my project itself a kind of human science, namely a kind of anthropology that studies humankind both from within and without, as Eric Wolf defined the discipline in 1964?[25] Am I arguing that, fundamentally, human being is rhetorical and should be studied as such? After reading my engagement with Foucault you should anticipate the answer is no—human nature, humankind, and even human being cannot be a starting place for scholarly inquiry where we then look to discover its qualities, even shifting over time and place. Instead, following Foucault, my approach is not historical but historiographic, meaning that my inquiry itself must already reside in some disciplinary formation, through which and against which it proceeds, even producing and reproducing humans (and other things) along the way. Not historical but historiographic, insofar as the very units of history themselves—historical periods and the objects of study that appear in history—are themselves the focal point: historiography makes arguments about how *the units themselves* appear as such. Specifically, in this case the disciplinary formation I work from is rhetoric, and the figure I'm arguing for is listening, while working against all sorts of disciplinary pressure that has pushed in the other direction through a distinctly modern trajectory, namely toward positive human science and its human being who speaks. Nevertheless, it is worth spending some time now on the relationship between rhetoric and the human science we now call anthropology—a relationship that goes back to the eighteenth century at least, though figured differently than the disciplinary relationships just described. Whereas pedagogy, politics, and psychology found in rhetoric an art of moving souls, anthropology found in rhetoric an approach that still resonates today.

Like the academic field anthropology, rhetoric figures distance. As competent researchers of those others with whom we are ultimately consubstantial, we first must carve out our field of study aesthetically, rendering certain subsets suitable representatives of the whole by way of *synecdoche*—showing for instance how detailed analysis of obscure seventeenth-century British texts on the art of listening to sermons will tell us something crucial about a distant culture that, ultimately, includes us. Likewise, we must mobilize figures such as *personification* to tell our story of a listening culture born with some distinctly Judeo-Christian characteristics and vanquished by the modern cult of agency, where it waits to be revitalized, resuscitated, reborn. As competent researchers we must at the same time consider our motivating *pathos* for carving up the world this way not that. How do sympathies and antipathies shape our project of study?[26] Which cultural investments and linguistic means, for instance, distance the ears of the parishioner at Blackfriars circa 1610 (whom we will meet below), and which draw them closer? What specific silences does this inquiry impose?

With regard to this project, recent German efforts in *Rhetorische Anthropologie* might appear counterproductive. Rhetorical anthropology built on the model of philosophical anthropology faces an inherent dilemma: what one hand wishes to deliver *homo rhetoricus* in terms of universal capacities, the other hand snatches away. By way of example, this tension shapes three fairly recent essay collections that share roots in the Seminar für Allgemeine Rhetorik in Tübingen, Germany, and that in combination mark what editor Josef Kopperschmidt considers the real reason for current interest in rhetoric: namely its anthropology, and especially its sophisticated treatments of "the whole man" constituted in a culturally situated language and in the interanimation of body and mind. After ambitiously titling his collection *Rhetorische Anthropologie: Studien zum Homo rhetoricus*, for instance, Kopperschmidt backpedals from the project's apparent "ontological ambitions" (22–23). Although, Kopperschmidt protests, the "homo-" formula, such as "homo-faber" and "homoludens," might imply claims about mankind's essential nature, it doesn't have to. We should simply consider *homo rhetoricus* one useful heuristic for characterizing humankind from a particular, and in this case rhetorical, perspective (22). Metzger and Rapp rightly insist that the rhetorically informed *homo inveniens* is a modern creature distinguished by a focus on the new and the creative, but they also must struggle against their essentializing rubric, as well as the contribution of someone like Peter L. Oesterreich, who flatly argues that man is a rhetorical being ideally subject to a universal, rhetorical anthropology (Kopperschmidt, 355).

Then the eclectic volume 23 of *Rhetorik: Ein internationales Jahrbuch* collected by Peter D. Krause under the rubric *Rhetorik und Anthropologie* introduces questions of appropriate scope. Is the "rhetoric of x" formula found in Matthias Bohlender's "Von der Rhetorik des Vertrages zur Rhetorik des Tauschs. Zur Anthropologie der 'Marktgesellschaft'" and Ursula Kocher's "Lügen brauchen gute Redner: Überlegungen zu einer Rhetorik der Lüge" enough to mark the project as an appropriate contribution to *rhetorische Anthropologie*? After all, what sort of communication doesn't have a "rhetoric" so conceived? And what about Renate Lachmann's essay on "Phantasia, imaginatio und rhetorische Tradition" (Kopperschmidt, 245–70) or Karl Mertens "Der Kairos der Rede als Ausdruck menschlicher Situiertheit" (Kopperschmidt 295–313): two essays that take up traditional rhetorical topics? Might rhetoricians dodge the pitfalls of "mere rhetoric" and expand the reach of their work—whether stylistic, argumentative, or historical—by simply hanging on it the meta-label "anthropology"? All people do rhetorical things. But that doesn't mean human being is essentially rhetorical. (People do supine things. But that doesn't mean human being is essentially supine). In a moment of reflection, anyone doing rhetoric should consider how this effort to substantiate the discipline continues the series traced by Dilip Parameshwar Gaonkar: Perelman and Valesio would have rhetoric become its traditional counterpart dialectic, Grassi would recast rhetoric as the seat of primordial poetic utterance and thus as the ground of philosophy, followers of Marx, Nietzsche, and Freud would equate rhetoric with a hermeneutics of suspicion, and so on. In each case a rhetorical project "supplemental" at its core appropriates the substance of its host thereby losing, ironically, its identity and its purpose. Moreover, as Immanuel Kant worried in his famous 1770s pre-critical lectures on philosophical anthropology, if we are unsystematic, we may grope haphazardly toward empirical claims. Now for the better alternative.

It turns out crucial limitations on rhetorical anthropology reside in Hans Blumenberg's 1970 essay, foundational for this subfield: "Anthropologische Annäherung an die Aktualität der Rhetorik,"[27] where he defines modernity as the turn from metaphysics to anthropology. This claim, reminiscent of Dilthey and of Blumenberg's own masterwork *The Legitimacy of the Modern Age* (1966), is then given a new twist: as God slowly retreats from the modern world, philosophical anthropology begins to generate rhetorics of human nature in place of God. Humankind has no unmediated or purely "interior" relationship to itself; indeed, no predetermined essence or nature whatsoever. Rhetoric provides compensation for this essential lack, creating the verbal institutions that give self and Other form. Hence, we find the historical subject defined by way of comparison, the school subject trained in the art of verbal delay, the religious subject formed in ritual prayer—a rhetorical act that is particularly meaningful to Blumenberg because of its massive historical scope (447).

Indeed, the most successful work in rhetorical anthropology refrains from filling in humankind with rhetorical as opposed to philosophical characteristics—say replacing logos with pathos as the essence of man—and instead learns from Blumenberg's rhetorically informed skepticism and historicism. Particularly compelling along these lines is the work of Gonsalv K. Mainberger, whose essay "*Homo rhetoricus* deskriptiv, konstitutiv, situativ: Kontroverse um Zivilisationsstile in Frankreich des 17. Jahrhunderts" (Kopperschmidt, 271–93) shows concretely that *homo rhetoricus* can only be found *en situation* (284). One way to characterize the virtues of Mainberger's work here and in his underutilized study *Rhetorica* is to emphasize historically how rhetoric is concerned with second nature not first.

When rhetorical anthropology compulsively rehearses its prehistory going back, say, to the *homo mensura* principle attributed to Protagoras (Kopperschmidt, 100), it imposes similarities over time that obfuscate more than they clarify. Alternatively, a Blumenbergian revision in the history of modern disciplines can provide the analytic clarity that defines new research programs. For instance, Tanja van Hoorn's essay "Affektenlehre—rhetorisch und medizinisch: Zur Entstehung der Anthropologie um 1750 in Halle" (Krause, 81–94) effectively mobilizes the eighteenth-century psychosomatics of Platner, Stahl, and Meier to argue for a clear distinction between anthropology and ethnology (84), and ultimately to rewrite the story of anthropology's birth as a discipline in Germany. Meanwhile Kevin F. Hilliard's "Rhetoric into Anthropology: Herder's Revision of the Theory of Invention" (Krause, 95–100) details convincingly in a mere six pages how, despite Herder's typically romantic rejection of school rhetoric, prescription in the art of rhetorical invention ultimately became description in Herder's ostensibly anti-rhetorical anthropology (100). With some qualification, John H. Zammito's research is also helpful in this disciplinary history. Despite his enthusiastic citation of the rhetorically informed critic of eighteenth-century literature Hans-Jürgen Schings, Zammito leaves out rhetoric from his index altogether, as well as from his list of inquiries that helped crystalize anthropology around the year 1772, which include the medical model of physiological psychology, the biological model of the animal soul, the pragmatic or conjectural model of cultural-historical theory, the literary-psychological model of the new novel including travel literature, and a philosophical model of rational psychology grounded in the quandaries of substance interaction. Indeed, the 1772 date is symptomatic of a justifiable but selective philosophical genealogy that would ignore an important element of Odo Marquard's article on "Anthropologie" in the *Historisches Wörterbuch der Philosophie*, which significantly credits the first anthropology lecture in Germany to a professional rhetorician, Gottfried Polycarp Müller (delivered in Leipzig, 1719).

One important thread that connects my archive-based, critical history of listening to ethnographic fieldwork is a similar commitment to local aesthetics. Just as I wish to mobilize meaningfully local topoi of gender in classical antiquity to denaturalize our communication commonplaces and offer new possibilities for inventive listening (chapter 4), a rhetoric culture theorist like Strecker mobilizes a meaningfully local topos such as "Rooks in the Mountains" to evoke the *genius loci* of Hamar.[28] When it comes to situating ways of communicating in ways of *being*, however, anthropologists are more than fellow travelers; they have some strategies that apply to a rhetorician.

Concerned, like Steven Tyler, that ethnographies lose their grip when held to the mathematizing standards of science and language philosophy (which typically prioritize literalness, symbolic reductions, and universal translatability), Strecker expands upon the rhetorical notion of genius loci as a guide for anthropologists.[29] Crucial to this concept for Strecker is the feeling for local realities—including physical landscape and social institution—which guides the inventive practices of a given culture and thus guides its anthropology. For instance, Strecker foregrounds Alfred Gell's essay "The Language of the Forest: Landscape and Phonological Iconism in Umeda" to explain how an "acoustic modality" characterizes the genius loci of Umeda forest culture, producing both the contours of Umeda language (shaped by metaphors of sound rather than vision), and thus Umeda anthropology (88–90). In turn, Steven Feld's seminal study *Sound and Sentiment: Birds, Weeping, Poetics, and Song in Kaluli Expression* grounds social institution in myth. While suggesting (like Gell) that the Kaluli of Papau New Guinea have a basic sound rather than sight orientation (61), Feld helpfully grounds social institution in a focal myth "The Boy Who Became a Muni Bird," which provides local contours that uniquely identify place and thereby provide the impetus for invention. By learning to listen to the Kaluli world through this focal myth where "social *sentiment*, mediated by *birds*, is metaphorically expressed in *sound*" (42), for instance, Feld invents his own ritual songs designed for ethnographic engagement.

As a rhetorician working primarily on listening culture, what I find useful in Strecker's genius loci is the feeling for place that grounds communication theory in local details and mythology impossible to specify in terms of the traditional rhetorical "situation" that includes speaker, auditor, message, and exigency.[30] Unsatisfied with general models coming from scientific psychology or the scientific field of interpersonal communication, I am interested here in models that can help us understand the cultural idiosyncrasies that "irrationally" constrain one's communication and at the same time provide opportunities for invention. Like Steven Feld working through the constraints and opportunities for communication in a Kaluli culture focused in the myth "The Boy Who Became a Muni Bird," I work through the constraints and opportunities for communication in a tradition focused, among other places, in gendered myths of speaking and listening. However, I depart from such cultural anthropology insofar as I pair invention with criticism in a Foucauldian vein.

In describing genius loci as "the concrete reality man has to face and come to terms with in his daily life" (Norberg-Schulz, quoted in Strecker 85), the anthropologist situates him or herself "within" the dominant culture however described, and thus misses opportunities for imminent criticism. "People perceive the characteristics of their environment as a kind of 'environmental image' that provides them with an orientation and a sense of security," continues Strecker (86); but I would ask, whose sense of security and at what price? What is the history of that orientation that necessarily privileges certain perspectives (and people) over others? From this perspective my project begins with the observation that certain gender myths such as Odysseus and the Harpies orient our speaking and listening, but in this case responsible invention—which is to say invention that goes beyond variations on a given theme—requires criticism. Since our gendered myths of activity and passivity shape communication fundamentally, we must distance ourselves from the reality these myths impose. For example, my larger project on the art of listening critically engages our received active/passive dyad in order to reshapes our auditory culture around publicity rather than intimacy. I am thus working outward from a moment when a significant element of our *counter*culture—meaning in this case auditory culture—enjoyed predominance, because that's where we can most readily mobilize language and sensibilities that carry critical weight in the present. In the section that follows, a rich auditory culture of the European Reformation provides a focal point for this particular project because, among other things, it serves as a counterpoint to the classical and modern communication cultures outlined above.

IV. SACRED RHETORIC AND THE PUBLIC EAR

Simply listing some English sermon titles provides a sense for the auditory culture we have largely forgotten: Hugh Roberts, *The day of hearing* (1600), Robert Wilkinson, *A sermon of hearing, or, jewell for the ear* (2nd ed. 1602), Stephen Egerton, *The boring of the eare* (1623), William Harrison, *A plaine and profitable exposition, of the parable of the sower and the seede. wherein is plainly set forth, the difference of hearers, both good and bad* (1625), Thomas Shepherd, *Of Ineffectual Hearing the Word* (2nd ed. 1652).[31] Meanwhile natural-scientific treatises such as Richard Brathwaite's *Essaies upon the Five Senses* (1620) and contemporaneous dramatic works including Shakespeare's acoustically paranoid *Othello* set the stage for a culture generally interested in "the other side of language." Indeed as Kenneth Gross suggests in *Shakespeare's Noise*, Renaissance drama revolves around the work of slander, hearsay, and other obvious forms of social audition that travesty "the common Renaissance emblem of the ruler as a Herculean rhetorician, able to draw those who hear him by fantastic chains that radiate from his mouth to their ears" (and here you might recall for example the frontispiece to Thomas Wilson's 1560 *Art of Rhetoric*, or the image of Hercules at the beginning of chapter 1). Moreover, in Renaissance drama and beyond, continues Gross, "The ear of the king, the confessor, the judge, the spy, the actor, the lover—each is different" (35), which again has ramifications for the rhetorician. Finally, with Neil Rhodes we should remember sensual hierarchy was an explicit concern of the period: for instance, Robert Robinson's (1617) *Art of Pronunciation* draws an anxious distinction between the *vox audienda* and *vox videnda*, where the first is the audible voice and the second a voice visible in writing.[32]

So how exactly does the ear figure differently in this literature? As the appendix to this book offers a tally of relevant Bible passages and themes, here I will highlight a few that are most important. Listening is not just the road to passive indoctrination. Nor is the reverse adequate: the active listener-as-judge tells only part of the story, which means that many of our more recent efforts to recuperate the agency of the auditor miss the point (chapter 4). Most importantly, listening in this literature is characterized explicitly as a public, not a private, act. Of course for the devout, listening to the Word of God is the acoustic event par excellence, which in turn poses a problem for our more recent social scientists of communication since from a secular perspective there would be nothing to hear, literally speaking: listening to the Word of God would have to be a metaphorical stand-in for an event of some other kind subject to social science, empirically understood. What, then, does it look like when a listening model is built around this nonevent? Significantly for these ministers of the Word, the privacy of the home is reserved for private prayer whereas *the public sphere is for listening*.[33] "Cannot we sit at home and read a Sermon?" asks an imaginary interlocutor in Jeremiah Burroughes's 1647 *Gospel-Worship . . . Hearing the Word*. No, because "the great ordinance is the preaching of the word, faith comes by hearing, the Scripture saith, and never by reading."[34] Several ministers later collect their advice in a treatise *Concerning Hearing the Word*, which dramatically qualifies what they call the "bare hearing" of sacred scripture "read in a more private Way, and by Persons of a private Character."[35] In sum, "hearing the Word preach'd is a social Duty" unlike prayer, which can be done in private (25). Fundamental in all of these accounts is the assumption that listening, like speaking, is a highly complex, rhetorical activity that warrants constant practice and reflection. Consistent with the nascent human sciences we have been tracking this far, early modern rhetoric as the art of listening is "meta-practical."

Along with scriptural injunctions to hear truly and not just barely, these Puritan treatises and sermons provide all sorts of practical injunctions. Prepare the soil by meditating upon Scripture and completing worldly business that might distract you; then in church continue to fight the enemies of attention such as stray thoughts, wandering eyes, needless shifting and stirring, irreverent talking and laughing; come to church with something in your stomach but not too much, otherwise you'll doze off; remember to jostle your slumbering neighbors, and so on. After all, if one can stay awake for a play and thereafter repeat long discourses point for point, then certainly one should be able to do the same in church, observes Thomas Taylor.[36] For Stephen Egerton, the social character of hearing entails concrete social responsibility: the social body must be in place at the right time in order for the public ear to function, and therefore individuals have the responsibility to mobilize those who would otherwise be dismembered, namely children, the elderly, the infirm.

V. POETICS IN THE FIELD OF VISION

Now in terms of a broader architectonic for this chapter we seem to have just left behind human science in favor of preachers and poets, or for theology and what we now call the humanities. Indeed, that is one important point of my story at this juncture: when one does a careful history of rhetoric, the nineteenth-century division between humanities and human science achieves new clarity, as does their early modern confluence out of which the division arose. The most consequential figure in this division is the eye and the ear.

Why for us is the public ear so difficult to figure? We find another clue when one of these early modern preacher-poets like John Donne or George Herbert is read from the perspective of our contemporary literary criticism, which usually can't help but find—counterintuitively—a dominant figure of *vision* just as they listen to poetry. As we learned to live in modern regimes of vision that include print, panopticon, and spectacle, our literary criticism skewed in exemplary fashion toward vision at the expense of other senses, especially hearing; for a quick point of reference you might think of the grapheme in both New Criticism and deconstruction, or what Charles Bernstein calls the "Euclidean" prosody of most modern poetics.[37] Ironically we still see evidence for this hearing loss in literary criticism, where we would expect precisely the opposite, such as Richard Deming's 2008 *Listening on All Sides:*

Toward an Emersonian Ethics of Reading or Helen Vendler's 2005 *Invisible Listeners: Lyric Intimacy in Herbert, Whitman, and Ashbery*, which, by way of negation, inscribes a regime of vision into its very title ("invisible"). In fact, both fold listeners into readers with an aggressive form of synesthesia common in our critical moment when readerly interpretation, engagement, and understanding are usually figured visually. Despite the recent emergence of sound studies in the literary humanities by way of Charles Bernstein and Bruce Smith among others, the ear is still regularly collapsed into more sophisticated epistemologies and practices of the eye.[38] How, for instance, does George Herbert's poetry and neighboring sermonic literature defy Vendler's ocular criticism? We can best answer this question by outlining the basic communication models that compete in this case.

One basic problem with Herbert critics from Huxley to Vendler is that their communication model falls into the disciplinary subcategory called "interpersonal" (see chapter 3 for an extended discussion). Ultimately, according to Vendler, "Herbert's most credible dramatic model is one of almost horizontal intimacy with the God who writes, or speaks, as a friend" (16). And why would Herbert address this "invisible" friend rather than a visible one? To escape the complications of actual communication and to generate an ethical abstraction (if we accept such an oxymoron) that re*vises* everyday life. Thus Vendler:

> In actual worldly relations—and Herbert had close relations with his birth family, his wife and nieces, his friends and parishioners—there occur countless obstacles to intimacy: age, circumstance, illness, overwork. An invisible addressee or listener, by contrast, makes the poem resemble one of those "pure" problems posed by mathematics, where one assumes the absence of friction, or postulates an absolute vacuum, or inscribes a dimensionless point, or stipulates any number of other conditions impossible in reality. In the ether of the invisible, psychological models can be constructed unhindered by anything but the speaker's attitude toward the proposed relation, and so the conditions and hypotheses of intimacy ... can be explored freely, and a heart-satisfying ethics of intimate relation can be suggested. (26)

For a critic like Vendler, who considers Michael Schoenfeldt's psychoanalytic commentary on Herbert's "Love (III)" "a dubious form of critical assistance" (87n13) because it draws out the sexual resonance of "service," this reading is negligent when it comes to Herbert's "extrapersonal" communication, as we might call it, anticipating chapter 3.

For the esteemed critic Vendler, radical invisibility is a precondition for the ethical return to our everyday lives, where we are subject to a refreshed visibility, and where we can rebuild in language our house of being—not in the idiomatic sense of Heidegger but rather in the Kantian sense of a pure transcendental architecture wherein subjectivities can *appear* and then encounter one another as real people with, paradoxically, a greater degree of transparency. Heidegger or Foucault would probably consider this a metaphysics of presence in its most aggressive form: to be seen, Herbert's aural phenomenology must be transposed by Vendler into the spatial terms of Kantian epistemology. In fact, Heidegger works out a phenomenology of the ear in his 1924 lecture course on Aristotle's *Rhetoric*, and I think this early material helps us understand how Heidegger's later concept of *Lichtung*—the "clearing" that lets Being appear—can't be reduced to a condition of visibility. In contrast, Vendler's addressee is subject to a regime of visibility, even if that subjection comes by way of negation: "Although no one else is present in fact, the solitary poet is frequently addressing someone else, someone not in the room" (1). And this negative visualization finds good company in the critical thread William Waters identifies, for instance, in *Poetry's Touch: On Lyrical Address*, where the gesture of a poet "turning his back" on the listener defines lyric from at least Northrop Frye through Jonathan Culler's influential work on apostrophe.[39]

If Herbert wanted to write to a friend or family member *he would have*—and he did, addressing for instance his recently deceased mother in *Parentalia*. But a sample of first lines suggests a more diverse population including "my dear angry Lord," "poor Death," "Almighty Judge," "sacred Dove," "brave rose," "[sacred] book," "bright soul," "busy inquiring heart," "dear friend," "dear Mother," "Immortal Heat," "Immortal Love," "King of Glory," "all ye" [who pass by the crucified Jesus], "my God," "King of grief," "sacred Providence," "spiteful bitter thought," "peace prattler," "poor heart," "poor nation," "poor silly soul."[40] Communication with God, moreover, need not be divine inspiration in some simplistic sense. Instead, God's invocation—and this is the correct word insofar as it *does* something—materializes that domain between a speaking agent's absolute control and a patient serving simply as a vessel for God's Word. I am suggesting generally that Renaissance literature can help us recall a rich set of communicative modalities for this middle domain where we still spend most of our time.

This rich aural phenomenology, not Vendler's visual epistemology, informs a lyric poet such as George Herbert, including this passage from *The Temple*: "Though private prayer be a brave design, / Yet public hath more promises, more love: / And love's a way to hearts, to eyes a sign."[41] Instead of Vendler's "single voice, alone" (1), a voice "unhindered by anything but the speaker's attitude," we should consider this passage and others in light of Herbert's decidedly public orientation, without which the speech act we call a promise would fail. Indeed, this sentiment "public [prayer] has more promises, more love" epitomizes Herbert's lyric as linguistic activity, not solitary reflection. Certainly Herbert has wide range when it comes to a phenomenology of the five senses including taste and smell in "The Banquet" and all five senses in the strangely titled "The Odor. 2 Corinthians 2." The eyes figure explicitly in the passage just quoted ("to eyes a sign"), in a shape poem like "The Altar," obviously in "The Glance" and "The Glimpse," and unexpectedly in "Grief," where the eye is figured phenomenologically not as a reader of signs but rather as the weeping organ. However, we unnecessarily limit our critical sensibilities when these diverse sensual moments, including vision, are forced to appear against Vendler's "ether of the invisible," or for that matter any post-Enlightenment and post-Romantic epistemology of the eye.[42] We would do much better to consider Renaissance material on its own sensual terms and retain this robust sensibility into later periods where epistemologies of the eye often obscure more than they reveal. Finally this brings us straight back to Foucault and our initial discussion of being disciplined in the human sciences, or being-moved.

VI. IMPLICATIONS HISTORIOGRAPHIC AND BIOPOLITICAL

Why, ultimately, does the art of listening seem to us like a minor motif in the grand symphony of rhetorical speech, a reversal of the order of things where the major modern theme points with Foucault toward a convergence of secular powers realized in the social body? In fact, during the latter part of his career Foucault worked on transformative arts of the soul, which is when he discovered, not coincidentally, rhetoric as the art of listening in the second sophistic. To cite one example from a late lecture published as *Technologies of the Self*, Philo of Alexandria's interpretation of the Bible provides a very precise indication of the way people must listen. At this point, Foucault's thesis is that oral rhetoric (including dialogue) as a civic art gives way to new technologies of the self, including writing and listening, where self-exploration and self-mastery (even subjection) are more important than mastery in a civic domain: "In Plato the themes of contemplation of self and care of self are related dialectically through dialogue. Now in the imperial period we have the themes of, on the one side, the obligation of listening to truth and, on the other side, looking and listening to the self for the truth within. The difference between the one era and the other is one of the great signs of the disappearance of the dialectical structure" (32–33). However, Foucault the philosopher (of a sort) never systematically revisited *The Order of Things* with these practicalities at hand; we therefore are left with epistemic projects of biopolitical management. That said, in 1978 Foucault does come very close to a basic revision, so it is worth concluding this section with a reminder why, although Foucault knew something substantial about rhetoric, his philosophical orientation misled ultimately.

Security, Territory, Population is about how early modern governmentality emerged out of the Christian pastorate that has roots in Saint Gregory Nazianzen echoing up through the eighteenth century and the familiar traditional form of *regimen animarum* or the "government of souls" (151)—a power exercised not on unified territories but on "a multiplicity on the move" (126). Rhetoric, we might reasonably think? No says Foucault, and he says exactly that:

> Finally, and above all ... and it is this that I would like to stress, is that in Christianity the pastorate gave rise to an art of conducting, directing, leading, guiding, taking in hand, and manipulating men, an art of monitoring them and urging them on step-by-step, an art with the function of taking charge of men collectively and individually throughout their life and at every moment of their existence. For the historical background of this governmentality that I would like to talk about, this seems to me to be an important, decisive phenomenon, no doubt unique in the history of societies and civilizations. From the end of antiquity to the birth of the modern world, no civilization or society has been more pastoral than Christian societies. And I do not think that this pastorate, this pastoral power, can be assimilated to or confused with the methods used to subject men to a law or to a sovereign. Nor can it be assimilated to the methods used to train children, adolescents, and young people. It cannot be assimilated to the formulae employed to convince, persuade, and lead men more or less in spite of themselves. In short, the pastorate does not coincide with politics, pedagogy, or rhetoric. It is something entirely different. It is an art of "governing men." (165)

I am suggesting that we take up this project Foucault never completed for broadly philosophical reasons, returning to the scene where our modern scientific disciplines emerged, and figure out more accurately how different our world looks when the rhetorical origins of the human sciences are revitalized.

A traditional "ought" discipline instead of a social scientific "is" discipline, rhetoric provides an especially useful analytic because it catalogs compensatory models calibrated to the fragments of a particular age wherein, for instance, the "good man speaking well" implicates people who will never be up to the task, as well as fragile institutions that cannot be realized without training designed to overcome initial conditions of physical immaturity, inarticulateness, incompetence, and ethical inadequacy: vanishing points of original sin. In fact, we have seen how the human sciences have an altogether different genealogy discernible by way of sacred rhetoric, or the art of moving souls gracefully. And this genealogy has implications for rhetorical theory that now is interested in the political arts of life management or biopower.

Also, now we can better understand what Martin Heidegger was up to in his crucial 1924 lecture course on Aristotle's *Rhetoric*, which does not follow the later tradition of grouping that work with the logics and the *Poetics*, but rather counterintuitively with the *Physics*, *On the Soul*, and *On the Movement of Animals*. Situating rhetoric with physics actually has a substantial tradition going back to Aristotle, as Heidegger demonstrated with dramatic flair in his SS 1924 lecture course, which was delivered at the same time that he was working intensively on Luther's phenomenology of the passions and engaging Wilhelm Dilthey's rhetorically sensitive work on the human sciences, where Melanchthon played an important role. Heidegger, in these 1924 lectures, resituates Aristotle's *Rhetoric* in the Aristotelian corpus understood very differently in comparison to his academic contemporaries: not as bifurcated projects with natural sciences on one side and human sciences on the other, but rather as methodologically continuous with Aristotle's *Physics* providing many of the basic concepts. It is in this scholarly context where rhetoric is rediscovered by Heidegger: *beings in the how of their being-moved*.

Rhetoric is dependent upon what kind of life one lives, which might be, for instance, blessed or ungodly in religious terms, praise- or blameworthy in ethical terms, friendly or unfriendly in political terms. And although Heidegger offers a strong critique of the human sciences divided along the lines of *Geisteswissenschaften* / *Naturwissenschaften*—he is determinedly not a scientist of rhetoric, nor is he an intellectual historian—Heidegger's interest in sacred rhetoric as it reorients disciplinary history winds up looking very much like the story we have told insofar as *movere* becomes central to his reorganization and revitalization of Aristotle. From a rhetorical perspective, in short, the history of the human sciences cannot be understood primarily by way of bare-life technologies after Foucault. Instead they must be understood by way of the life that can be lived one way or another, which means that persuasive technologies matter profoundly. In the language of early modern disciplinarity, therefore, rhetoric's proper domain is second nature, not first, and its purpose is to move people, not just know them.

Rhetorical genealogy thus also provides a contrast to Giorgio Agamben's oft-cited *Homo Sacer: Sovereign Power and Bare Life* to the extent that his work relies in this characteristic passage upon Foucault's biopower: as the territorial State passes into the "State of population," man is subject to bestialization achieved through the most sophisticated political techniques. "For the first time in history, the possibilities of the social sciences are made known, and at once it becomes possible both to protect life and to authorize a holocaust."[43] Again it is crucial to distinguish rhetorical studies from Foucault and Agamben on biopower, which has been explained in the following way. First Agamben reminds us that "The Greeks had no single term to express what we mean by the word 'life.' They used two terms that, although traceable to a common etymological root, are semantically and morphologically distinct: ζωή [zōē], which expressed the simple fact of living common to all living beings (animals, men, or gods), and βίος [bios], which indicated the form or way of living proper to an individual or a group" (1). Modernity for Agamben is then marked precisely by the collapse of this distinction whereby ζωή is politicized: "the politicization of bare life as such ... constitutes the decisive event of modernity and signals a radical transformation of the political-philosophical categories of classical thought" (4). At this point, my argument is that we must keep more careful track of the qualified life—βίος for Aristotle and *vita* for Augustine—if we are to understand the early modern human sciences. And to do this rhetoric, not philosophy, is the most helpful disciplinary tool. With

Augustine one replies: not just life but "a life worth living," a life qualified and distinguishable not only from death.[44] Or in contrast to Foucault and some of his most important interpreters, including Giorgio Agamben, Roberto Esposito, and Ian Hacking, not just the territorial state or the state of population where our creaturely life is primary, but the state of our souls—and I do mean that practically.[45]

Before closing, I wish to address some doubts about the redemptive aura my genealogical argument might have generated thus far. Is this life worth living just "affirmative biopolitics," as it has been criticized to great effect by Afro-pessimists Fred Moten, Frank Wilderson, and Jared Sexton among others? Michael Hardt offers an example of affirmative biopolitics when he writes in the *New Left Review* that "Biopolitics is the realm in which we [like Foucault's Cynics] have the freedom to make another life for ourselves, and through that life transform the world."[46] For instance, I think that Sexton would critique Hardt's affirmative and specifically pre-racial interpretation of Foucault and Agamben: "The affirmation of blackness, which is to say an affirmation of pathological being, is a refusal to distance oneself from blackness in a valorization of minor differences that bring one closer to health, to life, or to sociality."[47] In other words, to affirm our being gone awry is sometimes precisely to demonstrate pessimism toward a normative being as such, understood (perhaps incorrectly) as "bare life." I also like to think that the "life worth living" is composed of rhetorical projects that appear in their very failure to train successfully—hence the ear as a welcome defacement of the rhetorical tradition where the voice is primary. After all, transformative projects of the human sciences cannot, by definition, succeed completely and for that we should be grateful.

Finally, those who are less inclined toward genealogical work might still retain some increased degree of skepticism toward brilliant intellectual projects like Foucault's, which may do many things well, but lose track of key rhetorical threads on their way toward philosophy. Sometimes we can do more useful work by asking questions about modern subjectivity consistently and pursuing the answers in rhetorical terms, without giving way to the momentum behind some of the leading analytics of our day—not only Foucault's *parrēsia*, but also his discipline and disciplinarity, govermentality, biopolitics, and biopower. Although the issues raised by these Foucauldian lines of inquiry may be important, and his methodology powerful, we would do well to see his work itself as the product of particular disciplinary formations, as we can draw from different resources altogether.

CHAPTER THREE

Face-to-Face Communication, Disfigured

Why do we need a thorough reconfiguration of the ear? How and when was the ear disfigured, and what communication alternatives languish as a result? In this chapter I answer first by way of a critique of "interpersonal communication" in its typical twentieth-century form, which established the ear as a physical organ for hearing significant sounds, including most importantly the verbal expressions of others who communicate information. Emphasizing instead the tradition of ἄτεχνοι πίστεις (atechnoi pisteis), or unartful means of persuasion that are not provided by us but are given, I outline a genealogy of "extra-personal" communication, pivoting around Sigmund Freud and his persuasive contrivances, or *Veranstaltungen*, which he grounded in sacred practices where the ear is fundamental.

I. THE CRITIQUE OF INTERPERSONAL COMMUNICATION C. 1924

A now familiar type of interpersonal communication emerged in the early part of the twentieth century as an impoverished humanism where the basic problem is bridging the gap between individual agents who appear to take turns as speaker and listener. As far back as 1927

Martin Heidegger was exasperated with this model, as he insists in a series of *Being and Time* passages aimed at empathy, along with the very idea of communication that makes such emotion transfer possible in principle: "This phenomenon, which is none too happily designated as '*empathy*' [*Einfühlung*], is then supposed, as it were, to provide the first ontological bridge from one's own subject, which is given proximally as alone, to the other subject, which is proximally quite closed off" (162).[1] Indeed, without a communication model that presupposes voice-to-ear transactions between subjects who are first isolated from one another emotionally and otherwise, the very idea of empathy, or literally in German "feeling-into" another, would be more recognizable as a second-order phenomenon dependent both practically and logically upon a prior "being-with" (*Mitsein*). Here is Heidegger on the very idea of communication:

> As we have already indicated in our analysis of assertion, the phenomenon of *communication* must be understood in a sense which is ontologically broad. "Communication" in which one makes assertions—giving information, for instance—is a special case of that communication which is grasped in principle existentially. In this more general kind of communication, the Articulation of Being with one another understandingly is constituted. Through it a co-state-of-mind [*Mitbefindlichkeit*] gets "shared," and so does the understanding of Being-with. Communication is never anything like a conveying of experiences, such as opinions or wishes, from the interior of one subject, into the interior of another. Dasein-with is already essentially manifest in a co-state-of-mind and a co-understanding. In discourse Being-with becomes "explicitly" *shared*; that is to say, it *is* already, but it is unshared as something that has not been taken hold of and appropriated. (219)

My key term *extrapersonal communication* thus echoes a critique of interpersonal communication initiated here by Heidegger, though it winds up moving in a very different direction along with the history of rhetoric that predates Heidegger substantially. For it turns out that Heidegger, by the time he published this critique in 1927, had already abandoned rhetoric along with all other practicalities tied too closely to disciplinary history and their regional concerns. Whereas in 1924

Aristotle's *Rhetoric* offered an interpretation of concrete being-there, or Dasein, Heidegger's subsequent pursuit of Being as such rendered the practical trio of politics, ethics, and rhetoric obscure. At that point ethics was reconstrued by Heidegger according to the more primordial structural totality of "care," that comes before every factical situation—political action included. A primordial phenomenon such as "guilt" was formalized so that ordinary phenomena related to the law or social values—phenomena related to our concernful being with others—would *"drop out"* (238). In *Being and Time* Aristotle's *Rhetoric* is still mentioned in passing as "the first systematic hermeneutic of the everydayness of Being with one another" (178), but by that point such everydayness meant merely preliminary.

So my term *extrapersonal communication* turns decidedly un-Heideggerian after his critique. It is ontologically broad, as Heidegger might say, refusing to take for granted the entities that show up in rhetoric handbooks: most obviously in this chapter human agents speaking and listening. How then does the history of rhetoric shift accordingly? First, we continue to work around "voice," which offers itself relentlessly in a kind of positive history of rhetoric where the powers that be, or their antagonists, assert vocal agency. Focusing on the ear instead, we once again find ourselves in the 1920s, when the interpersonal model of communication shaped up definitively, along with its constitutive critique à la Heidegger and Freud as we will see in a moment. Finally, this historical pivot point in the 1920s allows us to revisit the history of rhetoric differently, in a manner more "ontologically broad." Now, instead of rhetoric focusing primarily on Aristotle's *artful* means of persuasion as they recur across history, we instead tell a story about ἄτεχνοι, or *unartful*, means of persuasion that confound agency in its recent forms. Not surprisingly, this very debate around communicative common sense plays out tellingly in the discipline so named: communication studies.

In their authoritative textbook *Engaging Theories in Interpersonal Communication*, Leslie A. Baxter and Dawn O. Brathwaite outline how this particular subfield emerged from speech education in the first half of the twentieth century, from postwar analysis of communication gone horribly awry, from everyday language rediscovered by Wittgenstein and Austin. Interpersonal communication is thus a subfield characteristically woven into some typical secular concerns of the middle twentieth century: How is communication tragically distorted, and, practically speaking, what can be done about it? Absent sacred rhetoric, we should notice, a typical mise-en-scène appears reassuringly as a cottage industry, and I quote: "[I]nterpersonal communication is the production and processing of verbal and nonverbal messages between two or a few persons" (6). Moreover, this perfectly reasonable field of study speaks loudly to our secular common sense, where we now most often think of communication more broadly just in this way: I say this, you say that. The basic model of interpersonal communication thus prevails as one moves into related subfields of communication studies, where I say/you say essentially scales up to groups and to organizations, with special attention paid to channels of communication and the noises involved: so scaled, the relevant professional organization officially calls this the "transactional model of communication." In December 2016, the National Communication Association homepage specified the model in an image and in this definition (see figure 2): "The transactional model of communication is a graphic representation of the collaborative and ongoing message exchange between individuals, or an individual and a group of individuals, with the goal of understanding each other. A communicator encodes (e.g., puts thoughts into words and gestures), then transmits the message via a channel (e.g., speaking, email, text message) to the other communicator(s) who then decode the message (e.g., take the words and apply meaning to them)."[2]

At the same time, over the last couple of decades, communication scholars, including most notably John Durham Peters, have criticized this interpersonal model in just those ways that quietly reintroduce the sacred. In his landmark 1997 book *Speaking into the Air: A History of the Idea of Communication*, Peters starts with a genealogical critique of communication understood as mutual communion of souls (1), as the transfer of

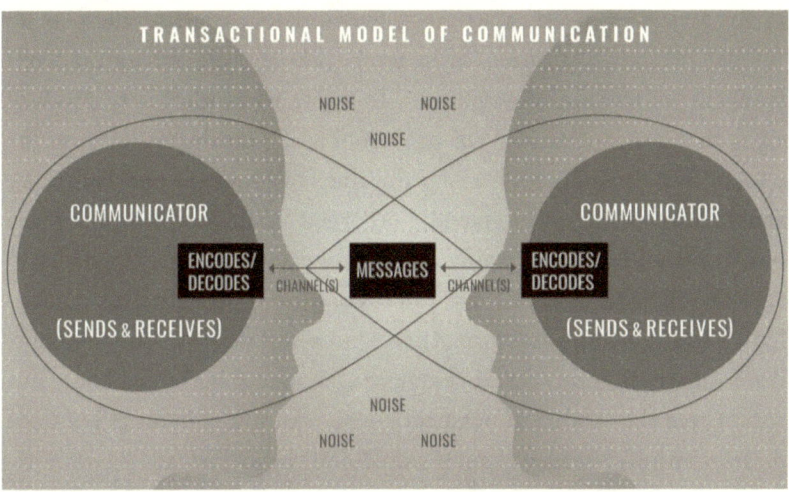

Figure 2. A special case of communication. Reprinted with permission from the National Communication Association. All rights reserved.

psychical entities such as ideas, thoughts, or meanings (John Locke through Ogden and Richards in 1923), as a therapeutic response to solipsism or misunderstanding (12) through Carl R. Rogers (26), as information processing (22). Like I do in this chapter, Peters pays special attention to the 1920s interwar culture insofar as it marks the moment when communication as person-to-person activity becomes thinkable in the shadow of mediated communication. "Mass communication came first" (6) Peters asserts, and the interwar culture is where we can best see "isolation and propaganda as two sides of the same coin" (15, referring to Lukács's *History and Class Consciousness* of 1923). Also like my work here on the extrapersonal, Peters tracks "beyond the merely human world," as he treats communication with animals, extraterrestrials, and smart machines (2). But what about rhetoric per se? Communication is not exactly the same thing as rhetoric, and therefore, to grasp sacred rhetoric we must distinguish it from prevailing models of extrahuman communication going back to the parable of the sower and what Peters ultimately calls "free dissemination."

By way of contrast, a strictly rhetorical focus means there is no "model of communication in general" (118) that Peters extrapolates from the text/reader interaction. "To speak to another is to produce signs that are independent of one's soul" (118), he rhapsodizes on the way to free dissemination along the lines of Emerson and James: we should acknowledge "the splendid otherness of all creatures that share our world without bemoaning our impotence to tap their interiority" (31). The rhetorician, I offer by way of contrast, is already situated ecologically among cultural formations with a certain force, among political formations with a certain exigency, among things beyond our control.[3] From the rhetorical perspective, one doesn't even dream of "free dissemination" because the job would end there; instead, the rhetorician has no stable ground to judge, which isn't to say the position is indifferent. We are already embedded in the analytics of power, and it is from these analytics we speak for worse and for better. In traditional terms, then, we have Aristotle's rhetorician who "sees the available means of persuasion in each case"—a definition I'll depersonalize below—as opposed to Peters's communication theorist concerned with relations as mediated, or Baxter's interpersonal communication theorist concerned with a subset of those relations that appear most prominently face-to-face. Thus, in terms of subfield affiliation, I approach "communication" in this chapter from the perspective of rhetorical studies, as opposed to interpersonal communication and media studies.[4]

At the heart of this chapter I will work through the late-modern fate of extrapersonal communication by way of an essential case study, namely Sigmund Freud's "magic words" that intuitively challenge our commonsense, transactional model of interpersonal communication. As Jacques Lacan later summed up this achievement, "the Freudian discovery leads us to hear in discourse this speech which reveals itself through, or even in spite of, the subject."[5] But I will emphasize how Freud, in his analysis of magic words, inadvertently exceeds his rhetorically sensitive interpreters including Jacques Lacan and Mikell Borch-Jacobsen, insofar as he analyzes Veranstaltungen, cleverly translated by Strachey as persuasive adjuncts or contrivances, which quietly persist in the orbit of religious practice broadly understood, and which find their theoretical justification in Aristotle's rhetoric. For Freud, as we will see, certain images contextualized appropriately, certain sorts of language like the divine promise, and certain ritual experiences like the pilgrimage, as well as sacred relics per se, *persuade*—even after the obvious religious aura fades. In fact, Freud's contrivances, I argue, should be counted as inartistic means of persuasion, or what Aristotle calls in his *Rhetoric* ἄτεχνοι πίστεις: laws, witnesses, contracts, testimony of slaves taken under torture, supernatural evidence, "and such like." With Freud's contrivances, in other words, we identify precisely how sacred rhetoric and the extrahuman more broadly shape up in modern form.

In terms of field scholarship, then, such an account helps us see differently a range of rhetorical theory including that of Kenneth Burke, who was an avid reader of Freud.[6] And even closer to home, my account complements the work of Christian Lundberg, who is interested in how the early Lacan frames the psychoanalytic project as a response to impoverished models of communication, for example in *Psychoses*, where Lacan writes, "The phenomenon of speech can't be schematized by the image that serves a number of what are called communication theories—sender, receiver, and something that takes place in between. It seems to have been forgotten that among many other things in human speech, the sender is always a receiver, and at the same time, that one hears the sound of one's own words. It's possible not to pay attention to it, but it is certain that one hears it."[7] Ultimately, however, my work here on Veranstaltungen moves toward object orientation, not what Lundberg calls the science of rhetoric (in this case figures and tropes). Most broadly, in the end, this chapter is about how we find and treat our objects when sacred rhetoric persists.

II. SACRED RHETORIC AND THE MYTH OF RE-ENCHANTMENT

Sometimes a story needs to be told just so that we can grasp what is already on hand. Such is the case with sacred rhetoric, which persists and imposes itself upon us at every turn, while at the same time remaining difficult to grasp in terms of the modern academy, where rhetoric has prevailed primarily as a secular art. In most undergraduate writing and speaking classrooms, for instance, rhetoric is a type of know-how designed to enhance a student's capacity for communicating in a variety of secular circumstances typically including other classrooms, public arenas, and professions. Meanwhile, for the same students, activities like preaching, praying, and parsing sacred texts happen somewhere else, like over lunch with friends (as I've witnessed regularly at the UC Irvine Student Center), or at home and in religious services over the weekend. At more advanced levels of scholarship, including graduate and professional, rhetoric is primarily a type of knowledge tied again to the classroom, but also to neighboring fields that sometimes need to know about their historical ties to rhetoric—as in the case of literary studies, law, or education—or to know about their limitations, as in the rhetoric of science. Preaching, praying, pilgrimage, sanctuary, renewing the self, or studying sacred texts might very well be at issue in these higher faculties. But they are grasped primarily through the sciences and their softer neighbors, in terms of aggregate cultures and individual behaviors. Or in terms of form. Or in terms of history. As the story has been told for over a century, going back at least to Weber's progressive disenchantment thesis (always bonded with re-enchantment as many forget), the sacred per se has been banished from the secular academy, and along with it has gone our grasp of sacred rhetoric.

More recently, however, a broad pushback in the academy is evident, for instance, in the title of an influential 2009 essay collection edited by Joshua Landy and Michael Saler, *The Re-Enchantment of the*

World: Secular Magic in a Rational Age. Indeed, as this book and others have argued, a powerful counter-tendency has always run alongside the push to secularize, producing "an array of strategies for re-enchantment, each fully compatible with secular rationality."[8] But we have only just begun to retell this story in rhetorical studies, which means that we don't yet have a good sense for what the strategies look like in this case, or what appear as "sacred rhetoric" in the first place. Hence one goal of this chapter: it tells this "re-enchantment" story from the perspective of rhetoric per se so we can simply grasp what is already on hand. But in doing so my work as a rhetorician winds up differing from cultural histories of the sort just mentioned, and in ways that are significant both in terms of methodology and in terms of the objects studied. Rhetoricians approach the matter in a way that is fundamentally different from cultural historians like Landy and Saler, whose re-enchantment fills a "God-shaped void" and hence is zero-sum on balance.[9] Rhetoricians first interrogate the very distinction: how it appears historically, how and to what end the arguments function, and what is at stake even when it comes to the naming of things. That is to say, from a rhetorical perspective, no calculation could ever lay out a balance sheet of dis- and re-enchantment. Saintly relic or statue? Prophecy or prediction? As we will see in the analysis that follows, these are not only questions about what sort of belief system prevails at a certain time and place—for instance, premodern religiosity or modern rationality, with named items lining up on one side or the other. Rather, it is fundamentally a question of who's saying what, when, and to what end. We have trouble grasping sacred rhetoric because our dominant ways of knowing in the academy make it difficult to pick out sacred things in the first place.

Exacerbating this difficulty is the confluence between a commonsense and a field-driven set of assumptions about who's in the room, so to speak. Typically, communication is not "extrapersonal," as I introduce on the way to a different room where sacred rhetoric might feel more at home. Instead it is essentially "interpersonal," which means that only you and I are in the room conversing while everything else, including the gods, doesn't register. Mistakenly, such disenchantment is often attributed to Sigmund Freud, who is in fact a key figure in the rediscovery of sacred rhetoric, and with it the art of listening in its broadest sense. Indeed, when it comes to the art of listening, expertise has been lodged historically in three areas that tell a story when assembled: in musicology; in sacred rhetorics, as discussed here and in the previous chapters; and, not unrelatedly, in the twentieth-century art/science of psychoanalysis established by Freud.

III. FREUD'S CONTRIVANCES

In a short piece on psychical treatment (or *Seelenbehandlung*) composed in the 1890s but first published in 1905, and importantly confluent with his late work on group psychology in the 1920s, Freud provocatively rehabilitates magic words on the way to justifying and qualifying his early theory of therapeutic hypnosis:

> A layman will no doubt find it hard to understand how pathological disorders of the body and mind can be eliminated by "mere" words. He will feel that he is being asked to believe in magic. And he will not be so very wrong, for the words which we use in our everyday speech are nothing other than watered-down magic. But we shall have to follow a roundabout path in order to explain how science sets about restoring to words a part at least of their former magical power.[10]

This moment is cleverly seized upon by Borch-Jacobsen in his 1990 essay "Analytic Speech: from Restricted to General Rhetoric,"[11] where science generally recuperates the power of persuasion abandoned to magicians, preachers, and healers (130–31), and where Freudian psychoanalysis is explicitly grounded in the rhetorical tradition understood as the art of moving souls. Originally in verbal hypnosis and later in nonverbal transference, Borch-Jacobsen identifies the persistent Freudian interest in affectability (136), classically categorized under the objectives of rhetorical invention; the end of rhetoric is *fidem facere et animos impellere* ("to instill confidence and move souls"). At the same time, we cannot help but notice how Freud's article on psychical treatment contributes to a general project of disenchantment that relocates certain supernatural powers, including rhetorical, in the affective margins of psychic life:

> The affects in the narrower sense are, it is true, characterized by a quite special connection with somatic processes; but, strictly speaking, all mental states, including those that we usually regard as "processes of thought," are to some degree "affective," and not one of them is without its physical manifestations or is incapable of modifying somatic processes. Even when a person is engaged in quietly thinking in a string of "ideas," there are a constant series of excitations [*Erregungen*], corresponding to the content of these ideas, which are discharged into the smooth or striated muscles. These excitations can be made apparent if they are appropriately reinforced [*geeignete Verstärkung*], and certain striking and, indeed, ostensibly "supernatural" phenomena can be explained by this means. Thus, what is known as "thought-reading" [*Gedankeneraten*] may be explained by small, involuntary muscular movements carried out by the "medium" in the course of an experiment. ("Psychical Treatment," 288)

But at the same time that Freud extends psychic life into the natural world and beyond, claiming even supernatural phenomena through his critique of the pathetic fallacy—these phenomena are merely projections—those same phenomena fold in and around the psyche by way of Veranstaltungen: persuasive adjuncts, contrivances, or events that cannot be reduced to mere thought however expressed.

I now propose that Freud's distinction between sanctioned rhetorical interactivities of psychic life and unsanctioned rhetorical interactivities that rely upon persuasive adjuncts (exemplified below) bears a meaningful relationship to a key classical distinction most famously articulated by Aristotle. And because Freud's model of psyche dominated before the recent rise of behavioral and cognitive sciences, it provides at the same time an ideal research domain as we try to gain some perspective on our current common sense: How is the scene set? What is given? Who are the characters? What is communicable and how?

IV. BACKGROUND I: ARISTOTLE'S ARTLESS
MEANS OF PERSUASION

Aristotle distinguishes between ἔντεχνοι πίστεις, or artful means of persuasion that can be prepared by the speaker, and ἄτεχνοι πίστεις, or artless means of persuasion that are given to the speaker. The first category may be more familiar, and it includes those that foreground the character (or ethos) of the speaker, those that dispose the listener (pathos), and those inherent to the structure of the argument, reasonably explicated (logos). The second category, artless, may be less familiar and it includes for Aristotle laws, witnesses, testimony of slaves taken under torture, contracts, "and such like" (*Rhetoric* 1.2.2).[12] Here are a few key examples from Aristotle: Antigone argues that the burial of her brother may have violated Creon's law, but it did not violate natural law (1.15.6); the Athenians "used Homer as a witness in their claim to Salamis" (1.15.13); Themistocles used the "wooden walls" oracle from Delphi to persuade Athenians that a sea battle and not a land battle would defeat the Persians (1.15.14). So, respectively, natural law, cultural authority, and oracle: three artless means of persuasion that Aristotle sees originating elsewhere before they are placed in the hands of a litigant. And although we can learn how to manipulate such givens, according to Aristotle, it is the ἔντεχνοι πίστεις that are trainable, and therefore they receive the most attention in the *Rhetoric* and in subsequent handbooks under his influence.

Or consider the professional litigant Demosthenes, a contemporary of Aristotle, plying his rhetorical trade in politics. Before Philip of Macedon was perceived as a major problem to the Athenians, Demosthenes argued probability, a form of logos, whereby Philip's future campaigns appeared to grow out of his demonstrated tendencies, and whereby the Lacedaemonians offered a different but comparable threat. By the time of the second Philippic six years later, however, self-referential passages appear artless: "That is what I said to [the Messenians], and they shouted their approval" (*Dem.* 6.26).[13] When Demosthenes cites himself, is that a character appeal constitutive of the argument and hence legitimately rhetorical, or is he introducing material extrinsic to the argument per se, namely a witness who happens to be himself? That depends upon the prevailing theory of argumentation and the prevailing scope of agency. Or is it enough simply to say that because it has rhetorical force it is therefore, by definition, artful? No, because that would be an attribution error—Nietzsche would later call it a metaphysical error built into our grammar—that we frequently suffer in our scholarship and in our classrooms, where we incorrectly assume that a rhetorical event requires a human agent. Despite our best efforts students tend to write, "Author X uses rhetorical device Y to persuade her audience of Z." And they do so because we give students conflicting messages about which means of persuasion lie in the rhetor's hand and which do not. What is the source of this ongoing confusion? In the case of Demosthenes, a line between artful and artless means of persuasion is not fixed, nor is it arbitrary. And we should consider this kind of example central, not marginal, to the tradition.

Typically, to this day we learn about the artful means of persuasion; the five canons of rhetoric from invention to delivery; and the genres deliberative, forensic, and epideictic. Typically, we do not learn about the rhetorical force of what is given; see for instance Corbett and Connors, *Classical Rhetoric for the Modern Student*; the index to Bizzell and Herzberg, *The Rhetorical Tradition: Readings from Classical Times to the Present*; Crowley and Hawhee, *Ancient Rhetoric for Contemporary Students*; the synoptic outline of contents in Thomas Sloan, *Encyclopedia of Rhetoric*; the Tübingen *Grundriss der Rhetorik*; and so on through the vast majority of rhetoric textbooks and handbooks published in the last decades.[14] In his *Introduction to Rhetorical Theory*, Gerald A. Hauser marks the point where, apparently, one's job as a rhetorician and as a teacher of rhetoric runs into a wall: "Whenever the facts 'speak for themselves,' we have sufficient grounds to make a decision without rhetoric."[15] My point here is contrary: when facts speak for themselves they speak rhetorically.

Where in the classical examples do we find most prominent the rhetorical force of what is given? In divine testimony or what is sometimes called supernatural evidence. That is where the secular handbook tradition fails most dramatically, as it gives way to sacred rhetoric, which prevails after the golden age of classical rhetoric primarily by way of preaching and biblical hermeneutics.[16] But first here is the Greek-influenced Roman rhetorician Quintilian[17] on supernatural evidence treated forensically under the heading *probatio inartificialis*:

> If to this kind of evidence [Quintilian lists: decisions of previous courts (5.2), rumors (5.3), evidence from torture (5.4), documents (5.5), oaths (5.6), and witnesses (5.7)] anyone should wish to add evidence of the sort known as supernatural, based on oracles, prophecies and omens, I would remind him that there are two ways in which these may be treated. There is the general method, with regard to which there is an endless dispute between the adherents of the Stoics and the Epicureans, as to whether the world is governed by providence. The other is special and is concerned with particular departments of the art of divination, according as they may happen to affect the question at issue. For the credibility of oracles may be established or destroyed in one way, and that of soothsayers, augurs, diviners and astrologers in another.[18]

Striking for us in this passage is how Quintilian takes for granted supernatural evidence even as it appears in a practical arena like the courtroom. What matters to Quintilian is not *whether* supernatural evidence should be admissible, but rather *how* it can be argued variously: in general, at the level of providential theory, or specifically in terms of divination and its various departments. Concretely, we should remember that Quintilian was thinking of Socrates at this point, who at his trial had to mitigate verbally the force of his own Delphic oracle proclaiming the wisdom of Socrates; you may anticipate how artless proofs would come to dominate sacred rhetoric from at least Paul's epistles on.[19]

Noteworthy for our purposes is how sacred rhetoric—broadly (and anachronistically) understood in this instance as divine—as opposed to the secular rhetoric of courtroom documents like a contract, will pivot differently around what is considered given and what is not, thereby shifting what counts in the discipline and what does not. "I call God as my witness" (μάρτυρα τὸν θεὸν) offers Paul in 2 Corinthians 23, as he provides evidence that his ministry is efficacious. Terribly inconvenient in this case, evidence is not delivered by the hand of a courtroom clerk. Instead it materializes with respect to a range of environmental affordances that include genre—the apologetic form of the letter—and the rich apparatus of authority that makes this particular call consequential: factors available to rhetoricians working beyond the Aristotelian handbook tradition.[20]

Hence a pedagogical point by way of example: Whereas in our day a religious arena may allow for supernatural evidence, a secular venue won't. Thinking about our basic communication students preparing for a presentation on animal rights or euthanasia, for instance, we might patiently remind them that supernatural evidence has a place in the heart or at church, but not in our classrooms. That is to say, in making a classroom argument about euthanasia, a sacred text like the Bible can appear to document community norms and their history; it can't appear as ultimate authority. In this example, a prototype for proof that resides outside of the argument—namely supernatural evidence—now becomes prototype for proof that resides inside the argument, as it is crafted by the student "alone." So, is the appeal to God as my witness artful or artless? The answer to this question depends completely upon the prevailing theory of argumentation, and the prevailing scope of rhetorical agency, which is to say historiographic concern subject to basic research. Note as well how the very idea of communication, as speaking and listening, depends in this example upon how the scope of rhetorical agency is decided. Under what conditions does the student speak his or her mind? Is God audible? Though these are complex questions that ask us to step outside of the narrow argumentative frame, the answers tend in predictable directions, as the student ultimately needs to be graded against institutional norms. In an everyday assignment of this sort we think we know what it sounds like when a student speaks his or her mind, and we assume that we can grade accordingly (sans God, it goes without saying). That is to say, when it comes to speaking and listening, the transactional model of communication prevails.

Though artless because it originates beyond the apostle himself, nevertheless the call of supernatural evidence did not then, nor does it today, fall on deaf ears. But to hear it takes some effort. No doubt, as Quintilian recognized, supernatural evidence is subject to spin: this can be a trivial observation that everything can be indexed and treated as such by the rhetorician. "Everything's an Argument," to cite the title of one popular textbook. However, this trivial observation obscures how in this case, as in many others, supernatural evidence carries a rhetorical force that resides beyond the rhetorician's hand. Where does it reside exactly? This is a deep concern for Renaissance rhetoricians as the classical distinction artful/artless came under new pressure.[21] Thus far in our classical material the distinction has hinged upon words spoken by the orator and words given to the orator, with the clerk's hand figuring mediation. But when this mediating figure gives way to books and to the growing domain of printed material, to the Church and its vexed canons of interpretation, even to the book of nature itself that speaks alongside ancient wisdom, then the distinction between artful and artless means of persuasion must shift as well, along with the discipline, rhetoric, that would mark its distinctions.

V. BACKGROUND 2: ARTLESS MEANS OF PERSUASION IN THE RENAISSANCE

Quintilian sanctions beyond Aristotle the rhetorical concern for artless means of persuasion and later influences Renaissance rhetoricians deeply interested in *probatio inartificialis* as they find a home, among other places, in blossoming citational practices that culminate in the commonplace book[22] and in the *cento*, composed entirely of quotations taken from other authors.[23] In our age of Turnitin.com we may find amusing this Renaissance example of shameless unoriginality. We might think of such proofs not only as artless, to use Aristotle's term, but also as "supplementary" in the Derridian sense, which finds some justification in the language of Anaximenes: *epithetoi pisteis* ("supplemental proofs").[24] For the supplement—in this case the citation—has subsumed the original reference point, namely the author. But is it so strange? What kind of proofs are we asking our students to produce in the blossoming citational practices of the research presentation composed, if not entirely at least to a significant degree, by quotations and opinions taken from other authors? Are these really the rhetorically sanctioned, artful means of persuasion—ethos, logos, pathos—that can be "prepared by the student alone," or are they artless means of persuasion that reside "outside" of the student? As the scope of rhetoric expands beyond the courtroom, this hard distinction becomes difficult to sustain.

As Quintilian suggests to us in his treatment of supernatural evidence, and later the English humanist Thomas Wilson explains about the argumentative place called "authoritie," artless means of persuasion run deeper than one might think. For authority, Wilson clarifies, pertains not only to God given voice by the Holy Ghost, nor only to noblemen and the learned philosophers given voice by their "stoute captaines." In fact the artless means of persuasion that we have at our argumentative disposal run so deep in "commune life," in the "lawes in anie realme," in "saiynges," in the "judgmentes of learned men," in the "commune opinion of the multitude," in "old custome," in "aunciaunt fashions, or anie suche like" that excluding artless means of persuasion from the so-called actual powers of the rhetorician can only be retained as a fantasy.

What, for example? The Decalogue's "Honoure thy father, & thy mother" is an opinion "naturally fastened" in man's heart, Wilson explains, and thus presumably, it can in turn anchor an argument that is not theological per se. So, is that argument artful because it lies in our hands and in our hearts, or is it artless because it is given to us by common sense, not to mention scripture? You can see how the pivot point shifts along with the figure of mediation: now what is given to us already resides in our heart, or to put this another way the domain of the given has dramatically expanded so the rhetorician spends less time fabricating and more time demonstrating what should already be self-evident.²⁵ Hence Wilson's definition: "Rhetoric is an art to set forth by utterance of words matter at large, or as Cicero doth say, it is a learned, or rather an artificial, declaration of the mind in the handling of any cause called in contention, that may through reason largely be discussed."²⁶ So according to Wilson, rhetoric is an artful declaration of the mind where the recognized domain of common sense has expanded markedly; or put another way what the mind artfully declares has been for the most part already given without art, incorporated.²⁷ Obviously relevant are also parameters of the "common," which is to say rhetorical argumentation depends upon what is shared, and by whom.

To summarize at this point: The commonplace and the cento make little room for the original author as we imagine *creator ex nihilo*; a certain strain of Renaissance humanism has pushed art toward common sense; and then, with Ramus, rhetorical art finally runs like sand through the rhetor's fingers.

Ramus notoriously divided arguments into two types: artful and artless, or in the translation of Dudley Fenner, the artificial and the inartificial argument, which "argueth of it self."²⁸ The former were demonstrable to the observer by the plain facts of the question at hand, while inartificial arguments, such as the resurrection of Christ, had to be taken on faith. Thus, the principles of "art" were not inherent human capacities (δυνάμεις), let alone categories of the mind. They were rather statements that pertain to a world beyond the human. In fact, no means of persuasion are left in the hands of a rhetorician, who has now given way to the logician and the theologian respectively. Artificial arguments demonstrate the correspondence between laws of nature and the ordered hierarchy of ideas existing in the mind of God. Inartificial arguments are a matter of faith, which troubled neo-Aristotelians to no end because they feared it would bring all authority to the bar of criticism, as Perry Miller once put it.²⁹ In *The Massacre at Paris* (1593) Christopher Marlowe represents the Duke of Guise accusing Ramus of appealing to artless testimony in his purely private attack on the learned:

Excepting against doctors' axioms,
And *ipse dixit* with this quiddity,
Argumentum testimonii est inartificiale
["argument from testimony is artless"].
To contradict which, I say, *Ramus* shall die.
                    The Massacre at Paris, scene 7, 31–34[30]

With Ramus the line between artful and artless means of persuasion has shifted once again and this time the results are deadly. Where once with Aristotle artless arguments from testimony might have waltzed into the courtroom under the guise of sanctioned authority, now they are condemned as quintessentially private at the *expense of* authority.[31] Ramus was dangerous politically because he undermined the role of church authorities, removing them completely from the sacred scene, and replacing them solely with logos-first-scripture and pathos (the soul that responds faithfully).

No doubt the neo-classical tradition has always explained how givens can be handled by the rhetorician one way or another: remember Quintilian on supernatural evidence in the Stoic or Epicurean treatment, for instance. However, the Aristotelian handbook tradition has not always provided meta-analysis that would explain how the sphere of givens is distinguished in the first place and how that sphere is subject to systematic reconfiguration. Fundamentally, this would be historiographic work, and it is not completely absent in the tradition, since we have that Renaissance threshold figure most prominently, Giambattista Vico.

Vico is a sensitive *historian* of rhetoric for whom the available means of persuasion exceed face-to-face communication to include cultural formations with a certain force.[32] So, complementing David Marshall's thesis in *Vico and the Transformation of Rhetoric in Early Modern Europe*, we might say that Vico generated his history of rhetoric in part by extending temporally Quintilian's discussion of artless means of persuasion, including (1) Quintilian's Supernatural Evidence, which Vico figures as Divine Providence in civic institutions like marriage initiated by huddling against the terrible gods; (2) the ancient Witness, whom Vico figures not in the testimony of a real person, Homer, but rather in "the true Homer," best understood as an "idea" of Grecian men whose characters inadvertently provide a key to historic time; and finally (3) Law, which becomes concrete analysis of the Twelve Tables that defined legitimate human being against forms of illegitimacy, including "monstrous" children born of uncertain unions. Each one of these artless means of persuasion function beyond the interpersonal situation, beyond the powers of any particular rhetorician, and can only be understood as such.

This is one way to measure Vico's contribution to the history and theory of rhetoric. He takes modular components of the rhetorical handbook—in this case ἄτεχνοι πίστεις—and shows how they take historical form. The historian of rhetoric can then, really for the first time, research the rhetorical forms of history and not just the speeches of famous rhetoricians documented in the historical record. Put differently, Renaissance rhetoric culminating in the work of Nicholas Caussin and later Giambattista Vico, initiates the historicist inquiry that made this particular profession possible, and it did so by reversing Aristotle's priority outlined above. Though Vico cut his teeth on a relatively conventional rhetoric handbook named after Quintilian's, the *Institutiones oratoriae* (1711), Vico ultimately prioritized artless means of persuasion in his *New Science* because he understood how historical givens shape us profoundly and therefore must be analyzed rhetorically.

For historians of rhetoric teaching in history departments, this attitude might seem intuitive. But as instructors teach the practicalities of analysis and persuasion, one would do well to remember Vico's example and think critically about what is given (to the rhetorician) and what is not.

VI. ARTLESSNESS IN FREUD AND BEYOND

So how exactly do ἄτεχνοι work for Freud? Discussing supernatural phenomena, including miraculous cures, Freud initially retreats from extra-psychic and extrapersonal analysis to a degree that justifies a predictable humanism: "There is no need ... to bring forward anything other than mental forces in order to explain miraculous cures.... Indeed, the power of religious faith is reinforced in these cases by a number of eminently human motive forces" ("Psychical Treatment," 290). Freud's hyperbole is figured by way of intensification, his metaphor in English is magnification—whereby the extrahuman finds its familiar seed, and I quote: "The individual's pious belief is intensified [*Verstärkung*] by the enthusiasm of the crowd of people in whose midst he makes his way as a rule to the sacred locality. All the mental impulses of an individual can be enormously magnified [*gesteigert*] by group influence such as this" (290). But I argue that without the adjuncts, contrivances, and events that exceed the psyche in this example and others—let's call them inartistic means of persuasion—psychic experience would be impossible to identify; indeed, there would be no psyche at all. And without psyche, or "mind" as we call it, to avoid the odor of antiquity, there would be no speaking understood as mental expression, and no listening understood as mental perception. After all, what is the mind completely detached from the world? Impossible to say.[33] Instead Freud explains in this key passage:

> The most noticeable effects of this kind of expectation coloured by faith are to be found in the "miraculous" cures which are brought about even today under our own eyes without the help of any medical skill. Miraculous cures properly so-called take place in the case of believers under the influence of adjuncts suitable to intensify religious feelings [*Veranstaltungen, welche geeignet sind, die religiösen Gefühle zu steigern*; Strachey translation slightly modified]—that is to say, in places where a miracle-working image is worshipped, or where a holy or divine personage has revealed himself to men and has promised them relief from their sufferings in return for their worship, or where the relics of a saint are preserved as a treasure. Religious faith alone does not seem to find it easy to suppress illness by means of expectation; for as a rule other contrivances [*Veranstaltungen*] as well are brought into play in the case of miraculous cures. The times and seasons at which divine mercy is sought must be specially indicated; the patient must

submit to physical toil, to the trials and sacrifices of a pilgrimage, before he can become worthy of this divine mercy. ("Psychical Treatment," 289–90)

Psyche is in the world concretely, and thus its treatment must also run through the things of this world in all of their historicity. So what significant shape do these contrivances take?

In his work on group psychology, Freud specifies that just like hypnosis, so-called "artificial groups"—for example the Catholic Church—put the object, Jesus, in the place of the ego ideal. However, in the group dynamic of the Church, as opposed to the military, Freud qualifies, it is not enough for the Christian to love Christ as his ideal and feel himself united with all other Christians by the ties of identification. He also has to "identify himself with Christ and love all other Christians as Christ loved them."[34] Indeed, where there is identification in Christ, object-love must be added, which "evidently goes beyond the constitution of the group" (*Group Psychology*, 86) to include a variety of extrinsic objects that we have just called Veranstaltungen: for instance certain reified images, certain sorts of language like the divine promise, certain ritual experiences like the pilgrimage, as well as sacred relics per se; Lacan would later identify the *objet petit-a* that, among other things, must be incorporated by the analyst as the figure of transference. So it is not enough to impose doctrine from above or give lip service from below—this religious world must be completely renatured, human being completely renewed, and community completely reconstituted as evangelical. Antonio Gramsci would analyze cultural hegemony of the Catholic Church; in 1921, Freud concludes rather unsatisfactorily that "all the ties that bind people to mystico-religious or philosophico-religious sects and communities are expressions of crooked cures of all kinds of neuroses."[35]

So, next to Quintilian's famous neologism *probatio inartificialis*, now sometimes misunderstood as "brute fact,"[36] I place Freud's Veranstaltungen. Why this particular word?[37] *Stalt* is an abstract from the verb *stellen*, to stand, and hence we get the root word *Anstalt* or establishment, institution, something stood up and mobilized by the prefix *ver-*. It is related to the verb *veranstalten*, which means to host, to arrange, to stage, to prepare, to contrive, to institutionalize, but in Freud's case the verb is nominalized so human agency is incorporated, and we are left with Strachey's persuasive adjuncts or contrivances, even social events with a particular duration and purpose, like a religious pilgrimage in this case. Freud's point: strictly speaking there is no such thing as a *magic* word without Veranstaltungen. Let's just say there is no such thing as a *persuasive* word—no rhetoric with its speaking and listening—without Veranstaltungen, otherwise known to the classical rhetorician as inartistic means of persuasion.

Clearly modern theorists of rhetoric have done some of this work already.[38] Not surprisingly given his Freud affinity, Kenneth Burke was onto something similar despite his penchant for symbolization that returns extrapersonal considerations back to people. For instance, military force, Burke argues in *A Rhetoric of Motives*, "can persuade by its sheer 'meaning' as well as by its use in actual combat."[39] Think about all the rhetorical work done by a standing army implicated in an ever-changing calculus of deterrence: let's call this very inartistic means of persuasion. Likewise, "recalcitrance" is a Burkean concept that objectifies rhetoric throughout his career: it "refers to the factors that *substantiate* a statement, the factors that *incite* a statement, and the factors that *correct* a statement."[40] So, for instance, the pseudo-statement "I am a bird" is revised into a complete practical statement when we can say "I am an aviator," but both, Burke argues, are simply statements insofar as the person who says them must take certain orders of recalcitrance into account.[41] Like Freud's magic words that are meaningless without Veranstaltungen, Burke's statements are meaningless without the world and its objectivity.[42] No doubt Burke's world and its objectivity are not that of science per se: "The magical decree is implicit in all language; for the mere act of naming an object or situation decrees that it is to be singled out as such-and-such rather than as something-other" (4). But just as Freud's magical words are materialized, Burke's "true" or "correct" magical decree doesn't escape the world and its recalcitrance—for example, the laws of motion—that are suspended only by "false" magic and by poetry writ large.

Words of whatever kind do nothing by themselves even accompanied by the psychoanalytic arts of personal interactivity, and this Freud knew well enough. His analysis of aphonic Dora initiates in part because "favorable" family circumstances have not desiccated her homosexual feelings the way they normally would, and her therapy founders, supposedly, on the object relation he calls transference.[43] Meanwhile, as Diane Fuss describes in her wonderful book *The Sense of an Interior: Four Writers and the Rooms That Shaped Them*, Freud's Berggasse 19 enacted the therapeutic session by way of precise spatial arrangement of objects and furniture (80): of course the famous couch that renders the patient supine with all that implies (90), the Etruscan mirror that opens a window onto immortality as a mythological scene reflects off the engraved surface (85), the bas-relief Gradiva who offers patient and doctor these instructions: "look, but not with bodily eyes, and listen, but not with physical ears." Poet H. D. recalls of her first visit, "The statues stare and stare and seem to say, what has happened to you?" (97). Miracle workers need their contrivances, including a certain disposition of time and place organized around a transferential object, as Freud would call it. Likewise, rhetoricians need their contrivances, including a certain disposition of time and place sometimes organized around a transferential object, which Freud's contemporary Siegfried Kracauer called in the context of Weimar culture the "human ornament," like the massive configurations at Nuremberg.[44] The job of the rhetorician is not to study words (*verba*) as one imagines at the height of 1980s linguistic constructivism, or things (*res*) as one imagines at the height of our current object-oriented theory, but rather the precise historical relation that gives this point of intersection force.

Hence a historical thesis. The modern project of dis- and re-enchantment has its ambiguity that rhetoricians should find deeply interesting because its resolution one way or another can determine our historiography. That is to say, the ambiguity around things that may or may not appear sacred—statues/relics, birds/auspices, walks/pilgrimages, pills/cures, words and spectacles human or divine—depend completely upon historically informed rhetorical analysis for their disambiguation. It's not that once in ancient times there were enchanted relics, auspices, pilgrimages, and divine interventions, whereas now under the weight of modernity there isn't (disenchantment). Nor is it adequate to reverse the progression, so that now the world can appear enchanted once again. Instead the project is rhetorical which does not mean secular, as there have long been historians of rhetoric who worked comfortably within a religious framework, like the early modern figure Nicholas Caussin through the late modern figure Richard Weaver: in each case the work is still historical and it argues a point. Or as Quintilian implied even earlier with respect to supernatural evidence, what matters is not whether the evidence is "really" supernatural or not: theoretically that would be argued earlier at the level of a definitional stasis determining in this case what sort of evidence is admissible in a court of law. For Quintilian teaching rhetoric, it's not a matter of whether the Delphic Oracle has authority in the courtroom, or, say, for us, how seriously we should take the aura of authority when it comes to an expert witness. Instead, Quintilian is locally concerned with the ways in which oracles can be handled more or less competently given the rhetorical situation. Likewise, we should not get hung up on the sacred/secular distinction per se along with its cognates, but should rather spend our time researching and analyzing how these distinctions play out. A final example referencing Freud.

In this passage Freud exemplifies how a certain kind of secular rhetoric works by way of fashion, within a distinctly bourgeois topography: once again, time and place appear disenchanted. But note how Freud's historiographic ambiguity is provisionally settled by way of figurative identity, or "complete" substitution, undone by alien material reminiscent of our contrivances as they approach a sacrament or holy communion, κοινωνία: the rhetorical contrivance par excellence.[45] Freud continues:

In their case reputation and group-influence act as a complete substitute for faith. There are always fashionable treatments and fashionable physicians, and these play an especially dominant part in high society, where the most powerful psychological motive forces are the endeavour to excel and to do what the "best" people do. Fashionable treatments of this kind produce therapeutic results which are outside the scope of their actual power, and the same procedures effect far more in the hands of a fashionable doctor (who, for instance, may have become well-known as an attendant upon some prominent personality) than in those of another physician. Thus there are human as well as divine miracle-workers. ("Psychical Treatment," 298)

In this case, "therapeutic results" however tenuous, are the materials produced outside the scope of actuality; faith is erased by reputation at the same time that faith—now completely extrinsic—provides a cure under the sign of reputation. Begged is the question of actuality, since the therapeutic results achieved in this case are by definition virtual. One job of the rhetorician—and we see that Freud was himself deeply insightful along these lines—is to explain what it means to be a human miracle worker in this instance, and how the job gets done, persuasive contrivances and all. To reiterate, in this case from Freud, the persuasive contrivance is "reputation" in terms of one lexicon, sacrament in terms of another. Freud's singular accomplishment in this instance is his demonstration of how exactly these two terms are related.

I will conclude with the unsexy recommendation that we continue to sidestep the disenchantment–re-enchantment narrative enabled by Freud and his earlier cohort, while foregrounding instead some new work on inartistic means of persuasion. That means at least two things methodologically. (1) To analyze rhetorically we always need some historical perspective on what is "given" to the rhetorician and what is not, for example, in this chapter, God's word given to the apostle Paul who listened in just the right way. Or a scientifically sanctioned cure given to Freud and his cohort, and then given subsequently to Freud's psychoanalytic patients, including Dora, who evidently listened with some skepticism. Then (2) because there is no such thing as a persuasive word without contrivances, we need to know in each case what these contrivances are, such as Paul's epistles in the first instance, or a reputation in the second. This methodology is traditional insofar as we should continue to ask, like Aristotle, "Which appeals are artful and thus in the hands of the rhetorician, and which appeals are artless?" But unlike Aristotle, whose objectives in that famous treatise were very different, our answer to this question will depend upon the prevailing theory of argumentation and the prevailing scope of rhetorical agency, which is to say historiographic concerns subject to basic research. Hopefully the preceding has shown how much can be gained by doing this kind of historical work, as our interest now turns to extrapersonal communication in all of its ecological, historical, and socio-political richness, while rejecting the primordial *homo religiosus* who, Agamben reminds us, "exists only in the imagination of scholars."[46]

CHAPTER FOUR

Passive Voices, Active Listening

A Case Study in Rhetoric and Composition

"Don't stop for anything!" urges the guru of "expressivist" writing Peter Elbow in his post-6os classic *Writing without Teachers* (1973). And with this directive Elbow aligns his own writerly voice with certain classical advice for cultivating vocal masculinity—most important is simply to press onward without worrying too much about what one says. Moreover, this unintentional alignment nevertheless points to something essential about our current communicative norms as they inform both writing and speech instruction. Hence the arc of this chapter. First, I draw from a range of Roman sources to demonstrate how voice, whether in speech or in writing, carries with it a masculine legacy that persists even now with some surprising consequences for thinking about the public sphere and its accessibility. Then, drawing from Augustine, who was originally trained in this Roman tradition of civic rhetoric, I sketch the alternative habits of an ear tuned to the Word of God. In terms of scholarship, I hope to show how work in the history of rhetoric is essential if we wish to address some of the puzzles of contemporary scholarship, including the decisionism of Krista Ratcliffe's work on rhetorical listening and the ambivalence around voice in composition studies after the feminist and race-critical responses to Elbow. More broadly and beyond the scholarly debates, we will see how this genealogy of communicative organs sharpens our sensitivity to certain composition issues, down to the fundamentals of grammar, where a regular distaste for the passive voice finds unlikely support in antiquated models of gender. Once again, a methodological point is that historical work is integrated with everyday life—in this case even the smallest units of our writing and speech instruction today.

It is no accident that the ideal orator-rhetorician after Cicero insists upon a virility that would mask a dramatic subjection to language, a subjection that threatens to return in the form of logorrhea traditionally known as "mere ornamentation" or its opposite: passive listening imagined as the catatonic condition suffered when one finally stops talking in the plain style. Plutarch, for instance, recommends continuous vocalization as a conduit for masculine vitality, while Lucian advises in his satirical *Rhetorum Praeceptor* that the only rule is not to be silent; press onward! For men, according to Plutarch, "the daily use of the voice in speaking aloud is a marvelous form of exercise, conducive not only to health but also to strength" (*Mor.* 130 AB; qtd. in Gleason), whereas for a woman, warns the gynecologist Soranus, speaking too much precipitates a dangerous decline in menses.[1]

But when, like Lucian, we disparage passive listeners, don't we always condemn ourselves? After all, who are those pathetic auditors at the other end of a rhetor's message? Not me! Who is persuaded by the rhetor's message? Anyone but me! I typically admit to my undergraduates that I can't recall being convinced of anything, although I have changed my mind aplenty. If we are writing teachers, moreover, we make a mistake when we comfortably endorse the active locution "I changed my mind" because it apparently lines up an agent with the subject of the sentence. In fact, I don't change my mind, though sometimes I'd like to think so; the passive construction "my mind was changed" is more appropriate conceptually. By what mechanisms, then, does our imaginary identification so consistently line up with the agent of an utterance rather than the patient?

Symptomatic of a discipline loath to deflate its constituting figure of the ideal orator, rhetoric scholars can learn more from scholars of classical antiquity, including most importantly Maud Gleason and Erik Gunderson, who have plausibly characterized classical rhetoric as a calisthenics of manhood focalized in the voice (Gleason, xxii). Downplaying rhetoric as some historically transcendent language art, Gleason and Gunderson treat rhetoric as a cultural formation that tells us about the classical performance of masculinity first and foremost. Seneca's ideal orator—the "good man speaking well" (*vir bonus decendi peritus*)—is not a neutral person expressing good moral character. Not only is speaking itself tied to virility as a physical act, moral character takes distinctly masculine form when it is tied to public activity. As one stoically inclined Christian, Clement of Alexandria, put it, "To do (*to dran*) is the mark of the man; to suffer (*to paschein*) is the mark of the woman" (Gleason, 70). Indeed, as Gleason points out, the very word that Plutarch selects to characterize a woman speaking is not the basic Greek word for talking (*legein*), but what linguists call a marked form that connotes "babble" or idle chatter: *lalein* (98).[2] Interestingly, my focal icon of late twentieth-century writing instruction, Peter Elbow, complicates the same gender dynamics insofar as he advocates *explicitly* for "babble" as a vocal exercise.

In any case, these initial tropes connecting gender to voice are anything but ancient history. Here are some passages from Elbow's work that start to demonstrate how so: "In your natural way of producing words there is a sound, a texture, a rhythm—a voice—which is the main source of power in your writing. I don't know how it works, but this voice is the force that will make the reader listen to you, the energy that drives the meaning through his thick skull."[3] Then we get these passages of anxious onanism that could only come from those auspicious years when Elbow's "expressivist" model of writing and writing instruction could appear in quite this form. And though it is an affront to our current political sensibilities, it is worth noting that Elbow remains to this day a much-cited icon in writing studies despite such dated formulations:

> There's something scary about being as strong as you are, about wielding the force you actually have.... Therefore, practice shooting the gun off in safe places. First with no one around. Then with people you know and

trust deeply. Find people who are willing to be in the same room with you while you pull the trigger. Try using the power in ways where the results don't matter.[4]

Try to *feel* the act of strength in the act of cutting: as you draw the pencil through the line or paragraph or whole page, it is a clenching of teeth to make a point stick out more, hit home harder. Conversely, try to feel that when you write in a mushy, foggy, wordy way, you must be trying to cover something up: message-emasculation or self-emasculation. You must be afraid of your strength. Taking away words lets a loud voice stick out. Does it scare you? (41–42)

Finally reflecting on his own phallic methodology: "It's scary. I think I'm developing a dependency on this prosthesis for the mind.... I just write flabby, mushy, soupy. No backbone in my head. I'll go blind and insane if I indulge myself in this easiness—if I continue to use this crutch, my organs will dry up and atrophy" (65).

Admittedly my argument in this chapter isn't distinguished by noticing how gender and sexuality work in Elbow's early material. Who could miss it? These issues have been addressed, among other places, in Amy Spangler Gerald's "An Uneasy Relationship: Feminist Composition and Peter Elbow," in James V. Catano's "The Rhetoric of Masculinity: Origins, Institutions, and the Myth of the Self-Made Man," and in "Feminism and Composition: The Case for Conflict," where Susan Jarratt critiques the traditionally gendered distribution of speaking and listening in Elbow's composition theory. And we should not overlook the fact that Elbow himself writes critically about gendered metaphors as far back as 1973, when he decides to tone down for the sake of his emerging professional community (*Everyone Can Write*, 147). Finally, we should carefully consider the positive resonance of Elbow's voice theory and pedagogy with the feminist and race-critical stance of scholars including Carol Gilligan, bell hooks, and June Jordan, whose work is central to the collection *Landmark Essays on Voice*, edited by Elbow himself.

"[T]*here is no passive construction possible in Black English*," declares June Jordan in a famous piece of hyperbole republished by Elbow (italics in the original). Since, according to Jordan, Black English is a language produced by people who constantly need to assert their existence in the face of annihilation, Black grammar insists on "the human being who is here and now/the truth of the person who is speaking or listening," and consequently, ideas expressed in Black English "will necessarily possess that otherwise elusive attribute, *voice*."[5] Not surprisingly, this rule of Black grammar is violated just a few passages later when Jordan cites from a student essay: "That pear tree beautiful to Janie, especially when bees fiddlin with the blossomin pear there growin large and lovely. But personal speakin, the love she get from starin at that tree ain the love what starin back at her in them relationship" (67). Now consider this same passage in so-called standard academic English that mechanically uses the active voice, where an agent performs the action expressed in the verb: "Janie finds the pear tree beautiful, especially when bees fiddle with the pear blossoms growing large and lovely. But ultimately Janie discovers love not in the trees, but in personal relationships." This time, the agent Janie asserts her existence (grammatically) as she "finds" and "discovers," but of course the complexity and the charm of the original passage—not to mention its common sense—dissipate completely. Who says a greater truth is captured or a more durable agent asserted when Janie acts on the pear tree with her faculty of judgment, rather than being affected by it? Is more lost than gained when we delete the apparent redundancy (another Black English allowance) "personal speakin" that confuses what Elbow might call the resonant voice of the student writing with the dramatic voice of the character written about by Hurston?[6] And finally, who is the proper agent of love not as an object found, but rather as a transitive verb? This question in fact drives much of Zora Neale Hurston's *Their Eyes Were Watching God*, and it is captured beautifully in the Black English of Jordan's student writing about the novel, a student who evades the simple formulation "Janie loves x" or absurdly "the tree loves x," settling instead on a subtle formulation where Janie *gets* love not from some obvious subjective agent, but rather in a complex interanimation that involves a range of creatures from trees to bees to others-in-relation. While the ordinary passive construction uses the auxiliary *be* as in "Janie is charmed by the pear tree," *get* is another common auxiliary, as in *get married, get paid, get involved*, and *get caught*, that avoids the passive construction syntactically while semantically exploiting a recipient subject, thereby frustrating those like Jordan who dislike the passive because they ostensibly want agentive subjects. Sometimes it is fair to say I marry you or you marry me, but usually it makes more sense to say that we got married, which captures the appropriate distribution of agency across an event that includes you, me, and the complex social institution without which the act is impossible. So, far from avoiding passive constructions as required by Jordan's language theory in that instance, actual student writing here and elsewhere in the essay uses mediopassive constructions ingeniously. And one would expect as much from a cultural critic like Jordan ultimately interested not only in the truth of the person speaking, but also the truth of the person listening.

In an online "Language Log" entry (accessed August 28, 2008) about the *Dummies* advice to authors Avoid Passive, noted linguist Arnold Zwicky recounts a darkly humorous anecdote from Dr. Alan Rubin, author of *Diabetes for Dummies*, who discussed with his editors the passive-voice rule: "Sometimes I'll write something like 'the patient was comatose and was given thyroid hormone,' and they'll change that to 'the patient was comatose and took thyroid hormone.' ... I have to tell them these are extremely sick patients, they can't take care of themselves, they have to be passive whether Wiley likes it or not."[7] In another entry, "When Men Were Men, and Verbs Were Passive," linguists Mark Liberman and Arnold Zwicky discuss "America's growing anxiety about passivity," which they specify as the verbal voice, not the attitude toward life, though, complains Zwicky, "the composition mavens sometimes get the two mixed up." Zwicky finds the "avoid passive" rule originated in US composition handbooks early in the twentieth century—first in Strunk's hugely popular 1918 *Elements of Style*—along with a metaphorical association between passive verbs and weakness or irresponsibility. And

I would add that scholars of early American composition theory move the timeline back. For instance, Jay Fliegelman wrote about the vocal imperatives of John Wilkes: "The success of a composition rests not on the beauty of its ordered (and, as Wilkes implies, effeminate and class-specific) expression, but on the degree to which its 'nervous [vigorous] manly sense' is permitted to break through the linguistic surface. It is not the admiration of the reader or auditor that one seeks to call forth, but captivated surrender to his or her passions."[8]

No doubt many of our respected venues for grammatical advice such as Purdue's OWL no longer condemn the passive wholesale, choosing instead to clarify the rhetorical implications of passive and active sentence constructions.[9] But Zwicky's criticism still accurately indicts a tradition that includes Elbow himself in *Landmark Essays*, where he discusses the pointed irresponsibility of language that aligns the syntax with the semantics of passivity. Of course Elbow, Jordan, and others are right when they question why we so often find it useful "to produce a voiceless, faceless text—to give the sense that these words were never uttered by a human being but rather just exist with ineluctable authority from everywhere and nowhere ('All students will . . .')—and thus try to suppress any sense that there might be a voice or person behind them" (xxxvii). But Zwicky is also right that distrust of passivity regularly confuses grammatical categories with dubious ethics, sometimes reaching hysterical pitch that improves neither. He rightly questions, for instance, the assumption that "energetic action, strength, and emphasis (rather than reserve) are unalloyed goods." "These are conventionally taken to be MASCULINE qualities," continues Zwicky, "so that a bit of linguistic ideology (about the values of the active vs. the passive) plugs into a bit of non-linguistic ideology (about the values of the masculine vs. the feminine)."[10] In turn, a rhetorician as opposed to a linguist assumes that the fundamentals of language instruction are bound up in particular ways of understanding and being in the world: following Nietzsche and Paul de Man, grammar *is* rhetoric—and not just a propaedeutic *to* rhetoric—insofar as grammar activates subjects and objects in particular situations.[11] Hence the importance of historical work for compositionists and others even when basic grammar is at issue: certain practical challenges in composition pedagogy can only be addressed by historical work that critically frames current practices, while mobilizing latent alternatives. Though admitting he is no cultural historian, Zwicky muses that the priority of a "spare and forceful" active voice in the early twentieth century is connected to "wider social values of the time."[12] But a genealogical outline of voice and ear substantially predates the culture of 1918 Strunk.[13]

A case in point would be the easily exploited confusion we have already seen between grammatical voice and voice as human pronunciation. As John Lyons explains in his canonic *Introduction to Theoretical Linguistics*, the term "voice" (Latin *vox*) was originally used by Roman grammarians in two distinguishable, but related senses: (1) in the sense of "sound" translating the Greek term *phōnē* and (2) in the sense of the "form" of the word: what the word "sounds" like. In turn, this second sense, according to Lyons, has disappeared from modern linguistic theory, giving way to a third sense ultimately derived from it, namely, in reference to the active and passive "forms" of the verb (replacing the Greek rhetorical and musical term *diathesis*). And though Lyons reassures us that there is minimal danger of confusing the phonological with the grammatical sense of "voice" (372), our technical and popular literature on language suggests otherwise. Traditional linguistics explains that the first voice is called active because "the action notionally devolves from the standpoint of the most dynamic, or active, party involved in the situation, typically the Agent," whereas the second voice is called passive because it "encodes action which notionally devolves from the standpoint of a nondynamic, typically static participant in a situation, such as the Patient of a transitive verb."[14] Thus, we are tempted to collapse grammatical agent and patient with the phonological voice that articulates their relationship.

Recommendations for powerful writing—whether from grammarians or compositionists or cultural critics—regularly exploit this confusion when our investments in active voice as the vehicle for agency entails suspicion of passive voice as the vehicle for subjection. Like the younger Seneca, who writes to Lucilius, "as a man speaks, so he lives" (*Epistles* 114.1), we assume that verbal style implicates character: resolute, for instance, in the face of annihilation, as an African American student writes in the active voice (Jordan), or complicit with bureaucracy, as one writes in the passive voice (Elbow). In other words, one important reason why we continue to suspect passive sentence construction despite its stylistic and conceptual advantages is because it supposedly obscures a speaking agent we can aspire to, or judge—which boils down to the same thing in the imaginary register—while foregrounding what we fear, namely the recipient whom we disavow as the abject other who is ultimately ourselves. Meanwhile, that recipient who is most appropriately characterized as the listener—conceived as the passive recipient of someone else's voice—can be reconceived by way of this history of linguistic categories, or alternatively by way of the history of rhetoric and composition.

Among other things this brief tour through linguistic voice illustrates, surprisingly, how the important feminist critique of Elbow shares something crucial with the equally important feminist and race-critical *endorsement* of Elbow's voice work exemplified in Lizbeth A. Bryant's *Voice as Process* and David G. Holmes's *Revisiting Racialized Voice: African American Ethos and Language and Literature*, namely, an insufficiently historicized anxiety that we are patient to someone else's agency, whether that means that we obey without the power to resist, agree without the power to decide for ourselves, get without the power to give back in kind, or listen without the power to speak.[15] Historical work not only identifies more precisely the legitimate grounds for such anxiety in the institutional priority of certain agencies over others, which in turn can generate the rejoinder that winds up in something like Jordan's grammatical imperative. Historical work can also help us identify where a persistent model—in this case a binary model that prioritizes masculine/active/voice over feminine/passive/ear—fails to capture living phenomena such as June Jordan's student essay, or a student essay of our own. Or to put this methodological point in terms of a physics metaphor: the analytics of current culture establish the field empirically—what we see and don't see and in what quantities—while historical work gives us force, allowing us to make claims about where the data is going.

On first glance it might appear that proper morality in classical antiquity divides along gender lines with men as speaking agents in the public sphere and women as subjects listening in private. But it's not so simple. To equate the public voice with masculinity and the private ear with femininity would be misleading, since most obviously women spoke in classical cultures while men listened appropriately, without either suffering the supposed indignities of gender transgression. So how do we distinguish? Gleason provides us with some initial clues when she explains the distinction between vocal exercises for men such as practicing scales and delivering speeches, and vocal exercises for women such as practicing scales and singing or reciting poetry, which was supposed to dry and warm a woman's natural constitution (94–98). However, in emphasizing the mimetic function of listening, whereby the male auditor participates in a spectacle of manliness (Gunderson, *Staging Masculinity* 135), Gunderson joins Gleason in downplaying the masculine auditor as *judge*.

In turn, we might understand the academic prestige of writing-as-criticism—vs. low-status composition—in terms of classical anxieties surrounding agency and the fixation on judgment.[16] Just as we champion active listening over passive listening that would somehow render us suggestible to bad teachers and charlatans from the world of politics and advertising, classical rhetoricians prophylactically invoke the figure of auditor-as-judge. Whether Aristotle's courtroom judge deciding the fate of a plaintiff, or Seneca the Elder's young charge judging deportment in a declamation exercise, passive listening is obscured in the figure of auditory agency. It is honorable to listen and then to judge. It is an exercise of our critical capacities instead of our bodies. It is an affirmation of our civic duties whether explicitly in the public forums of law and politics, or implicitly in ceremony and declamation, where our public persona iterates under the guise of mere theatrics. And to claim honor in judging, to exercise these critical capacities, to thereby affirm our civic duties, is naturally to affirm at the same time our age and our class status (e.g., citizen or foreigner), not to mention our manhood, presuming these claims are available in each case. After all, who in the classical context has access to this honorable disposition of the judge? Generally speaking, not children, slaves, foreigners, or women. Moreover, it is worth considering what price is paid when we valorize "active listening" as the self-evident antidote to passive listening, active voice as the antidote to a writerly passive voice. For the classical response suggests that a dysfunctional gender dynamic remains unresolved when the ear achieves agency only as a vehicle for judgment.

Though Krista Ratcliffe's award-winning book *Rhetorical Listening: Identification, Gender, Whiteness* underscores the "stance of openness" that a person may choose to assume in relation to any person, text, or culture, her inattention to this classical genealogy produces some familiar problems, including most importantly the unnecessary decisionism built into this very definition that emphasizes agency as conscious choice (26). Why must openness take cover in this distinctly modern form of autonomy where we were once directed, in the language of 1990s MTV, to choose or lose? And why not develop a more appropriate language and conceptual scheme of interdependence and responsibility, patience (to exploit a meaningful homonym), even subjection? It appears classical prejudices are built into the defensive posture still operative today in rhetorical theory and practice that urge us respectively to think critically, act up.[17] When Ratcliffe opens her introduction with an epigraph from Jacqueline Jones Royster, "How do we translate listening into language and action ... ?" (1), she helpfully turns our focus to the ear, while at the same time folding that focus back into our familiar action/passion topos, complicit with the US cultural bias identified by popular author Deborah Tannen, where speaking is gendered as masculine and valued positively in a public forum, while listening is gendered as feminine and valued negatively (21). But aren't writing instructors in a different position than critics insofar as one's job is more midwifery and mediation than self-assertion? Or at least shouldn't that be the case? No doubt these are provocative claims in the wake of social movements where autonomy, agency, and voice have been key terms for real political gain. The suggestion is simply that these concepts carry overlooked cultural baggage that sometimes hinder those same social movements, whereas listening-as-patience (instead of agency) and passivity (instead of activity) should be reconsidered potentially rich postures. So what are some of the alternatives? In what follows I will outline one leading alternative drawn from the tradition of sacred rhetoric I've tracked through this book.

· · ·

Parable of the Sower, Matthew 13.9, "He who has ears, let him hear," draws a crucial distinction between the physiological capacity to hear and more subtle inflections of listening that compose the human soul. And when the Jewish philosopher Philo of Alexandria describes the gender-neutral listening practices of the ascetic Therapeutae ("His audience listens with ears pricked up and eyes fixed on him always in one and the same posture, signifying understanding and comprehension by nods and glances" [*The Contemplative Life*, 77]), he introduces an important contrast between superficial and deep listening that we will see again in Augustine. Meanwhile, in this same treatise on the contemplative life, Philo introduces practical strategies for auditory self-mastery that would seed the Christian practices discussed to great effect by Michel Foucault: as civic oratory in the Greek tradition gave way to Roman technologies of the self, Foucault argues, advice for speakers gave way to advice for writers and listeners (chapter 2). Finally, the early Church Father Origen is significant for his Commentary on the Song of Songs, where he elaborates for the first time in the

Christian tradition the union of the bridal soul with the bridegroom Word, thereby complicating easy identification of the ideal subject and the ideal orator. But it is another Church Father and rhetorician in the wake of the Second Sophistic, Augustine of Hippo, who clearly articulates a rhetoric of listening including dimensions of passivity beyond Philo's silent virtuosity.

In his masterpiece on sacred rhetoric, *De doctrina Christiana* (*On Christian Doctrine*), Augustine invokes the listener as the traditional target of discourse—in this case homiletics—though he shows a special sensitivity to the listener's predispositions:

> Just as the listener is to be delighted if he is to be retained as a listener, so also he is to be persuaded if he is to be moved to act. And just as he is delighted if you speak sweetly, so is he persuaded if he loves what you promise, fears what you threaten, hates what you condemn... takes pity on those whom you place before him in speaking as being pitiful, flees those whom you, moving fear, warn are to be avoided; and is moved by whatever else may be done through grand eloquence toward moving the minds of listeners, not that they may know what is to be done, but that they may do what they already know should be done. (4.12.27)

Although the rhetorician as absolute master appears first, this passage ends with the conscience of the listener predisposed for virtue despite the inevitable filters of sin. Sacred eloquence, moreover, will appear for Augustine in the passive voice because ultimately the speaker is not the origin of eloquence. The eloquent words of Scripture, for instance, "seem not to have been sought by the speaker but to have been joined to the things spoken about as if spontaneously, like wisdom coming from her house (that is, from the breast of the wise man) followed by eloquence as if she were an inseparable servant who was not called" (6.10). In other words, sacred eloquence doesn't speak in the active voice but is rather spoken in the passive, at least seemingly. Like his pagan master Cicero, Augustine subordinates feminine eloquence to masculine wisdom and in doing so destabilizes the point of enunciation. But unlike Cicero the model of communication is radicalized by Augustine to the point where the human speaking agent is completely subsumed into a being-spoken: "Whether one is just now making ready to speak before the people or before any other group or is composing something to be spoken later before the people or to be read by those who wish to do so or are able to do so, he should pray that God may place a good speech in his mouth" (30.63).

Also, unlike Cicero or secular rhetoricians of the Second Sophistic, Augustine explicitly takes up the position of the listener as he articulates in great detail how he is subject to Logos, whether that means learning to speak as a child by imitating adult sounds in context (1.8.13), straining out the divine clamor of things in his profane juvenilia *De pulchro et apto* (4.15.27), or traveling by way of the gospel from the exterior to the interior ear, where the voice of the bridegroom can finally be heard: "There it is that I hear Your voice, Lord, telling me that only one who teaches us is speaking to us, and that whoever does not teach us may be speaking, but not to us. Yet who teaches us save Truth unchanging? When from changing creatures we learn anything, we are led to Truth that does not change: and there we truly learn, as we stand and hear Him and rejoice with joy for the voice of the bridegroom, returning to the Source of our being" (*Conf.* 11.8.10). Thus, at the core of our being is a voice, according to Augustine, but that voice is not our own. It is not our personal essence waiting for expression, nor is it our vehicle for the resilient type of agency invoked by June Jordan. Rather, it is the voice of the Other—in this case God—through which we are spoken.[18] Finally, this distinct passivity is articulated at the level of Augustinian grammar. In the tenth book of the *Confessions* 33, for instance, Augustine defends Church music by observing that he is moved "not by the singing but by the things that are sung" (*non cantu, sed rebus quae cantantur*). So, without the passive voice in its grammatical and physiological dimensions, we would have no way to properly articulate the transaction between God and the human soul, and hence no way to live that sacred transaction at all.

Ultimately, then, my project is selectively sympathetic with early Elbow—originally trained as a medievalist—insofar as he accounts for the gendered anxieties of persuasion much like Augustine, where our susceptibility to language is dramatized through competing religious and secular rhetorics. "I think we all fear, to a greater or lesser extent, being taken over, infected, or controlled by a bad or wrong idea," worries Elbow as he takes aim at Western agonistics of the sort we find in the Greek rhetorics of classical antiquity. In contrast, Elbow's "believing game" asks us, as it were, "to sleep with any idea that comes down the road. To be promiscuous. We will turn into the girl who just can't say no. A yes-man. A flunky. A slave. Someone who can be made to believe anything. A large opening that anything can be poured into. Force-fed. Raped" (*Writing without Teachers*, 185).

Well my word.

Now it is difficult to read these words without dismay. But at the same time, these words should not be dismissed, as they grope toward a dramatic history of writing and speaking still at work today, even if we have lost our grasp on exactly how so. In fact, sacred rhetoric through at least the Renaissance encourages a passive disposition toward God's Word-as-truth, with ecstasy replacing Elbow's anxiety. Recall, for instance, the famous formulation from twice-born-again John Donne's *Holy Sonnets* of 1609: "Take me to you, imprison me, for I, / Except you enthral me, never shall be free, / Nor ever chaste, except you ravish me." Or second-wave German reformer Sebastian Franck's bridal soul: "If I let hands and feet droop, despair in myself... cling to and squeeze myself, totally resigned under God and surrender to his almighty work which works in me, courts me and desires to impregnate me, and if I surrender—like Mary—that it might do with me according to its will, suffer patiently and without will, I shall instantly be clothed, overshadowed, slept with and impregnated by the power from on high."[19] Likewise from Elbow we get a masculine, or better a hermaphroditic birth, when he elaborates free writing as "internal cooking" that produces more force and voice in the words and where every cell of the final product contains a microcosm or "gene" of the whole (*Writing without Teachers*, 66). After all, we expect receptivity as the basic disposition of the student we address with our stylistic suggestions, including the paradoxical injunction "avoid passive." And how would we learn such a rule in the first place if we hadn't ourselves been subject to the instruction of others? Finally, we should remember that renaturing in the passive mode need not be apolitical. Elsewhere I have written about the explicitly passive posture that generates Puritan revolutionaries; in modern terms you might think of Gandhi's *satyagraha*. We should remember, moreover, that Elbow's "self revealed in words" (a perfect example of middle voice construction) was originally tied to a passive posture with important political consequences in the larger world: he was a draft counselor supporting conscientious objectors in their efforts to convince draft boards of their sincere opposition to serving in the military.[20] Isn't conscientious objection in times of war a perfect example of how our world can be transformed by way of directed passion-as-suffering, or in Stoic terms, directed inaction?[21]

No doubt, as Gunderson points out and as I have documented throughout this book, a commonplace of rhetorical theory characterizes the orator as a master of other men's hearts and passions (134), while a long tradition associates oratory with either a martial or magical metaphor of compelling the audience (Gleason, 123). But active listening, as it is understood by theoreticians and practitioners of persuasion from classical antiquity through today, only takes off at dusk like Hegel's owl of Minerva, leaving behind obscurities of our daily lives including our susceptibility to advertising, our political apathy, our immersion in commonsense, our lovely credulity, our vulnerability to others, our very capacity to learn and change. We have much work ahead when it comes to the theoretical and practical nuances of listening in its passive dimensions.

APPENDIX

THE ART OF LISTENING IN SELECT ENGLISH MANUALS AND SERMONS, 1582–1665

	Gifford *Parable of the Sower* 1582	Perkins *Foundation of Christian Religion* 1591	Roberts *The Day of Hearing* 1600	Wilkinson *A sermon of hearing* 1602	Harrison *Parable of the Sower & the Seed* 1625	Parr *Grounds of Divinitie* 1625	Taylor *Parable of the Sower & the Seed* 1634	Younge *Victory of Patience* 1636	Burroughes *Gospel-worship* 1647	Shepherd *Ineffectual Hearing of the Word* 1652	Mason *Hearing and Doing* 1656	Younge *Proof of a Good Preacher* 1665
Exodus 5.2 Who is this Lord, that I should obey his voice					p. 48							
Exodus 20.19 Talk with us, and we will hear			p. 4									
Lev. 10.13 I will be sanctified in those that come nigh me									Main theme of the text			
Deut. 5.1 Hear, O Israel, the statutes and judgements										p. 386		
Deut. 5.25, 27–29 Go thou near, and bear all that the Lord our God shall say							p. 157				p. 637	

Deut. 6.6 And these words will be thine in thy heart	pp. 173, 198	
Deut. 28.15 If thou wilt not hearken unto the Lord, all these curses will fall upon you	p. 36	
Deut. 32.46 Moses tells the people to set their hearts to his word		p. 171
Ezra 10.2,3 Story of Shechaniah & Ezra		p. 183
Job 33.16 Then he openeth the ears of men, and sealeth their instruction	p. 64	
Psalms 49.4 I will incline mine ear to a parable	p. 9	

(continued)

	Gifford Parable of the Sower 1582	Perkins Foundation of Christian Religion 1591	Roberts The Day of Hearing 1600	Wilkinson A sermon of hearing 1602	Harrison Parable of the Sower & the Seed 1625	Parr Grounds of Divinitie 1625	Taylor Parable of the Sower & the Seed 1634	Younge Victory of Patience 1636	Burroughes Gospel-worship 1647	Shepherd Ineffectual Hearing of the Word 1652	Mason Hearing and Doing 1656	Younge Proof of a Good Preacher 1665
Psalms 51.8 Make me to bear joy and gladness							p. 324					
Psalms 81 Hear, O my people, and I will testify unto thee												p. 31
Psalms 95.7–10 Harden not your hearts			p. 53		p. 53		p. 110					
Psalms 119 Thy word I have hid in my heart	C						pp. 156, 159, 324			p. 164	pp. 138, 168, 384	
Psalms 138.2 Thou hadst magnified thy word above all thy name									p. 182			
Prov. 1 Because I cried and you did not hear, you will cry and I will not hear									p. 207			

Prov. 2.1–2 Incline thy words to my wisdom	p. 24	pp. 172, 175, 191
Prov. 2.6 Wisdom & knowledge shall preserve		p. 185
Prov. 3.3 Write my mercy upon thine heart	p. 60	
Prov. 4.4–5 Let thine heart retain my words; Neither decline from the words of my mouth	pp. 60, 123, 156	
Prov. 7.24–27 Because I have called and ye refused, I will laugh at your destruction	Ciii	
Prov. 18.9 He that shall turn his ear away from God…	p. 67	

(continued)

	Gifford *Parable of the Sower* 1582	Perkins *Foundation of Christian Religion* 1591	Roberts *The Day of Hearing* 1600	Wilkinson *A sermon of hearing* 1602	Harrison *Parable of the Sower & the Seed* 1625	Parr *Grounds of Divinitie* 1625	Taylor *Parable of the Sower & the Seed* 1634	Younge *Victory of Patience* 1636	Burroughes *Gospel-worship* 1647	Shepherd *Ineffectual Hearing of the Word* 1652	Mason *Hearing and Doing* 1656	Younge *Proof of a Good Preacher* 1665
Prov. 28.9 *He that turneth away his ear from the law shall be abomination*							p. 4					
Isa. 2.3 *Let us go to the mountain of the Lord and be will teach us his ways*		C							p. 170			
Isa. 6.1 *Make our hearts fat, our ears heavy*			p. 57						p. 205	pp. 164–65		
Isa. 6.9, 10 *Open their hearts, ears, and eyes*												
Isa. 30.31 *The Voice of the Lord smote with a rod*					p. 189							
Isa. 42.18–20, 23 *Hear for the time to come*									pp. 156, 190		p. 480	

Reference					
Isa. 55.11 *My word shall not come back to me void*			p. 323		p. 158
Isa. 66 *Poor souls tremble at my word*				p. 181	p. 611
Jer. 4.3 *Let's go to the mountain of the Lord; he will teach us*				p. 168	
Jer. 4.4 *Plow up your fallow fields*	Bviii				
Jer. 6.17 *They said, we will not hearken*			p. 326		
Amos 8.11 *I will send a famine of the hearing of the word*		Ciii			
Matt. 7.26 *For those who hear these things and do them will not be considered foolish*					p. 393

(continued)

	Gifford *Parable of the Sower* 1582	Perkins *Foundation of Christian Religion* 1591	Roberts *The Day of Hearing* 1600	Wilkinson *A sermon of hearing* 1602	Harrison *Parable of the Sower & the Seed* 1625	Parr *Grounds of Divinitie* 1625	Taylor *Parable of the Sower & the Seed* 1634	Younge *Victory of Patience* 1636	Burroughes *Gospel-worship* 1647	Shepherd *Ineffectual Hearing of the Word* 1652	Mason *Hearing and Doing* 1656	Younge *Proof of a Good Preacher* 1665
Matt. 10.14–16 *Those that do not bear disciples' word face grave consequences*							p. 4		p. 200			Title Page?
Matt. 13.20 *He that received the seed into stony places, the same is he that heareth the word and with joy receives it*							p. 63					
Matt. 22.22 *When they heard these words they marveled*							p. 161					
Matt. 28.18, 19 *All power is given unto me; go forth and teach*									p. 201			

Mark 4.24 *Unto you that hear more shall be given*					p. 17	
Mark 8.17–21 *Why do you perceive and not understand; Is your heart hardened?*						p. 162
Mark 13 *Parable of the Sower*	Main theme of the text	B3$_v$	Main theme of the text		p. 168	p. 168
Mark 16.15,16 *Go into the world and preach God's word*					p. 196	
Luke 2.51 *Mary kept these things in her heart*		C		Main theme of Text		pp. 476, 533
Luke 6.48–49 *He that beareth and not doeth is like a man that builds a house without a foundation*		Ci$_v$	p. 188	p. 156	pp. 60–61	pp. 295–96, 711 p. 527

(continued)

	Gifford Parable of the Sower 1582	Perkins Foundation of Christian Religion 1591	Roberts The Day of Hearing 1600	Wilkinson A sermon of bearing 1602	Harrison Parable of the Sower & the Seed 1625	Parr Grounds of Divinitie 1625	Taylor Parable of the Sower & the Seed 1634	Younge Victory of Patience 1636	Burroughes Gospel-worship 1647	Shepherd Ineffectual Hearing of the Word 1652	Mason Hearing and Doing 1656	Younge Proof of a Good Preacher 1665
Luke 8.4 Hearing they might not understand							p. 1					
Luke 8.10 In seeing they might not see, and in hearing they might not bear										p. 157	p. 244	
Luke 8.13 They are on the rock who receive the word of God with joy	Biii_v				B							
Luke 8.18 Take heed, therefore, how you bear				Aiiii_v	Title Page, p. 20	p. 17			pp. 161, 208		p. 443	
Luke 10.18 He that beareth you, beareth me, despiseth you, despiseth me			p. 4									

Luke 10.16 *He that heareth you heareth me*		p. 35				
Luke 11.28 *Blessed are they that bear the word of God and keep it*	p. 189					pp. 2, 298
Luke 12.41 *Story of Martha & Mary*			p. 174			
Luke 16.31 *If you hear not Moses, prophets, you will not be convinced by Christ*				p. 202		
John 2.14 *Word of God abides in you*					p. 191	
John 5.37 *Ye have neither heard his voice, nor seen his shape*						p. 153
John 6.45 *Every man that hath heard, come unto me*						pp. 158, 170

(continued)

	Gifford *Parable of the Sower* 1582	Perkins *Foundation of Christian Religion* 1591	Roberts *The Day of Hearing* 1600	Wilkinson *A sermon of bearing* 1602	Harrison *Parable of the Sower & the Seed* 1625	Parr *Grounds of Divinitie* 1625	Taylor *Parable of the Sower & the Seed* 1634	Younge *Victory of Patience* 1636	Burroughes *Gospel-worship* 1647	Shepherd *Ineffectual Hearing of the Word* 1652	Mason *Hearing and Doing* 1656	Younge *Proof of a Good Preacher* 1665
John 10.27 *My sheep bear my voice*							p. 31					
John 12.48 *He that rejecteth me, and receive not my words, hath one that judge him*											p. 478	
John 15 *If you abide in me, my words in you, you shall have what you ask*	Ciii_v									p. 168		
John 17.20 *I shall pray for those who come unto me through the word*					p. 42							
John 32.34 *That which I know not teach me*									p. 170			

Acts 2.37 When they heard they were pricked in their hearts	p. 182		
Acts 2.41 Converts gladly receiving the word		p. 185	
Acts 3.6 People give heed to what Philip spake			p. 172
Acts 4.20 For we cannot but speak the thing which we have seen and heard		p. 91	
Acts 10.33 Now therefore are we all here present before God, to hear all things that are commanded thee of God	p. 48	p. 325	

(continued)

	Gifford *Parable of the Sower* 1582	Perkins *Foundation of Christian Religion* 1591	Roberts *The Day of Hearing* 1600	Wilkinson *A sermon of hearing* 1602	Harrison *Parable of the Sower & the Seed* 1625	Parr *Grounds of Divinitie* 1625	Taylor *Parable of the Sower & the Seed* 1634	Younge *Victory of Patience* 1636	Burroughes *Gospel-worship* 1647	Shepherd *Ineffectual Hearing of the Word* 1652	Mason *Hearing and Doing* 1656	Younge *Proof of a Good Preacher* 1665
Acts 13.18 Gentiles heard the word and were glad									p. 209			
Acts 13.48 Word of God is glorified									p. 193			
Acts 16.14 Opening of Lydia's heart to the word of God		C			p. 173		pp. 328–29		p. 171		pp. 6, 610	
Acts 17.11 Nobleness of receiving God's word with a readiness of mind									p. 165			
Acts 17.20–21 Thou bringest certain, strange things to our ears							p. 69				p. 514	

Acts 20.32 God's word will give you an inheritance among those who are sanctified	p. 195	
Rom. 1.16 Christ's word is salvation to everyone who believeth		p. 478
Rom. 2.13 The bearer and the doers are just before God		p. 477
Rom. 10.4–5 The word is nigh thee	p. 210	
Rom. 10.9 If you believe, you will be saved	p. 212	
Rom. 10.14 How shall they believe who have not heard? How shall they hear without a preacher?	pp. 23, 324	

(continued)

	Gifford *Parable of the Sower* 1582	Perkins *Foundation of Christian Religion* 1591	Roberts *The Day of Hearing* 1600	Wilkinson *A sermon of hearing* 1602	Harrison *Parable of the Sower & the Seed* 1625	Parr *Grounds of Divinitie* 1625	Taylor *Parable of the Sower & the Seed* 1634	Younge *Victory of Patience* 1636	Burroughes *Gospel-worship* 1647	Shepherd *Ineffectual Hearing of the Word* 1652	Mason *Hearing and Doing* 1656	Younge *Proof of a Good Preacher* 1665
Rom. 10.17–19 *So then faith cometh by hearing, and hearing by the word of God*			pp. 56, 67	Theme of the sermon	p. 42					p. 157		
Rom. 11.8 *God hath given them the spirit of slumber, eyes that they should not see, and ears that they should not hear*										p. 164		
1 Cor. 1.21 *It pleased God by the foolishness of preaching to save them that believed*					p. 45		p. 324					
2 Cor. 4.3–5 *If the gospel is hid, it is hid to all the lost*									p. 202	pp. 159, 169		

Ephes. 1.13 If you bear the gospel of salvation, you are sealed with the Holy Spirit	p. 135
Phil. 2.16 Hold fast to the word of life	pp. 193, 214
1 Thess. 1.5 With the word comes power	p. 213
2 Thess. 2.10 Men give over to spiritual delusion for not receiving truth with love	p. 185
1 Thess. 2.13 Not the word of man, but the word of God	p. 166
2 Thess. 3.1–2 Pray that the word of God has free course among us	pp. 193, 209

p. 43

(continued)

	Gifford *Parable of the Sower* 1582	Perkins *Foundation of Christian Religion* 1591	Roberts *The Day of Hearing* 1600	Wilkinson *A sermon of hearing* 1602	Harrison *Parable of the Sower & the Seed* 1625	Parr *Grounds of Divinitie* 1625	Taylor *Parable of the Sower & the Seed* 1634	Younge *Victory of Patience* 1636	Burroughes *Gospel-worship* 1647	Shepherd *Ineffectual Hearing of the Word* 1652	Mason *Hearing and Doing* 1656	Younge *Proof of a Good Preacher* 1665
2 Tim. 4.3–4 *For the time will come when they have itching ears*											p. 427	
Tit. 1.9 *Hold fast to the faithful word you've been taught*									p. 191			
Heb. 1.1,3 *God speaks to us through his son; the son is better than angels*									p. 173			
Heb. 2.1 *Give more earnest heed to the things which we have heard, lest at any time we should let them slip*							p. 156				p. 714	

Reference							
Heb. 3.7–11 *If today you bear his voice, harden not your hearts*	theme of first sermon	p. 53	p. 113				
Heb. 3.15 *If today you bear his voice, harden not your hearts*							p. 482
Heb. 5.11 *Ye are dull of hearing*	theme of second sermon						
Heb. 4.2 *Word not profitable if not mixed with faith*				p. 43	p. 177		
Heb. 4.12 *Word of God quick & powerful*						p. 196	
Heb. 6.4–8 *It is impossible for those who were once enlightened, once tasted the good word, if they should fall away, to renew themselves to repentance; Word compared to Rain*					p. 121		p. 203

(continued)

	Gifford Parable of the Sower 1582	Perkins Foundation of Christian Religion 1591	Roberts The Day of Hearing 1600	Wilkinson A sermon of hearing 1602	Harrison Parable of the Sower & the Seed 1625	Parr Grounds of Divinitie 1625	Taylor Parable of the Sower & the Seed 1634	Younge Victory of Patience 1636	Burroughes Gospel-worship 1647	Shepherd Ineffectual Hearing of the Word 1652	Mason Hearing and Doing 1656	Younge Proof of a Good Preacher 1665
Heb. 12.19 Which voice they heard intreated that the word should not be spoken to them anymore										p. 159		
Heb. 12.25 What can we escape if we do not bear God's word							p. 4, 36		p. 197			
Jam. 1.19 Let every man be swift to bear		C										
Jam. 1.21 Receive with meekness the word to save your soul							pp. 179, 187			p. 168	pp. 134, 564	
Jam. 1.22 Faithful doer of the word blessed in his deed		Ciii$_v$		Civ					p. 191		p. 394	

Jam. 1.25 *One who is not a forgetful bearer and a doer of the word is blessed indeed*		p. 179
1 Pet. 2.1–2 *The word is a milk you may grow by*	p. 170	
2 Pet. 1.18,19 *This voice in heaven which we have heard*	p. 172	p. 564
Story of David	p. 1	
Parable of the Talents	B	p. 171 p. 176–77

Lessons of the Preachers

	Gifford *Parable of the Sower* 1582	Perkins *Foundation of Christian Religion* 1591	Roberts *The Day of Hearing* 1600	Wilkinson *A sermon of hearing* 1602	Harrison *Parable of the Sower & the Seed* 1625	Parr *Grounds of Divinitie* 1625	Taylor *Parable of the Sower & the Seed* 1634	Younge *Victory of Patience* 1636	Burroughes *Gospel-worship* 1647	Shepherd *Ineffectual Hearing of the Word* 1652	Mason *Hearing and Doing* 1656	Younge *Proof of a Good Preacher* 1665
Listening and Worship												
Many come into church ready to listen, but they only hear non-descript sound, humming, or follow not because they do not hear what came before; this is the work of the Devil; the Devil might take the word from your heart	Avii$_v$ & Aviii				p. 5, 34							
Hearing God's word a part of our worship									p. 162			

A3

Hearing is a duty commanded by God, enjoined by Christ, required by the apostles, and practiced by all good people		
Through listening, we profess our dependence on God for knowing his mind and the way to eternal life	p. 163	
In listening, we come to wait upon God in a way of ordinance	p. 163	
When all the congregation is of one mind, focused on his word, God will send his spirit	p. 64	p. 20
There's but one day a week appointed to listen to God. Don't abuse it by turning your hearing elsewhere	p. 72	

(continued)

	Gifford *Parable of the Sower* 1582	Perkins *Foundation of Christian Religion* 1591	Roberts *The Day of Hearing* 1600	Wilkinson *A sermon of hearing* 1602	Harrison *Parable of the Sower & the Seed* 1625	Parr *Grounds of Divinitie* 1625	Taylor *Parable of the Sower & the Seed* 1634	Younge *Victory of Patience* 1636	Burroughes *Gospel-worship* 1647	Shepherd *Ineffectual Hearing of the Word* 1652	Mason *Hearing and Doing* 1656	Younge *Proof of a Good Preacher* 1665
Active hearing is God's work and we owe Him our wholehearted effort											p. 771	
Your hearts must be continually sown so that you'll have a fruitful harvest at the end of time; multiple hearings may ultimately yield fruitfulness					p. 12					p. 163	p. 376	
How One Should Prepare to Listen												
The profit of hearing depends on the manner of hearing					A5, p. 26						pp. 415–16, 424, 603, 605	
Good hearing requires patience					p. 210							
Prepare yourself to struggle with the Devil's distraction	Aviii_v					p. 40		p. 48				

Being distracted even once is detrimental				p. 7		
Prepare your soul; for you will be hearing the word of God, not merely a man speaking		pp. 3, 68	p. 12	p. 19	p. 166	pp. 603, 642 p. 32
Plow up the fallow ground of your hearts	Bviii	p. 74	p. 17			p. 189
Humble your soul to hear God				pp. 28, 153	p. 168	p. 189 p. 533
Be humbled to your ignorance; you know little of God's mind			p. 17		p. 168	
Create a stillness in your heart	Bvi$_v$			p. 17	p. 168	
Labor to rid the heart of thorns (lust, sins)		pp. 102–3, 151		p. 168		pp. 469–70
Come with the resolution to yield to whatever God has in mind	Aviii$_v$	p. 61		p. 168	pp. 149, 153	pp. 533, 592
					p. 170	

(continued)

	Gifford Parable of the Sower 1582	Perkins Foundation of Christian Religion 1591	Roberts The Day of Hearing 1600	Wilkinson A sermon of hearing 1602	Harrison Parable of the Sower & the Seed 1625	Parr Grounds of Divinitie 1625	Taylor Parable of the Sower & the Seed 1634	Younge Victory of Patience 1636	Burroughes Gospel-worship 1647	Shepherd Ineffectual Hearing of the Word 1652	Mason Hearing and Doing 1656	Younge Proof of a Good Preacher 1665
Pray to God to open your eyes, mind, and your heart				Cii	p. 29	p. 20			p. 171	p. 188	pp. 328, 754	
Come to the word with a hungry heart		C					p. 66		p. 173			
Fight those enemies of attention: straying thought, wandering eyes, needless shifting and stirring of the body, irreverent talking and laughing, sleeping				Bvi$_v$–vii	pp. 30–31	p. 17	pp. 39, 326					
Even if you have good intentions and think of yourself as prepared, and yet hear not, you are not ready; God will not understand							p. 27					

Everyday, exercise yourself in reading the word, meditating on it, conferring and talking of it; also prayer and fasting	p. 30	p. 710
If you don't understand something, ask the learned to explain it	p. 32	
Bring to the word wisdom fitting of your state		p. 603
Come to the word refreshed and ready to do the work of the soul		p. 542
Worldly concerns may keep a man from hearing at all; also keep men from preaching and hinder their prayer and preparation	p. 109	p. 540
	pp. 179–80, 202	

(continued)

	Gifford Parable of the Sower 1582	Perkins Foundation of Christian Religion 1591	Roberts The Day of Hearing 1600	Wilkinson A sermon of hearing 1602	Harrison Parable of the Sower & the Seed 1625	Parr Grounds of Divinitie 1625	Taylor Parable of the Sower & the Seed 1634	Younge Victory of Patience 1636	Burroughes Gospel-worship 1647	Shepherd Ineffectual Hearing of the Word 1652	Mason Hearing and Doing 1656	Younge Proof of a Good Preacher 1665
How One Should Receive / Respond to God's Word												
One must be patient to hear the word of God					pp. 5–6							
You must hide or lock away the word of God in your heart (like a jewel)	Aviii$_v$ C		Aiii$_v$	pp. 5–6, 48	p. 26							
You must set your heart unto it				Bvi								
Not enough to hear; one must hearken, set the word to his/her mind									p. 171			
Give the greatest of that which it seeks												
Understand: your soul depends on it									p. 173			
Open your heart to God	Biiii								p. 174			
									p. 175			

Be careful how you apply God's word						p. 175		
Mix faith with the word; otherwise it is no good						p. 177		
One must hear God's word with a heart trembling in fear	Biiiᵥ C	p. 181						
Your hearts must bow to/lie under the word; must be received with humility, meekness			p. 56			pp. 179, 183		pp. 38–39
Word must be received with love, joy, thanksgiving					p. 5, 66	p. 184		
One must receive the word with an honest heart			pp. 5–6			p. 186	p. 179	
Be not only a hearer of the word, but a doer and save your soul	Cii	p. 172		p. 193	p. 40	p. 25	p. 468	pp. 179, 395, 437
We must keep the word to reap its benefits			p. 194	p. 182				p. 368

(continued)

	Gifford *Parable of the Sower* 1582	Perkins *Foundation of Christian Religion* 1591	Roberts *The Day of Hearing* 1600	Wilkinson *A sermon of hearing* 1602	Harrison *Parable of the Sower & the Seed* 1625	Parr *Grounds of Divinitie* 1625	Taylor *Parable of the Sower & the Seed* 1634	Younge *Victory of Patience* 1636	Burroughes *Gospel-worship* 1647	Shepherd *Ineffectual Hearing of the Word* 1652	Mason *Hearing and Doing* 1656	Younge *Proof of a Good Preacher* 1665
Understand the Word might not have a consistent effect on a hearer										p. 174		
A good hearer continues to hear afterward							p. 156					
The word is a seed and takes time to germinate; the word is rain							pp. 111, 126–27			p. 171	p. 533	
Not retaining the word is the difference between a godly man and a hypocrite							p. 157					
If there is difficulty with the word, the problem lies with the hearer, not the preacher							p. 113				p. 424	p. 15

Power of the Word				
There is more dreadfulness in God's name in the word than in all his works		p. 182		
The word of God makes one tremble	p. 47	p. 157	p. 163	
The word is immortal nourishment		p. 25	pp. 181–82	
God's word is a sword of the spirit and kills our corruptions				p. 39
God speaks directly to the hearer and tailors its message to the hearer		p. 2	pp. 166–67	
Nonbelievers and Sinners: The Effect of the Word upon Them and Questions They Must Ask				
Word too good for a wicked man to know or understand		p. 12		

(continued)

	Gifford Parable of the Sower 1582	Perkins Foundation of Christian Religion 1591	Roberts The Day of Hearing 1600	Wilkinson A sermon of hearing 1602	Harrison Parable of the Sower & the Seed 1625	Parr Grounds of Divinitie 1625	Taylor Parable of the Sower & the Seed 1634	Younge Victory of Patience 1636	Burroughes Gospel-worship 1647	Shepherd Ineffectual Hearing of the Word 1652	Mason Hearing and Doing 1656	Younge Proof of a Good Preacher 1665
The word is given to you in the name of God; is that not an adequate source?									p.178			
If all that I hear spoken against sin and its consequences is true, what state will I be in then?									p.178			
I may question these things now, but what if I were dying?									p.178			
In not believing the words which the very devils fear am I worse than devils?									p.178			
There's a distemper in those with a troubled conscience; when the word comes close to their conscience this distemper rises against God									p.180			

There is a great distance between them and God					p. 159	
Satan has made them blind & deaf					p. 159	
They cannot hear because they are not elect					p. 160	
Putting worldly cares before the instructions of the word is a sign of a hard heart		p. 115				
People that can hear, but refuse are worse than those who cannot comprehend	p. 170					
Why God Is Sanctified in the Word						
Because there is so much of God in his word; God is truly revealed				p. 196	p. 157	
Effectual hearing attains God's heart and his will					p. 159	pp. 485–87, 509

(continued)

	Gifford *Parable of the Sower* 1582	Perkins *Foundation of Christian Religion* 1591	Roberts *The Day of Hearing* 1600	Wilkinson *A sermon of hearing* 1602	Harrison *Parable of the Sower & the Seed* 1625	Parr *Grounds of Divinitie* 1625	Taylor *Parable of the Sower & the Seed* 1634	Younge *Victory of Patience* 1636	Burroughes *Gospel-worship* 1647	Shepherd *Ineffectual Hearing of the Word* 1652	Mason *Hearing and Doing* 1656	Younge *Proof of a Good Preacher* 1665
God appointed the word as a great ordinance to convey special mercies he intends for his people									p. 196			
God's word is twofold: the external voice and the internal voice which speaks secretly to our hearts							p. 325			p. 157		
The word is quick and lively and works one into salvation or damnation									p. 196			
What One Loses by Not Sanctifying the Word of God												
Lose the greatest opportunity for joy/happiness							p. 130		p. 200			

Lose the mercy God's word holds for the elect				pp. 13, 114	p. 200
As the word is rejected, Christ is rejected	Cii				p. 201
Extremely hard of heart will never be convinced by the word	Avi		p. 42	pp. 13, 31, 110, 114	p. 202
It is a sign of reprobation		C	p. 74	pp. 14, 130	p. 202
Nothing can be sanctified to those who do not sanctify God's name in the word	Bv	p. 15		p. 203	
You'll be susceptible to cursing					p. 203
God gave his word for salvation; if not sanctified, this promise will be reversed		C	p. 102		p. 205 p. 164
No comfort in the word on the day of affliction					p. 206

(continued)

	Gifford Parable of the Sower 1582	Perkins Foundation of Christian Religion 1591	Roberts The Day of Hearing 1600	Wilkinson A sermon of hearing 1602	Harrison Parable of the Sower & the Seed 1625	Parr Grounds of Divinitie 1625	Taylor Parable of the Sower & the Seed 1634	Younge Victory of Patience 1636	Burroughes Gospel-worship 1647	Shepherd Ineffectual Hearing of the Word 1652	Mason Hearing and Doing 1656	Younge Proof of a Good Preacher 1665
The Lord will one day make good on his word							p. 14		p. 207			
The word you reject will be the word that judges you							p. 14		p. 207		p. 478	
An evil heart cannot apply the word because it does not hear to know; cannot pray beforehand so it loses all the power of the word							pp. 327–28					
You will be blasted and come to nothing					A3$_v$	p. 208						

How the Hearer of the Word Is Rewarded						
As long as man keeps God's word In their ears, they cannot fully fall away			p. 190			
All the good, joy, peace of the world is yours		p. 172	p. 324	p. 210	pp. 132, 136	
It is certain evidence of your election	C	A3$_v$	p. 213		p. 134	
No better proof of a man's faith than to give care to God's words, understand it, carry it away, and joy in it; faith comes through hearing	Biii$_v$	A3$_v$, p. 41	p. 155	pp. 57, 108		
The word will comfort you in the day of affliction and save you		pp. 21, 196	p. 61		p. 214	p. 39
You will be the glory of the ministers of God at the day of judgment			p. 324		p. 214	

(continued)

	Gifford Parable of the Sower 1582	Perkins Foundation of Christian Religion 1591	Roberts The Day of Hearing 1600	Wilkinson A sermon of hearing 1602	Harrison Parable of the Sower & the Seed 1625	Parr Grounds of Divinitie 1625	Taylor Parable of the Sower & the Seed 1634	Younge Victory of Patience 1636	Burroughes Gospel-worship 1647	Shepherd Ineffectual Hearing of the Word 1652	Mason Hearing and Doing 1656	Younge Proof of a Good Preacher 1665
A good heart hearing the word will increase one's appetite for the word							p. 324				p. 22	
A good heart cannot hear the scriptures without great reverence							pp. 321–22					
Preaching reveals the unsearchable riches of Christ							pp. 322–23					
Preached word brings spirit of God							pp. 322–23					
The word is power against sin										p. 183		

Miscellaneous Information

	Gifford Parable of the Sower 1582	Perkins Foundation of Christian Religion 1591	Roberts The Day of Hearing 1600	Wilkinson A sermon of hearing 1602	Harrison Parable of the Sower & the Seed 1625	Parr Grounds of Divinitie 1625	Taylor Parable of the Sower & the Seed 1634	Younge Victory of Patience 1636	Burroughes Gospel-worship 1647	Shepherd Ineffectual Hearing of the Word 1652	Mason Hearing and Doing 1656	Younge Proof of a Good Preacher 1665
Cannot we stay home and read a sermon? "the great ordinance in preaching of the word, faith comes by hearing, the Scripture faith, and never by reading..."									p. 167		p. 218	
Sermons can, as they say, go in one ear and out the other	Avi											
Private prayer is reserved for the home; the public sphere is for listening			pp. 63–64									
If you have trouble listening, pay attention from the beginning to end; you will come away with some good lesson			p. 73									

(continued)

	Gifford *Parable of the Sower* 1582	Perkins *Foundation of Christian Religion* 1591	Roberts *The Day of Hearing* 1600	Wilkinson *A sermon of hearing* 1602	Harrison *Parable of the Sower & the Seed* 1625	Parr *Grounds of Divinitie* 1625	Taylor *Parable of the Sower & the Seed* 1634	Younge *Victory of Patience* 1636	Burroughes *Gospel-worship* 1647	Shepherd *Ineffectual Hearing of the Word* 1652	Mason *Hearing and Doing* 1656	Younge *Proof of a Good Preacher* 1665
As the Israelites came prepared to hear God at Sinai, so must we				Aiii$_v$								
The hearer is a lock, and the speaker a key				Avi$_v$								
Ears as a sieve				Bvi$_v$								
It is unreasonable for us to expect God to hear us when we do not listen to him				Cii$_v$								
God bestows the gifts of a preacher according to the attentiveness of his audience				Ciii$_v$								
The papist see the mass and do not hear, even though Jesus and the prophets tell us otherwise					A4							
One publishes his sermons so that the simple (those who cannot hear well) can better understand					A5							

Three elements of hearing: Attention, Intention, Retention	p. 21		
A simple mind is no excuse for bad hearing		p. 41	
If you can go to a play and repeat long discourses point for point or stay awake for the performance, you can for the word		pp. 42, 49	p. 723
Riches choke the word in many ways: business keeps men from church, breed contempt for God & his word, make them too happy to seek joy in church, leave no room in heart for the spiritual, hinder profession & confession, hinder practice & obedience		p. 194	

(continued)

	Gifford Parable of the Sower 1582	Perkins Foundation of Christian Religion 1591	Roberts The Day of Hearing 1600	Wilkinson A sermon of hearing 1602	Harrison Parable of the Sower & the Seed 1625	Parr Grounds of Divinitie 1625	Taylor Parable of the Sower & the Seed 1634	Younge Victory of Patience 1636	Burroughes Gospel-worship 1647	Shepherd Ineffectual Hearing of the Word 1652	Mason Hearing and Doing 1656	Younge Proof of a Good Preacher 1665
Marks of a man in whom the world choketh the word: desires after goods rather than grace, speaks more about the material, clogs himself with too much business, unjust in his getting or spending of riches, will not follow the word's instruction							p. 199					
Marks of a man who puts pleasures above the word: undervaluing of better pleasures such as those found in God's house, more joyful at his own tables than at God's, more joy in secular books & dice, delight more in gathering riches than grace, prefer empty							p. 231					

joy before fullness of joy, immoderate sorrow when he cannot obtain worldly pleasures, immoderate fear of death as it's the end of all pleasures	p. 428
You may applaud fine, witty phrases you hear, but like a Cypress tree, it is fine to see but bears no fruit	pp. 431–32
Popular preachers, who use fine turns of phrase only flatter the congregation and do not help them to salvation	p. 479
Five types of bad hearers: headless hearers, partial hearers, forgetful hearers, sensual hearers, and fruitless hearers	
If eating and drinking distract our hearing, we should forego them	p. 627

(continued)

	Gifford Parable of the Sower 1582	Perkins Foundation of Christian Religion 1591	Roberts The Day of Hearing 1600	Wilkinson A sermon of hearing 1602	Harrison Parable of the Sower & the Seed 1625	Parr Grounds of Divinitie 1625	Taylor Parable of the Sower & the Seed 1634	Younge Victory of Patience 1636	Burroughes Gospel-worship 1647	Shepherd Ineffectual Hearing of the Word 1652	Mason Hearing and Doing 1656	Younge Proof of a Good Preacher 1665
We must not measure God's hearing of our suit by his present suit and our sense of the answer								p. 251				
In our unfit supplications we are most heard when our requests are repelled								p. 241				
Good to hear those who recognize our faults whether they be friends or enemies								p. 93				
He who cannot endure words for Christ would never be able to endure wounds for him								p. 85				

NOTES

INTRODUCTION

1. Kenneth Cmiel summarizes:

   I do not see language as so opaque that it inevitably defeats critical reason, and would strongly contest Roland Barthes's assertion that language is essentially fascistic. Responsible language, I would claim to the contrary, is central to the possibility of an antiauthoritarian politics.... Ultimately my sympathies are with those who have worried about the erosion of public debate in the twentieth century, people as diverse as John Dewey, Jürgen Habermas, Hannah Arendt, and C. Wright Mills. Spirited and contentious public discussion by no means assures social harmony or that all interests will be appropriately rewarded, but I do believe that a lively public is a critical element of a flourishing democracy.

   Kenneth Cmiel, *Democratic Eloquence: The Fight Over Popular Speech in Nineteenth-Century America* (New York: W. Morrow, 1990), 18–19.

2. A quick guide to keywords: On apathy and the political virtues of passivity, including humility, see also Daniel M. Gross, *The Secret History of Emotion from Aristotle's "Rhetoric" to Modern Brain Science* (Chicago: University of Chicago Press, 2006), chapters 2–5; on attentiveness and paying attention, see also Susan Bickford, *The Dissonance of Democracy: Listening, Conflict, and Citizenship* (Ithaca, NY: Cornell University Press, 1996); on ignorance, see Jacques Ranciére, *The Ignorant Schoolmaster: Five Lessons in Intellectual Emancipation* (Palo Alto, CA: Stanford University Press, 1991) and Jack [Judith] Halberstam, *The Queer Art of Failure* (Durham, NC: Duke University Press, 2011); on dependency as a precondition for learning, see John Dewey, *Democracy and Education*

(New York: Macmillan, 1916); on belonging, see Aimee Carrillo Rowe, *Power Lines: On the Subject of Feminist Alliances* (Durham, NC: Duke University Press, 2008); on being oriented, see Sara Ahmed, *Queer Phenomenology: Orientations, Objects, Others* (Durham, NC: Duke University Press, 2006); on being addressed, see Darian Leader, "The Voice as Psychoanalytic Object," in *Analysis* 12 (2003), 70–82; on being held accountable and on vulnerability, see Judith Butler, *Giving an Account of Oneself* (New York: Fordham University Press, 2005).

3. Insofar as I work through the human sciences from the perspective of rhetoric, not philosophy, my project has some affinity with the Project on Rhetoric of Inquiry (POROI) initiated in the 1980s by economist Deirdre McCloskey and the political theorist John S. Nelson among others. In a summary piece, Nelson explains how his neighboring disciplines of history, law, literature, economics, anthropology, sociology, and psychology give poor accounts of their own inquiry methods because "each thinks that its rules or procedures of inquiry come fundamentally from philosophy (and, in some cases, secondarily from mathematics or statistics)" instead of rhetoric. My project differs from POROI insofar as I work primarily through disciplinary genealogies, not epistemology and methodology critique. See John S. Nelson, "Approaches, Opportunities and Priorities in the Rhetoric of Political Inquiry: A Critical Synthesis," in *The Recovery of Rhetoric: Persuasive Discourse and Disciplinarity in the Human Sciences*, ed. Richard H. Roberts and James M. M. Good (Charlottesville: University of Virginia Press, 1993), 165.

4. Hannah Arendt, *The Life of the Mind* (New York: Harcourt Brace Jovanovich, 1978), 110. Arendt comments upon Aristotle, *On Sense and Sensible Objects*, 437a4–17, which reads:

> Of these faculties, for the mere necessities of life and in itself, sight is the most important, but for the mind [*nous*] and indirectly [*kata symbebēkos*] hearing is the most important.... [It] makes the largest contribution to wisdom. For discourse, which is the cause of learning, is so because it is audible; but it is audible not in itself but indirectly, because speech is composed of words, and each word is a rational symbol. Consequently, of those who have been deprived of one sense or the other from birth, the blind are more intelligent than the deaf and dumb.

Arendt quips, "The point of the matter is that he [Aristotle] seems never to have remembered this observation when he wrote philosophy" (241n86).

5. For a discussion, see Eric Santner, Kenneth Reinhard, and Slavoj Žižek, *The Neighbor: Three Inquiries in Political Theology* (Chicago: University of Chicago Press, 2005), 12n3.

6. Arendt's footnote leads us to Hans Jonas, *The Phenomenon of Life: Toward a Philosophical Biology* (New York: Harper and Row, 1966) and to his 1934 work on Gnosis, *Gnosis und spätantiker Geist* (Göttingen: Vandenhoeck and Ruprecht, 1934).

7. Bryan Garsten, *Saving Persuasion: A Defense of Rhetoric and Judgment* (Cambridge, MA: Harvard University Press, 2006). See especially Garsten on Hobbes and Rousseau (25–84) who are accused of detaching rhetoric from the Ciceronian tradition of practical judgment (36). In contrast, Andrew Dobson "listens out for" speech rhetorically in his book *Listening for Democracy: Recognition, Representation, Reconciliation* (Oxford: Oxford University Press, 2014).

8. Don Ihde, *Listening and Voice: A Phenomenology of Sound* (Athens: Ohio University Press, 1976); David M. Kleinberg-Levin, *The Listening Self: Personal Growth, Social Change, and the Closure of Metaphysics* (London: Routledge, 1989); G. Corradi Fiumara, *The Other Side of Language: A Philosophy of Listening* (London: Routledge, 1990).

9. *Ars Amatoria* 1.509 quoted in John C. Flügel, *The Psychology of Clothes* (London: Hogarth, 1930), 103.

10. Flügel continues with the speculation that "it is perhaps no mere chance that a period of unexampled scientific progress should have followed the abandonment of ornamental clothing on the part of men at the beginning of the last century" (118). See also Flügel (120) on transvestism and aesthetic empathy.

11. Herbert A. Wichelns, "The Literary Criticism of Oratory," in *Studies in Rhetoric and Public Speaking in Honor of James Albert Winans*, ed. Alexander Magnus Drummond (New York: Century Co., 1925), 182–83.

12. Karen Tracy, James P. McDaniel, Bruce E. Gronbeck, *The Prettier Doll: Rhetoric, Discourse, and Ordinary Democracy* (Tuscaloosa: University of Alabama Press, 2007), 29–30.

> Their engagement began when Dewey reviewed two of Lippmann's books—*Public Opinion* (1922) and *The Phantom Public* (1925)—and took on more detail in Dewey's 1927 book, *The Public and Its Problems*. To Dewey, the patterns of social fragmentation combined with empowerment of economic and political institutions to produce the "eclipse of the public," and to counter them he imagined the cultivation of a social media apparatus that would perform time- and space-binding operations—bringing "the people" closer together and creating common resources of social knowledge—essential to constituting, maintaining, reproducing, and revising a large-scale democracy.... The attitude of Lippmann was far less optimistic. In *Phantom Public*, which marks the transition from agora to phantasmagoria that predominates much theoretical discussion today, Lippmann drew the picture of a society too vast and tangled for commoners to effectively think or talk about it in

determinative ways. In a prelude to detailing arguments for an extraordinary democracy built around a cult of expertise, premised on delegation of "the people's" power to technically competent decision-makers, he remarked: "I have not happened to meet anyone, from a President of the United States to a professor of political science, who came anywhere near to embodying the accepted ideal of the sovereign and omnicompetent citizen."

See also Hadley Cantril who uses Gustav LeBon in his foundational work on public opinion, "Social Psychology of Everyday Life," *Psychological Bulletin* 31 (1934), 297–330.

13. In his foreword, David E. Wellbery describes Kittler's approach:

While Kittler accepts the Lacanian dictum that the unconscious is the discourse of the Other, he reads this formula from the standpoint of Foucault. That is to say, the term *discourse* no longer refers, as in Lacan's rendering, to the linguistic and therefore abstract notion of extended speech, but rather to positive modes of existence of language as shaped by institutions of pedagogy, technical means of reproduction, storage and transfer, available strategies of interpretation, and so on. Likewise the Lacanian Other is for Kittler not the general and sovereign instance of the one Law, but rather (and again, with Foucault) the network of forces and resistances, commands and addresses, that constitute historically specific configurations of domination. (xxi)

14. In *Decolonizing the Mind: The Politics of Language in African Literature* (London: James Curry, 1986), 56–57, Ngũgĩ wa Thiong'o sets up a contrast with demystifying Kamiriithu theater: "Education, far from giving people the confidence in their ability and capacities to overcome obstacles or to become masters of the laws governing external nature as human beings, tends to make them feel their inadequacies, their weaknesses and their incapacities in the face of reality; and their inability to do anything about the conditions governing their lives. They become more and more alienated from themselves and from their natural and social environment. Education as a process of alienation produces a gallery of active stars and an undifferentiated mass of grateful admirers."

15. Ingeborg Bachmann, *Frankfurter Vorlesungen: Probleme zeitgenössischer Dichtung* (Munich, Piper: 1982) referencing Samuel Beckett's, "Dear incomprehension"; Mary R. Lea and Brian V. Street, "Student Writing in Higher Education: An Academic Literacies Approach," *Studies in Higher Education* 23, no. 2 (1998): 157–72; Jerry Won Lee, *The Politics of Translingualism: After Englishes* (New York: Routledge, 2018); Carla Mazzio, *The Inarticulate Renaissance: Language Trouble in an Age of Eloquence* (Philadelphia: University of Pennsylvania Press, 2009); Catherine Nicholson, *Uncommon Tongues: Eloquence and Eccentricity in the English Renaissance* (Philadelphia: University of Pennsylvania Press, 2014);

Jonathan Alexander, Susan C. Jarratt, and Nancy Welch, eds., *Unruly Rhetorics: Protest, Persuasion, and Publics* (Pittsburgh: University of Pittsburgh Press, 2018); Dina Al-Kassim, *On Pain of Speech: Fantasies of the First Order and the Literary Rant* (Berkeley: University of California Press, 2010); Cheryl Glenn, *Unspoken: A Rhetoric of Silence* (Carbondale: Southern Illinois University Press, 2004); Gayatri Spivak, "Can the Subaltern Speak? Speculations on Widow-Sacrifice," *Wedge*, nos. 7–8 (1985): 120–30.

16. See, for example, Susan Bickford, *The Dissonance of Democracy: Deliberation is "paying-attention-to"* (30). The need for attention to others is the very grounding of rhetoric according to Aristotle (41). "What lies between representative thinking on the one hand, and a kind of impossible empathy on the other, is listening" (87). The training of our imagination enables us to hear others better (90). See also Sophia Rosenfeld, "AHR Forum on Being Heard: A Case for Paying Attention to the Historical Ear" (316–34), *American Historical Review* 116, no. 2 (2001): 328 on "listeners rights."

17. For a complex discussion of feminist filmmakers including Mulvey, Ackerman, and especially Cavani, see Silverman, *The Acoustic Mirror*, 187–234. Silverman winds up emphasizing masculine renunciation à la Fassbinder instead of any simpler reversal of the classical cinema apparatus.

18. Gerda Lerner, *The Creation of Patriarchy* (Oxford: Oxford University Press, 1986); Evelyn Fox Keller, *Reflections on Gender and Science* (New Haven, CT: Yale University Press, 1985), plus a 1990 interview by Bill Moyers featuring "theoretical physicist Evelyn Fox Keller on the rhetoric of science"; Susan C. Jarratt, *Rereading the Sophists: Classical Rhetoric Refigured* (Carbondale: Southern Illinois University Press, 1991).

19. Mikkel Borch-Jacobsen contributes to this project in his essay "Analytic Speech: From Restricted to General Rhetoric," collected in John Bender and David E. Wellbery, *The Ends of Rhetoric: History, Theory, Practice* (Stanford, CA: Stanford University Press, 1990), 127–39, where Freudian psychoanalysis is grounded in the rhetorical tradition generally understood as the art of moving souls. In particular Borch-Jacobsen draws attention to Freud's 1890 article on "Psychical Treatment" (*Seelenbehandlung*), where science recuperates the power of persuasion abandoned to magicians, preachers, and healers (130–31). See also *The Emotional Tie: Psychoanalysis, Mimesis, and Affect* (Stanford, CA: Stanford University Press, 1992), 54; chapter 3 of this book.

20. Immanuel Kant, *Critique of Judgment* (Indianapolis, IN: Hackett, [1790] 1987), §53.

21. This argument is pursued in Frank Biess and Daniel M. Gross, *Science and Emotion after 1945: A Transatlantic Perspective* (Chicago: University of Chicago Press, 2014).

22. André Breton, "Manifesto of Surrealism," in *Surrealism*, ed. Patrick Waldberg (New York: Oxford University Press, 1965), 66.

23. Susan Buck-Morss offered this influential formulation in 1989: "Based on the writings of Max Weber, it has become a shibboleth in social theory that the essence of modernity is the demythification and disenchantment of the social world. In contrast, and in keeping with the Surrealist vision, Benjamin's central argument in the *Passagen-Werk* was that under conditions of capitalism, industrialization had brought about a *re*enchantment of the social world ... and through it, ... a 'reactivation of mythic powers.'" Susan Buck-Morss, *The Dialectics of Seeing: Walter Benjamin and the Arcades Project* (Cambridge, MA: MIT Press, 1989), 253–54. Overview can be found in Joshua Landy and Michael Saler, eds., *The Re-Enchantment of the World: Secular Magic in a Rational Age* (Palo Alto, CA: Stanford University Press, 2009). "What we aim to show, in this edited volume, is that modernity produces an entirely new array of strategies, *compatible with secular rationality*, for re-enchanting a disenchanted world. We perceive this as being an exciting new trend in current conceptualizations of Western modernity, particularly as exemplified in such recent works as Simon During's *Modern Enchantments: The Cultural Power of Secular Magic* (Harvard, 2002) and Jane Bennett's *The Enchantment of Modern Life: Crossings, Attachments, and Ethics* (Princeton, 2002)."

24. Principium eiusmodi debet esse ut statim apertis rationibus quibus praescripsimus aut benivolum aut adtentum aut docilem faciamus auditorem; at insinuatio eiusmodi debet esse ut occulte, per dissimulationem, eadem illa omnia conficiamus, ut ad eandem commoditatem in dicendi opere venire possimus (1.7).

25. Martin Heidegger, *History of the Concept of Time: Prolegomena* (Bloomington: Indiana University Press, 1992), 292.

26. Along with the seminal single-author work by Sterne noted above, an introduction to the field of sound studies should include at least the following. Jonathan Sterne, ed., *The Sound Studies Reader* (London: Routledge, 2012) along with deeper reading in the authors included; Michael Bull and Les Black, eds., *The Auditory Culture Reader* (New York: Berg, 2003); Veit Erlmann, ed., *Hearing Cultures: Essays on Sound, Listening and Modernity* (Oxford: Berg, 2004); Peter Szendy, *Listen: A History of Our Ears* (New York: Fordham University Press, 2008); Jean-Luc Nancy, *Listening* (New York: Fordham University Press, 2007);

Veit Erlmann, *Reason and Resonance: A History of Modern Aurality* (New York: Zone, 2010); Shane Butler, *The Ancient Phonograph* (New York: Zone, 2015); Michel Chion, *Sound: An Acoulogical Treatise* (Durham, NC: Duke University Press, 2016); James A. Steintrager and Rey Chow, eds., *Sound Objects* (Durham, NC: Duke University Press, 2019). See also Works Cited with Additional Suggested Readings for key monographs in sound studies.

27. Famously Karl Marx gives us the following in his *Economic and Philosophic Manuscripts of 1844*: "For not only the five senses but also the so-called mental senses, the practical senses (will, love, etc.), in a word, *human* sense, the human nature of the senses, comes to be by virtue of *its* object [durch das Dasein *seines* Gegenstandes], by virtue of *humanized* nature. The *forming* of the five senses is a labor of the entire history of the world down to the present."

28. Classic studies include Jacques Attali, *Noise: The Political Economy of Music* (Minneapolis: University of Minnesota Press, [1977] 1985); R. Murray Schafer, *The Soundscape: Our Sonic Environment and the Tuning of the World* (Rochester, VT: Destiny Books, [1977] 1994).

29. Lisbeth Lipari, *Listening, Thinking, Being: Toward an Ethics of Attunement* (University Park: Pennsylvania State University Press, 2014) is a book that is complementary to mine in some ways. Whereas I am working with Heidegger especially during the Marburg years midcareer, Lipari focuses on late Heidegger working around Heraclitus toward non-instrumental language as it calls: "being's poem, just begun, is man" (quoted on p. 101). I think the ethical attunement Lipari finds beyond Heidegger in a figure like Levinas actually does appear in its nascent form c. 1924, only to be abandoned by Heidegger soon thereafter, as we will see in chapter 1. Other recent works on listening and sound in rhetorical studies include Greg Goodale, *Sonic Persuasion: Reading Sound in the Recorded Age* (Urbana: University of Illinois Press, 2011); Byron Hawk, *Resounding the Rhetorical: Composition as a Quasi-Object* (Pittsburgh: University of Pittsburgh Press, 2018); Steph Ceraso, *Sounding Composition: Multimodal Pedagogies for Embodied Listening* (Pittsburgh: University of Pittsburgh Press, 2018). Again, it is the disciplinary history—and its consequences—that distinguishes my work on the art of listening.

CHAPTER ONE

1. Adam H. Müller, Dennis R. Bormann, and Elisabeth Leinfellner, *Adam Müller's Twelve Lectures on Rhetoric: A Translation with a Critical Essay* (Ann Arbor, MI: Published for University of Nebraska Press by University Microfilms International, 1978), 85.

2. Theodore Kisiel, *The Genesis of Heidegger's "Being and Time"* (Berkeley: University of California Press, 1995), 296–301.

3. When it comes to Heidegger's lectures on Aristotle's *Rhetoric*, shaping his masterwork *Being and Time*, see Daniel M. Gross and Ansgar Kemmann, *Heidegger and Rhetoric* (Albany: State University of New York Press, 2005), especially my introduction "Being-Moved: The Pathos of Heidegger's Rhetorical Ontology," 1–45.

4. Martin Heidegger, *Basic Concepts of Aristotelian Philosophy*, trans. Robert Metcalf and Mark B. Tanzer (Bloomington: University of Indiana Press, 2009).

5. Stanley Rosen, "Phronesis or Ontology: Aristotle and Heidegger," in Riccardo Pozzo, ed., *The Impact of Aristotelianism on Modern Philosophy* (Washington, DC: Catholic University of America Press, 2004), 248. See also Franco Volpi, *Heidegger e Aristotele* (Padua: Daphne Editrice, 1984), 26. Strauss: "By speaking humanly about the human passions, Riezler lets us see incidentally the powerful reasons why he could not have been mistaken or misled about the meaning of 1933. His analysis of the passions are also meant as a critique of the 'narrow humanity' that informs Heidegger's analysis of *Existenz*; they point to the riddle posed by Heidegger's obstinate silence about love or charity on the one hand, and about laughter and the things which deserved to be laughed at on the other." Leo Strauss, *What Is Political Philosophy? And Other Studies* (Chicago: University of Chicago Press, 1959), 259–60.

6. Certain strains of classical and biblical aesthetics tend toward spiritual discernment, as in Proverbs 1.7: "The fear of the LORD is the beginning of knowledge [αἰσθήσεως], but fools despise wisdom and instruction." James I. Porter argues that there is a continuous strand of ancient Greek and Roman theory of art, poetry, and rhetoric that tends less toward intellectual understanding along formalistic lines à la Aristotle, and more toward sensible or "aesthetic" experiences, as they only appear in material objects and performance. *The Origins of Aesthetic Thought in Ancient Greece: Matter, Sensation, and Experience* (Cambridge: Cambridge University Press, 2010).

7. Kisiel, "Rhetorical Protopolitics in Heidegger and Arendt," in Daniel M. Gross and Ansgar Kemmann, eds., *Heidegger and Rhetoric* (Albany, NY: State University of New York Press, 2005), 144: "The rhetor demonstrates his mettle by demonstrating phronesis (practical wisdom, prudence) or resolute openness to the demands exacted by the situation of action, which in one formula in *Being and Time* is characterized as the capacity to listen to (heed, hear) the call of (communal) conscience." See also Michael J. Hyde's career-long work on Heidegger and the call of conscience, for example, *The Call of Conscience:*

Heidegger and Levinas, Rhetoric and the Euthanasia Debate (Columbia: University of South Carolina Press, 2001).

8. Romans 6.12: "Let not sin therefore reign in your mortal body, that ye should obey [ὑπακούειν] it in the lusts thereof." Here is Heidegger on "Phenomenology and Theology" in 1927, *Pathmarks* (Cambridge: Cambridge University Press, 1998), 59: "What does it mean to speak? Does language consist only in converting what is thought into vocables, which one then perceives only as tones and sounds that can be identified objectively? Or is the vocalization of speech (in a dialogue) something entirely different from a series of acoustically objectifiable sounds furnished with a signification by means of which objects are spoken about? Is not speaking, in what is most proper to it, a saying, a manifold showing of that which hearing, i.e., an obedient heeding of what appears, lets be said?"

9. "Therefore the irrational element also appears to be two-fold. For the vegetative element in no way shares in a rational principle, but the appetitive and in general the desiring element in a sense shares in it, in so far as it listens to and obeys it; this is the sense in which we speak of 'taking account' of one's father or one's friends, not that in which we speak of 'accounting' for a mathematical property. That the irrational element is in some sense persuaded by a rational principle is indicated also by the giving of advice and by all reproof and exhortation. And if this element also must be said to have a rational principle, that which has a rational principle (as well as that which has not) will be twofold, one subdivision having it in the strict sense and in itself, and the other having a tendency to obey as one does one's father." Aristotle, *Nicomachean Ethics*, in *The Complete Works of Aristotle*, rev. ed., edited by Jonathan Barnes (Princeton: Princeton University Press, 1984), 1102b34.

10. For example, *Rhetorica ad Herennium* 1.7: Verum hae tres utilitates tametsi in tota oratione sunt conparandae, hoc est, ut auditores sese perpetuo nobis adtentos, dociles, benivolos praebeant, tamen id per exordium causae maxime conparandum est. = "But though this three-fold advantage—that the hearers constantly show themselves attentive, receptive, and well-disposed to us—is to be secured throughout the discourse, it must in the main be won by the introduction to the cause." See also Marjorie Curry Woods, *Classroom Commentaries: Teaching the Poetria nova across Medieval and Renaissance Europe* (Columbus: Ohio State University Press, 2010), 11, on the craftsman metaphor in medieval pedagogy: shaping, fashioning, even violently.

11. Jeffrey Walker, *Rhetoric and Poetics in Antiquity* (Oxford: Oxford University Press, 2000), 9.

12. Thomas Conley, *Rhetoric in the European Tradition* (Chicago: University of Chicago Press, 1990), 178.

13. Brian Vickers, *In Defence of Rhetoric* (Oxford: Oxford University Press, 1988), 272.

14. Martin Heidegger, *Supplements: From the Earliest Essays to "Being and Time" and Beyond* (Albany: State University of New York Press, 2002), 106. Here Heidegger is referencing Martin Luther's "The Question of Man's Capacity and Will without Grace" of 1516.

15. Martin Heidegger, "Phenomenological Interpretations in Connection with Aristotle: An Indication of the Hermeneutical Situation," in *Supplements*, 126; "Phänomenologische Interpretationen zu Aristoteles: Anzeige der hermeneutischen Situation," in Martin Heidegger, *Phänomenologische Interpretation ausgewählter Abhandlungen Aristoteles zu Ontologie und Logik* (Frankfurt am Main: Vittorio Klostermann, 2005).

16. As quoted in Alan G. Gross and Arthur E. Waltzer, eds., *Rereading Aristotle's "Rhetoric"* (Carbondale: Southern Illinois University Press, 2000). Examples are numerous and here are a couple. Eugene Garver writes: "If Aristotle's *Rhetoric* did not exist, it would be hard to argue that the history of philosophy would be any different, since it has not figured in that history. The subject is outside the scope of my project, but it is worth noting that the history of rhetoric would not have been much different without Aristotle's *Rhetoric* either, since its influence even there has been marginal." *Aristotle's "Rhetoric": An Art of Character* (Chicago: University of Chicago Press, 1994), 3–4. Jonathan Barnes writes that "Modern philosophy does not greatly occupy itself with rhetoric" because it is "not an Aristotelian art." *The Cambridge Companion to Aristotle*, Jonathan Barnes, ed. (Cambridge: Cambridge University Press, 1995), 259, 275.

17. Ingemar Düring, *Aristotle in the Ancient Biographical Tradition* (Stockholm: Almqvist & Wiksell, 1957), 462. See also Ingemar Düring, *Aristoteles: Darstellung und interpretation des Denkens* (Heidelberg: C. Winter, 1966), 35ff.

18. Düring, *Aristotle in the Ancient Biographical Tradition*, 465.

19. Ibid., 67–69. See also Paul Moraux, *Les listes anciennes des ouvrages d'Aristote* (Louvain: Ed. Universitaires, 1951).

20. On the important ancient catalog of Diogenes Laërtius, for instance, see Ingemar Düring, *Aristotle in the Ancient Biographical Tradition*, 67–69.

21. Heidegger, "Phenomenological Interpretations," 139. Though Glenn W. Most mistakenly sees the Greeks replacing Christians in Heideggerian thought, he provides a typical and accurate description of Heidegger's distaste for all things Latin. Heidegger frequently denigrated the Latin language and

Roman culture "which he contests for being not only a Roman mediation (and hence betrayal) of Greek philosophy, but also a Christian and medieval Scholastic mediation of Greek paganism." Glenn W. Most, "Heidegger's Greeks," *Arion: A Journal of Humanities and the Classics* 10, no. 1 (2002): 87.

22. Joydeep Bagchee, in his *Bryn Mawr Classical Review* of *Basic Concepts*, provides a succinct summary of Heidegger's publication project around Aristotle.

> In the 1922 essay, Heidegger does not as yet specify Aristotle's *Rhetoric* as presenting us with such a text [that would link the interpretation of the hermeneutic situation to the destructive appropriation of the tradition] but, by the time of the 1924 lecture course, it has become evident that (the interpretation of) Aristotle's *Rhetoric* is to fulfill this precise function. The present work (which establishes the link between human existence and its self-addressing of itself in the Aristotelian *Rhetoric* and unfolds an interpretation of κίνησις from the *Physics*) thus constitutes the *key text* in this project. Indeed, together with his lectures on Aristotle's *Nicomachean Ethics* delivered in winter semester 1924/25 (published as the first half of *Plato's Sophist*), an interpretation of *Nicomachean Ethics* Z, and the text *Phänomenologische Interpretation ausgewählter Abhandlungen Aristoteles zu Ontologie und Logik* from summer semester 1922, an interpretation of *Metaphysics* A 1–2, it constitutes in essence the entire project as laid out in the 1922 essay. The final piece is a lecture course on Aristotle's *Metaphysics* Θ 1–3 given in summer semester of 1931.

23. Werner Jaeger, *Aristotle: Fundamentals of the History of His Development* (Oxford: Clarendon Press, 1934 [1923]), 5. Here is another influential but misleading scheme from Richard McKeon: "By means of their subject matter Aristotle differentiates three sciences: metaphysics, mathematics, and physical or natural science. The purpose of all three is simply knowledge, and they are therefore grouped together as theoretic sciences, to be distinguished by their purpose from the practical sciences, which are directed to action and conduct, and from the productive sciences, which are intended for the making of artificial things. These distinctions are amplified and applied in all of the works of Aristotle." Richard McKeon, *The Basic Works of Aristotle* (New York: Random House, 1941), xxii.

24. Hence also a recent uptake of Heidegger by the "new materialists" including Bruno Latour, and rhetoricians like Thomas Rickert, in his influential work of rhetorical theory *Ambient Rhetoric: The Attunements of Rhetorical Being* (Pittsburgh: Pittsburgh University Press, 2013).

25. Gross and Kemmann, *Heidegger and Rhetoric*, 50.

26. These questions are rhetorical, not the philosophical question of being posed by Heidegger in *Being and Time*, 21 ff.

27. Martin Heidegger, *Nietzsche*, vol. I (New York: Harper & Row, 1979), 48–49.

28. "For in what this will wills, we are only following the towering willing of our *Führer*.... To the man of this unprecedented will, to our *Führer* Adolf Hitler—a threefold 'Sieg Heil!'" (as translated in Bret W. Davis, *Heidegger and the Will: On the Way to Gelassenheit* [Evanston, IL: Northwestern University Press, 2007], 73).

29. In his discussion of fear Heidegger points out that Aristotle's enemy or *Feind* is typically reserved or ironic (257).

30. "In this view, 'epideictic' appears as that which shapes and cultivates the basic codes of value and belief by which a society or culture lives; it shapes the ideologies and imaginaries with which, and by which, the individual members of a community identify themselves; and, perhaps most significantly, it shapes the fundamental grounds, the 'deep' commitments and presuppositions, that will underlie and ultimately determine decision and debate in particular pragmatic forums.... When conceived in positive terms and not simply in terms of lack, epideictic discourse reveals itself (as Perelman recognized) as the central and indeed fundamental mode of rhetoric in human culture" (Walker 9–10); see also Chaïm Perelman and Lucie Olbrechts-Tyteca, *The New Rhetoric* (South Bend, IN: University of Notre Dame Press, 1971), 51.

31. Siegfried Landshut, a Jewish student of Heidegger, wrote in 1925 about a basic alienation of politics-as-human togetherness (*Miteinanderleben*) in the form of failed liberalism that depersonalized politics in the manner of Rousseau as a means for overcoming the contradictions that arise between sovereignty and equality. The result is human division and compromise: *Gegeneinandersein*, which can take the form of nationalist pathos. Siegfried Landshut, *Kritik der Soziologie und andere Schriften zur Politik* (Berlin: Luchterhand, 1969), 302. Also noteworthy in this context is Landshut's critique of mass-mediated public opinion (*öffentliche Meinung*) insofar as it subsumes discussion into the general form of a rhetorical question that takes for granted the shared ground of speaker and auditor (286).

32. The moment is captured by Peter Gordon, *Continental Divide: Heidegger, Cassirer, Davos* (Cambridge, MA: Harvard University Press, 2010), 7: "For Heidegger, human beings are understood to be defined first and foremost by our finitude, which is to say we discover ourselves in the midst of conditions we had no share in creating and cannot hope to control. To be human in Heidegger's view is to be gifted with a special sort of *receptivity*, or openness to the world. This phenomenon of disclosedness lies at the very core of human

existence, deeper than our rationality and before any and all practical action. Not infrequently, critics have noted that this image of human life has its roots in the religious experience of dependency upon God."

33. Rudolf Bultmann, *Faith and Understanding* (Philadelphia: Fortress Press, 1971), 291–92.

34. Heidegger, *Supplements*, 110.

35. "alle gewaltigen, weltumwälzenden Ereignisse nicht durch Geschriebenes, sondern durch das gesprochene Wort herbeigeführt worden sind.... Dabei handelt es sich nicht selten bei den Menschen um die Überwindung von Voreingenommenheiten, die nicht in ihrem Verstand begründet, sondern meist unbewußt, nur durch das Gefühl gestützt sind." Adolf Hitler, *Mein Kampf*, vol. 2 (Munich: Verlag Franz Eher Nachfolger, 1927), 525 and 527; also translated and excerpted in Anton Kaes, Martin Jay, and Edward Dimendberg, *The Weimar Republic Sourcebook* (Berkeley: University of California Press, 1994), 130–31.

36. For example, Jacques Derrida's subtle discussion of Heidegger's 1933 rectorial address ultimately finds refuge in a form of active listening.

> For in all honesty we must make clear the fact that at the very moment at which he runs the risk of placing this thematics of the *Führung* in the service of a determinate politics, Heidegger gives it to be understood that he is breaking in advance with any such service. In its spiritual essence, this free conducting must not give rise to any camp-following [*suivisme*], one should not accord it any following, any follower, any *Gefolgschaft*, any aggregation of disciples or partisans. One can naturally extend to the party what Heidegger says, to exclude them, of the School as academic study, technical apprenticeship, or professional training. Undoubtedly it will be difficult to understand what can be meant by a *Führung* which mandates, demands, or commands without being followed, obeyed, or listened to in any way. However spiritual it be, one will say, it must surely guide. Certainly, Heidegger would say here, but if one finds it difficult to understand, that means that one remains imprisoned in a logic of understanding and does not accede to this freedom of listening, to this fidelity or modality of following which would have no relationship to the mindless following of *Gefolgschaft*. Perhaps. But it is also the case that, on the other hand, if it is not further reduced to its discursive modalities or to interrogative utterances, this questioning belongs through and through, that is to say essentially, to will and to will as the will to know.

Jacques Derrida, *Of Spirit: Heidegger and the Question*, trans. Geoffrey Bennington and Rachel Bowlby (Chicago: The University of Chicago Press, 1989), 43–44.

37. Juan Donoso Cortés (1809–1853) Spanish author and diplomat, alarmed by the proceedings of the French Revolutionary Party 1848–49, denounced

free speech as the enemy of truth in *Ensayo sobre el catolicismo, el liberalismo, y el socialismo considerados en sus principios fundamentales* (Madrid: M. Rivadeneyra, 1851).

38. Compare *Being and Time* on responsibility: "'Being-guilty' also has the signification of *'being responsible for'* [*'schuld sein an'*]—that is, being the cause or author of something, or even 'being the occasion' for something. In this sense of 'having responsibility' for something, one can 'be guilty' of something without 'owing' anything to someone else or coming to 'owe' him" (327). Meanwhile here is a Schmittian passage on skirting responsibility: "Dasein, as a they-self, gets 'lived' by the common-sense ambiguity of that publicness in which nobody resolves upon anything but which has always made its decision. 'Resoluteness' signifies letting oneself be summoned out of one's lostness in the 'they'" (345).

39. Carl Schmitt, *Political Romanticism*, trans. Guy Oakes (Cambridge: MIT Press, 1986).

40. Carl Schmitt, *The Crisis of Parliamentary Democracy*, trans. Ellen Kennedy (Cambridge, MA: MIT Press, 1985), 6.

41. Upset that this postwar reissue appeared with no meaningful qualification of Heidegger's avowed National Socialism, twenty-four-year-old Habermas published a critique in the *Frankfurter Allgemeine Zeitung* (July 25, 1953): "Mit Heidegger gegen Heidegger denken. Zur Veröffentlichung von Vorlesungen aus dem Jahre 1935" ("Thinking with Heidegger against Heidegger. On the publication of lectures from 1935"). Soon thereafter, while working as Theodor W. Adorno's research assistant, Habermas developed contrarily a broad, social-modernization framework for understanding the relationship between the political failures of German philosophers—Heidegger, Schmitt, Jünger, Gehlen—and democracy movements that had taken root elsewhere in the West but not yet securely in 1950s Germany. Habermas drew important analytic distinctions between rational forms of social organization and "pathological" forms, with the root word *pathos* suggesting diagnosis and cure. Under what conditions, he asked, do public spaces and the political public sphere either "betray the pathological traits of anomie or repression," or, alternatively, provide the space for a complex society to cohere normatively, according to "the abstract, legally mediated form of solidarity among citizens?" (21–22). Habermas explains in a 2005 intellectual autobiography that this question motivated his abiding and influential pursuit of "communicative rationality" as a model for reconstructing the norms and procedures by which agreement might be reached by very different sorts of people. Jürgen Habermas, *Zwischen*

Naturalismus und Religion (Frankfurt am Main: Suhrkamp, 2005); translated as *Between Naturalism and Religion* (Cambridge: Polity, 2008).

42. Rudolf Augstein, Georg Wolff, and Martin Heidegger, "Nur noch ein Gott kann uns retten," *Der Spiegel*, May 31, 1976: 193–219. English translation in Thomas Sheehan, *Heidegger: The Man and the Thinker* (Piscataway, NJ: Transaction Publishers, 1981), 45–67.

43. John P. McCormick points us to this passage on modern phantasmagoria in the Susan Buck-Morss essay, "Aesthetics and Anesthetics: Walter Benjamin's Artwork Essay Reconsidered," *October* 62 (1992): "It has the effect of anesthetizing the organism, not through numbing, but through flooding the senses. These simulated sensoria alter consciousness, much like a drug, but they do so through sensory distraction rather than chemical alteration, and—most significantly— their effects are experienced collectively rather than individually." McCormick reminds us that Hobbes intended his automaton, his man-monster-machine to be a "visible Power to keep them in awe" (II, 17), in other words, a "sense-induced distraction of the masses." John P. McCormick, *Carl Schmitt's Critique of Liberalism: Against Politics as Technology* (Cambridge: Cambridge University Press, 1997), 284.

44. Heidegger writes,

> That means: Bolshevism is the "organic," i.e., organized, calculating (and as +) conclusion of the unconditional power of the party along with complete technization. The bourgeois world has not seen and in part still does not want to see today that in "Leninism," as Stalin calls this metaphysics, a metaphysical projection has been performed, on the basis of which in a certain way the metaphysical passion of the current Russian for technology first becomes intelligible, and out of which it brings the technological world into power. That the Russians, e.g., build ever more tractor factories is not what is *primarily* decisive, but instead that the total technological organization of the world is the metaphysical ground of planning and of all operations, and that this ground is experienced from the ground up and unconditionally into the working completion. Insight into the "metaphysical" essence of technology becomes for us historically necessary, if the essence of Western historical man is to be saved.

Martin Heidegger, *Parmenides* (Bloomington: Indiana University Press, 1992), 86.

CHAPTER TWO

1. Arthur E. Walzer, "*Parrēsia*, Foucault, and the Classical Rhetorical Tradition," *Rhetoric Society Quarterly* 43, no. 1 (2013): 1–21. Walzer's article also summarizes the uptake of Foucault and rhetorical studies per se. A lively "Forum

on Arthur Walzer's '*Parrēsia*, Foucault, and the Classical Rhetorical Tradition'" appears in *Rhetoric Society Quarterly* 43, no. 4 (2013): 355–81. Contributors include Pat J. Gehrke, Susan C. Jarratt, Bradford Vivian, and Arthur E. Walzer.

2. Michel Foucault, *The Order of Things: An Archaeology of the Human Sciences* (New York: Vintage, 1970 [1966]), 310.

3. Ibid., 318.

4. "To sum up, I think that if we look for the operator (*opérateur*) of transformation for the transition from natural history to biology, from the analysis of wealth to political economy, and from general grammar to historical philology, if we look for the operator that upset all these systems of knowledge, and directed knowledge to the sciences of life, of labor and production, and of language, then we should look to population." Michel Foucault, *Security, Territory, Population: Lectures at the Collège de France, 1977–1978* (Basingstoke, UK: Palgrave Macmillan, 2007), 78.

5. Michel Foucault, *The Government of Self and Others: Lectures at the Collège de France, 1982–1983* (Basingstoke, UK: Palgrave Macmillan, 2010), 335–36.

6. Paul Oskar Kristeller provides the sketch of early modernity dominant in intellectual history since at least the 1940s. His focus question: "What is the Renaissance philosophy of man?" As it turns out, medieval and Renaissance philosophies can be distinguished according to whether their view of human nature is pessimistic or optimistic. See Paul Oskar Kristeller, "The Dignity of Man," in *Renaissance Concepts of Man and Other Essays* (New York: Harper and Row, 1972), 5.

7. See especially Nancy Struever, "Garin, Camporeale and the Recovery of Renaissance Rhetoric," *Modern Language Notes* 119, no. 1 (2004): 47–55. Struever explains how the Italian program redid the history of philosophy "not as an internalist account of philosophy as a group of disciplines—logic, metaphysics, epistemology—but as responses to a broad range of cultural events" (48). I argue in this book that the rhetorical history of the human sciences has to first untie this rhetoric-philosophy knot, which Foucault also adopts counterproductively.

8. *Theologia rhetorica* lies at the heart of the Trinkaus essay entitled "Themes for a Renaissance Anthropology." The rhetorical theology Trinkaus finds most pronounced in the writing of Lorenzo Valla produced a new understanding of human nature by combining Sophistic-Ciceronian epistemology with the religious eroticism of Augustine. No longer was man a part of a great chain of being, a graduated scale of animal, human, and divine, each segment overlapping with the next; Platonic metaphysics had been definitively left

behind. See Charles Trinkaus, *The Scope of Renaissance Humanism* (Ann Arbor: University of Michigan Press, 1983), 390; A. O. Lovejoy, *The Great Chain of Being: A Study of the History of an Idea* (New York: Harper and Row, 1965). However Trinkaus ultimately treats human nature as a universal concept introduced in extant literature by the Sophists, revised in Plato's *Timeus*, rendered rhetorical in Cicero's *De officiis*, and restored to the Platonic model in the medieval Christian tradition (running through Nemesius of Emesa's fourth-century treatise *De natura hominis* to late medieval Scholasticism), before finding its modern expression in late Renaissance Humanism (343–96).

9. Thus, Stephen Greenblatt's *Renaissance Self-Fashioning*: "Perhaps the simplest observation we can make is that in the sixteenth century there appears to be an increased self-consciousness about the fashioning of human identity as a manipulable, artful process." Stephen Greenblatt, *Renaissance Self-Fashioning: From More to Shakespeare* (Chicago: The University of Chicago Press, 1980), 2. In a way, Greenblatt radicalizes Burckhardt's claim, arguing that the expression of human nature—its rhetoric—actually produced the Renaissance individual. In contrast to Greenblatt I focus on the disciplinary history of rhetoric.

10. The foremost challenger to rhetoric as architectonic of the human sciences is law. See Donald R. Kelley, *History, Law, and the Human Sciences* (London: Variorum, 1984) and *"Altera natura*: The Idea of Custom in Historical Perspective," in *New Perspectives on Renaissance Thought: Essays in the History of Science, Education and Philosophy*, ed. John Henry and Sarah Hutton (London: Duckworth, 1990). Schematically the difference between the two disciplines as architectonics of the human sciences is that rhetoric appeals, whereas law punishes and protects.

11. "Biopower" appears in the first volume of the history of sexuality, *La volonté de savoir* (1976), which translates to "the will to knowledge," significantly, since this subtitle highlights an epistemic and disciplinary analysis that originates in Foucault's earlier work on the human sciences and their institutions. Now biopower is contrasted with the subtractive powers of a sovereign in that the power to take life with the sword becomes one element among others working to "incite, reinforce, control, monitor, optimize, and organize the forces under it: a power bent on generating forces, making them grow, and ordering them." (136). And the two senses of "discipline," bodily control and academic study now merge in characteristic fashion. Though Foucault observes that the great technology of power only consolidates in the nineteenth century, most was in place earlier: "During the classical period, there was a rapid development of various disciplines—universities, secondary schools, barracks,

workshops; there was also the emergence, in the field of political practices and economic observation, of the problems of birthrate, longevity, public health, housing, and migration. Hence there was an explosion of numerous and diverse techniques for achieving the subjugation of bodies and the control of populations, marking the beginning of an era of 'biopower'" (140). Michel Foucault, *The History of Sexuality Volume 1: An Introduction* (New York: Vintage, 1980).

12. Georges Gusdorf, *Introduction aux sciences humaines; Essai critique sur leurs origines et leur développement* (Paris: Les Belles Lettres, 1960); Donald R. Kelly, "*Altera natura*: The Idea of Custom in Historical Perspective," in *New Perspectives on Renaissance Thought: Essays in the History of Science, Education and Philosophy*, eds. John Henry and Sarah Hutton (London: Duckworth, 1990); Roger Smith, *The Norton History of the Human Sciences* (New York: Norton, 1997); Fernando Vidal, *The Sciences of the Soul: The Early Modern Origins of Psychology* (Chicago: University of Chicago Press, 2011).

13. Sachiko Kusukawa, *The Transformation of Natural Philosophy: The Case of Philipp Melanchthon* (Cambridge: Cambridge University Press, 1995); Heinz Scheible, *Melanchthon: Eine Biographie* (Munich: Beck, 1997); Karl Hartfelder, *Philipp Melanchthon als Praeceptor Germaniae* (Nieuwkoop: Graaf, 1964); T. Muther, *Die Wittenberger Universitäts- und Facultäts-Statuten vom Jahre 1508* (Halle: Buchhandlung des Waisenhauses, 1867); C. Scheurl, *Briefbuch, ein Beitrag zur Geschichte der Reformation und ihrer Zeit*, ed. F. von Soden and J.K.F. Knaake (Aalen: Zeller, 1962); Lawrence D. Green and James J. Murphy, eds., *Renaissance Rhetoric Short-Title Catalogue 1460–1700* (Aldershot, UK: Ashgate, 2006).

14. Philipp Melanchthon, "De corrigendis adolescentiae studiis," *Melanchthons Werke in Auswahl: Studienausgabe*, ed. R. Stupperich (Gütersloh: Bertelsmann, 1963), 34–39.

15. τέχνη ἔστι σύστημα ἐγκαταλήψεων ἐγγεγυμνασμένων πρός τι τέλος εὔχρηστον τῶν ἐνὶ τῶι βίωι (Galen, *Definitiones medicinae*). Finem seu utilitatem in omnibus artibus in primis spectandam esse probat ex ipsius artis definitione, quae et Quintiliani causa fuit, cur rhetorices finem tam magna cura libro secundo capite decimo octavo quaesiverit. Philipp Melanchthon, "Praefatio in officia Ciceronis," *Corpus Reformatorum Philippi Melanthonis Opera quae Supersunt Omnia*, vol. II, ed. C.B. Bretschneider and H.E. Bindseil (Halle: C.A. Schwetschke, 1846), 257 (hereafter cited in text as CR).

16. For instance, Flacius Illyricus [Matthias Flacius], *Clavis Scripturae Sacrae, seu de Sermone Sacrarum Literarum*, in 2 vols. (Basel: Johannes Oporinus and Eusebius Episcopium, 1567); Salomon Glassius [Salomon Glaß], *Philologiae Sacrae, qua Totius Sacrosanctae, Veteris et Novi Testamenti, Scripturae, tum Stylus et*

Literatura, tum Sensus et Genuinae Interpretationis Ratio Expenditur, Libri Quinque: Quorum I. II. Generalia de S. Scripturae Stylo & Sensu; III. IV. Grammatica Sacra; V. Rhetorica Sacra, Comprehensa (Jena: Steinmann, 1668 [1623]).

17. Martin Luther, *Dr. Martin Luthers Werke, kritische Gesamtausgabe* (Weimar: Böhlau, 1883–1987), vol. 40/3, 59–60. In the original Latin:

> Recitius leguntur haec in futuro: "Non dabit, ut moveatur pes tuus, neque dormitabit, qui custodit te." Cohaeret autem hic versus cum superioribus. Quia enim instituit Propheta exhortationem ad finem, hoc agit, ut his ceu promissionibus instet, urgeat et hortetur ad retinendam illam fiduciam in auxilium divinum. Est autem summe necessarium adhortari et urgere non solum alios, sed etiam nos ipsos propter illa visibilia et instantia pericula et vexationes. Quia enim ista, quae contristant, praesentia sunt, contra quae consolantur, sunt absentia, ideo opus est, dum durant praesentia, quae vexant, ut verbo excitemur ad perseverantiam et patientiam. Est enim haec experientia coniungenda cum doctrina. Nam oculi nostri multo sunt obtusiores, quam ut possint ad invisibilia ista pertingere et finem praesentium afflictionum videre. Hinc fit, ut natura semper circumspiciat de modo, quo liberari possit, et dum eum non videt, sicut est absconditus et invisibilis, cruciatur. Opus est igitur adhortationibus, ut ista (liceat enim sic loqui) naturalis brevitas seu angustia cordis nostri dilatetur, magnificetur, ac prolongetur.... Rhetoricatur igitur Spiritus sanctus iam, ut exhortatio fiat illustrior.

Note the deponent form *rhetoricatur*, which has a passive form but an active meaning.

18. Klaus Dockhorn, "Rhetorica movet: Protestantischer Humanismus und karolingische Renaissance," in *Rhetorik: Beiträge zu ihrer Geschichte in Deutschland vom 16.–20. Jahrhundert*, ed. Helmut Schanze (Frankfurt am Main: Athenaion, 1974); "Luthers Glaubensbegriff und die Rhetorik," *Linguistica Biblica* 21–22 (1973): 19–39; and Dockhorn's famous review of Hans-Georg Gadamer's *Wahrheit und Methode*, in *Göttingische Gelehrte Anzeigen* 218 (1966): 169–206. For a bibliography on the topic of Luther and Rhetoric see Reinhard Breymayer, "Bibliographie zum Thema 'Luther und die Rhetorik,'" *Linguistica Biblica* 21–22 (1973): 39–44.

19. On this topic see especially Debora K. Shuger, *Sacred Rhetoric: The Christian Grand Style in the English Renaissance* (Princeton, NJ: Princeton University Press, 1988).

20. Alterum officium est postea inventa intelligere, agnoscere, et tanquam dictata accipere. Ab hoc officio nominatur intellectus patiens. Vidit Aristoteles in omni vita, in artibus, in consiliis publicis et privatis, in stratagematibus, in poëtica, in eloquentia, alios aliis perspicaciores esse, et inventione plus valere: Alios inventa intelligere, et suis cogitationibus anteferre, ut Themistocles suadens, ut cives relicta urbe naves ingrediantur, plus valet intellectu

faciente, quam alii, sed coeteri intelligunt consilium et adprobant. Philipp Melanchthon, *Liber de Anima*, CR Vol. 13, 148.

21. Erasmus's translation of Galen: Agite igitur, o pueri . . . ad cognoscendas artes animum appellite . . . scientes quaecunque artes nihil adferunt utilitatis ad vitam, has artes non esse. Quoted in Olaf Berwald, *Philipp Melanchthons Sicht der Rhetorik* (Wiesbaden: Harrassowitz, 1994), 12.

22. Daniel Georg Morhof, *Polyhistor Literarius Philosophicus et Practicus*, rev. ed. (Lubeck: Petri Bockmanni, 1714).

23. For the history of this distinction see Hans-Georg Gadamer, "The Significance of the Humanist Tradition for the Human Sciences," in *Truth and Method*, 2nd rev. ed. (New York: Crossroad, 1989), 3–42.

24. Richard McKeon, "Aristotle's Conception of Moral and Political Philosophy," *Ethics: An International Journal of Social, Political, and Legal Philosophy* 51, no. 3 (1941): 290. McKeon's influential *Basic Works of Aristotle* (New York: Random House, 1941) separates (1) natural sciences (2) moral and political philosophy—that is, the practical sciences—and (3) rhetoric and poetic.

25. Eric R. Wolf, *Anthropology* (New York: W. W. Norton, [1964] 1974), 88: "It is in part history, part literature; in part natural science, part social science; it strives to study men both from within and without; it represents both a manner of looking at man and a vision of man—the most scientific of the humanities, the most humanist of sciences."

26. See my article "Foucault's Analogies, or How to Be an Historian of the Present without Being a Presentist," *Clio: A Journal of Literature, History and the Philosophy of History* 31, no. 1 (2001): 57–82.

27. In Blumenberg, *Wirklichkeiten, in denen wir leben. Aufsätze und eine Rede* (Stuttgart: Reclam, 1981) 104–36. Partially translated as Hans Blumenberg, "An Anthropological Approach to the Contemporary Significance of Rhetoric," in *After Philosophy: End or Transformation?* ed. Kenneth Baynes, James Bohman, and Thomas McCarthy (Cambridge, MA: MIT Press, 1987), 433, 456.

28. See Ivo Strecker, "The *Genius Loci* of Hamar," *Northeast African Studies* 7, no. 3 (2000): 85–118.

29. A concept derived from Christian Norberg-Schulz, *Genius Loci: Towards a Phenomenology of Architecture* (London: Academy Editions, 1980); and Martin Heidegger, "Building Dwelling Thinking," translated in *Poetry, Language, Thought* (New York: Harper Colophon Books, 1971).

30. Or fleshed out in Lloyd F. Bitzer's seminal definition: "Rhetorical situation may be defined as a complex of persons, events, objects, and relations presenting an actual or potential exigence which can be completely or partially removed if discourse, introduced into the situation, can so constrain human

decision or action as to bring about the significant modification of the exigence." Lloyd F. Bitzer, "The Rhetorical Situation," *Philosophy and Rhetoric* 1, no. 1 (1968): 1–14. Critiques of Bitzer's rhetorical situation that emphasize the *production* of identities and social relations would also have a hard time articulating the kind of cultural history that I'm advocating here. See for instance Barbara Biesecker, "Rethinking the Rhetorical Situation from within the Thematic of 'Différance,'" *Philosophy and Rhetoric* 22, no. 2 (1989): 110–30.

31. On this literature see also Ceri Sullivan, "The Art of Listening in the Seventeenth Century," *Modern Philology* 104, no. 1 (2006): 34–71; Arnold Hunt, *The Art of Hearing: English Preachers and Their Audiences, 1590–1640* (Cambridge: Cambridge University Press, 2010); Wes Folkerth, *The Sound of Shakespeare* (London: Routledge, 2002), especially chapter 2, "The Public Ear," which begins with the appearance of that phrase in *Antony and Cleopatra* 3.4.5.

32. Neil Rhodes, *Shakespeare and the Origins of English* (Oxford: Oxford University Press, 2004); Robert Robinson, *The Art of Pronunciation* (Menston, UK: Scolar Press, 1969 [1617])

33. Here I have paraphrased Hugh Roberts, *The Day of Hearing* (London: J. Barnes, 1600), 63.

34. Jeremiah Burroughes, *Gospel-Worship, 1. Hearing the Word* (London: P. Cole and R. W., 1647), 167.

35. John Newman, B. Grosvenor, Thomas Bradbury, Jabez Earle, William Harris, and Thomas Reynolds, *Practical Discourses Concerning Hearing the Word; Preach'd at the Friday Evening-Lecture in Eastcheap* (London: Printed by J. Darby, 1713), 9.

36. Thomas Taylor, *The Parable of the Sower and of the Seed* (London: T. Purfoot, 1634), 42.

37. Charles Bernstein, ed., *Close Listening: Poetry and the Performed Word* (New York: Oxford University Press, 1998), introduction 3–16.

38. Ibid.; Bruce R. Smith, *The Acoustic World of Early Modern England: Attending to the O-Factor* (Chicago: The University of Chicago Press, 1999).

39. Waters does try with some success to rediscover the lyrical "touch," as he puts it, but his failure to situate this move in a critical history of the senses limits the impact.

40. George Herbert, *The Works of George Herbert* (Chestnut Hill, MA: Adamant Media, 2006).

41. Ibid., 16.

42. The leading intellectual history is Martin Jay, *Downcast Eyes: The Denigration of Vision in Twentieth-Century French Thought* (Berkeley: University of California Press, 1993).

43. Giorgio Agamben's *Homo Sacer: Sovereign Power and Bare Life* (Stanford, CA: Stanford University Press, 1998), 3.

44. See also Judith Butler on social death and a life worth living, including the interview with Fina Birulés, "Gender Is Extramoral," *MR Zine*, May 16, 2009, http://mrzine.monthlyreview.org/2009/butler160509.html.

45. Robert Esposito, *Bíos: Biopolitics and Philosophy* (Minneapolis: University of Minnesota Press, 2008); Ian Hacking sums up his own work: "I have long been interested in classifications of people, in how they affect the people classified, and how the affects [sic] on the people in turn change the classifications." In Hacking's "10 ways of making people" one can easily recognize Foucault's influence at the level of epistemology and his history of the human sciences: "1. Count! 2. Quantify! 3. Create Norms! 4. Correlate! 5. Medicalise! 6. Biologise! 7. Geneticise! 8. Normalise! 9. Bureaucratise! 10. Reclaim our identity!" Ian Hacking, "Making Up People," *London Review of Books* 28, no. 16 (2006): 23–26. See also Ian Hacking, *Rewriting the Soul: Multiple Personality and the Sciences of Memory* (Princeton, NJ: Princeton University Press, 1995).

46. Michael Hardt writes that Foucault needs the discovery of biopolitics to grapple fully with politics. Michael Hardt, "Militant Life," *New Left Review* 64 (2010): 159. He continues, "The militancy of the ancient Cynics, however, is clearly an entirely different politics of life. Biopolitics is the realm in which we have the freedom to make another life for ourselves, and through that life transform the world. Biopolitcs is thus not only distinct from biopower but also may be the most effective weapon to combat it" (159).

47. Jared Sexton, "The Social Life of Social Death: On Afro-Pessimism and Black Optimism," *InTensions* 5 (2011): 1–47.

CHAPTER THREE

1. Martin Heidegger, *Being and Time* (New York: Harper & Row, 1962), 219.

2. As of March 26, 2019, the caption loosens the interpersonal focus this way: "At its foundation, Communication focuses on how people use messages to generate meanings within and across various contexts, and is the discipline that studies all forms, modes, media, and consequences of communication through humanistic, social scientific, and aesthetic inquiry." http://www.natcom.org/discipline/.

3. My ecological rhetoric here is thus connected to Nathaniel Rivers and Ryan Weber, "Ecological, Pedagogical Public Rhetoric," *College Composition and Communication* 63, no. 2 (2011): 187–218; Jenny Edbauer, "Unframing Models of

Public Distribution: From Rhetorical Situation to Rhetorical Ecologies," *Rhetoric Society Quarterly* 35, no. 4 (2005): 5–24; Thomas Rickert, *Ambient Rhetoric: The Attunements of Rhetorical Being* (Pittsburgh: University of Pittsburgh Press, 2013).

4. For a breakdown of professional subfields see, for instance, the University of Iowa Communication Studies Department areas of specialization, or "clusters," which "cohere around understanding and explaining how different modes and media of communication shape people's everyday lives." The clusters are (1) interpersonal communication and relationships, (2) media studies, and (3) rhetoric and public advocacy. Peters and Baxter have both been distinguished professors in this department, representing media studies and interpersonal communication respectively. http://clas.uiowa.edu/commstudies/research. Website accessed March 28, 2019.

5. *The Seminar of Jacques Lacan: Book I, Freud's Papers on Technique, 1953–1954*, ed. Jacques-Alain Miller (Cambridge: Cambridge University Press, 1988), 266.

6. Kevin A. Johnson summarizes how Burke mentions a Freudian influence on the following concepts: rationalization vs. analysis, comic frame, audience persuasion, cluster criticism, surrealist ingredient in art, purposive forgetting, proportional strategy, matriarchal symbolizations, prayer and chart in literary criticism, occupational psychosis, scapegoating, perfection, terministic screens, the negative, the guilt cycle, beauty and sublimity, original sin, motive, and identification. Kevin E. Johnson, "Burke's Lacanian Upgrade: Reading the Burkean Unconscious through a Lacanian Lens," *KB Journal: The Journal of the Kenneth Burke Society*, 6, no. 1 (2009).

7. Quoted in Christian Lundberg, *Lacan in Public: Psychoanalysis and the Science of Rhetoric* (Tuscaloosa: University of Alabama Press, 2012), 60.

8. Joshua Landy and Michael Saler, eds., *The Re-Enchantment of the World: Secular Magic in a Rational Age* (Palo Alto, CA: Stanford University Press, 2009). See also for instance Morris Berman, *The Reenchantment of the World* (Ithaca, NY: Cornell University Press, 1981); Jane Bennett, *The Enchantment of Modern Life: Attachments, Crossings, and Ethics* (Princeton, NJ: Princeton University Press, 2001).

9. The game looks one way to dialecticians Horkheimer and Adorno and another way to Landy and Saler, who call their approach "antinomial" (3), but zero-sum it remains: "each time religion reluctantly withdrew from a particular area of experience, a new, thoroughly secular strategy for re-enchantment cheerfully emerged to fill the void" (1).

10. Sigmund Freud, "Psychical (or Mental) Treatment," in *The Standard Edition of the Complete Psychological Works of Sigmund Freud—Volume 7 (1901–1905)* (London: Hogarth Press, 1968), 283.

11. Collected in John Bender and David E. Wellbery's still provocative volume, *The Ends of Rhetoric: History, Theory, Practice* (1990). Via Borch-Jacobsen among others, including most importantly Emmanuel Levinas, Diane Davis develops a related post-Freudian rhetoric focusing on basic affectability and openness to the other, not contrivances that might just be things brought to bear. Diane Davis, *Inessential Solidarity: Rhetoric and Foreign Relations* (Pittsburgh: University of Pittsburgh Press, 2010).

12. Translations from Aristotle are from George A. Kennedy, *On Rhetoric: A Theory of Civic Discourse* (New York: Oxford University Press, 1991). For a discussion of this distinction before Aristotle, see David Mirhady, "Non-Technical Pisteis in Aristotle and Anaximenes," *The American Journal of Philology* 112, no. 1 (1991): 5–28. See also: Cicero, *De oratore*, 2.116; *De inventione*, 2.46; *Topica*, 24; *Partitione oratatoria*, 48; Quintilian 5.1–7. Christopher Carey, "'Artless' Proofs in Aristotle and the Orators," collected in Edwin Carawan, ed., *Oxford Readings in the Attic Orators* (Oxford: Oxford University Press, 2007), 231, explains: "Even 'artless' proofs allow scope for ingenuity, and we find the scope exploited in practice in Greek oratory in the fifth and fourth centuries, even if it is not enshrined in theory." Carey focuses on the ways in which the wording of a challenge became more significant at the same time that artificial proof assumed a dominant role in Athenian litigation (232); he also discusses drafting techniques (238), selective quotation (238) and arrangement (239). Kennedy (38) has this to say in a footnote about inartistic ethos, which also becomes a central concern for Renaissance rhetoricians: "Aristotle thus does not include in rhetorical ethos the authority that a speaker may possess due to his position in government or society, previous actions, reputation for wisdom, or anything except what is actually contained in the speech and the character it reveals. Presumably, he would regard all other factors, sometimes highly important in the success of rhetoric, as inartistic; but he never says so." Later (184) Kennedy admits, "In religious discourse unsupported maxims made by an authoritative teacher can be effective, as in the case of many sayings of Jesus." As I start with Aristotle, this project revises the perspective of Plett on intertextuality: "This concept [intertextuality] is not based on an interpretation of classical authorities such as Aristotle but is extracted from the commonplaces themselves." Heinrich F. Plett, "Rhetoric and Intertextuality", in *Rhetorica: A Journal of the History of Rhetoric* 17, no. 3 (1999): 316. See also Ann Moss, *Printed Commonplace-Books and the Structuring of Renaissance Thought* (Oxford: Clarendon Press, 1996).

13. See Gottfried Mader, "Foresight, Hindsight, and the Rhetoric of Self-Fashioning in Demosthenes' Philippic Cycle," *Rhetorica: A Journal of the History of*

Rhetoric 25, no. 4 (2007): 339–60. Mader analyzes Demosthenes's self-fashioning in the Philippic cycle as rhetorical process, focusing crucially "on the role of foresight as constituent of symbouleutic authority and justification for his uncompromising political line."

14. Edward P. J. Corbett and Robert J. Connors, *Classical Rhetoric for the Modern Student* (Oxford: Oxford UP, 1965); Patricia Bizzell and Bruce Herzberg, eds., *The Rhetorical Tradition: Readings from Classical Times to the Present*, 2nd ed. (New York: Bedford/Saint Martin's, 2000); Sharon Crowley and Debra Hawhee, *Ancient Rhetoric for Contemporary Students*, 5th ed. (Longman, 2011); Thomas Sloan, ed., *Encyclopedia of Rhetoric* (Oxford: Oxford University Press, 2001); Gert Ueding and Bernd Steinbrink, *Grundriss Der Rhetorik: Geschichte, Technik, Methode* (Stuttgart: Metzler, 1986).

15. Gerald A. Hauser, *Introduction to Rhetorical Theory*, 2nd ed. (Long Grove, IL: Waveland, 2002), 120. Hauser favors the language of "internal" and "external" appeals.

16. An early and still visionary scholarly book along these lines is Debora K. Shuger, *Sacred Rhetoric: The Christian Grand Style in the English Renaissance* (Princeton, NJ: Princeton University Press, 1998).

17. Quintilian, *The Orator's Education*, ed. and trans. Donald A. Russell (Cambridge, MA: Harvard University Press, 2002), 5.1:

> To begin with it may be noted that the division laid down by Aristotle has met with almost universal approval. It is to the effect that there are some proofs adopted by the orator which lie outside the art of speaking, and others which he himself deduces or, if I may use the term, begets out of his case. The former therefore have been styled ἄτεχνοι or *inartificial* proofs, the latter ἔντεχνοι or *artificial*. To the first class belong decisions of previous courts, rumours, evidence extracted by torture, documents, oaths, and witnesses, for it is with these that the majority of forensic arguments are concerned. But though in themselves they involve no art, all the powers of eloquence are as a rule required to disparage or refute them. Consequently in my opinion those who would eliminate the whole of this class of proof from their rules of oratory, deserve the strongest condemnation.

18. Quintilian, *The Orator's Education*, 5.7.35–36. Augurs interpret auspices, which are signs like the flight patterns of birds, as opposed to oracles which are supposed to be unmediated.

19. Quintilian (ibid., 5.11.42) knows this tradition of Socrates's oracle; he also relates Cicero's use of divine testimony. See Fredrick J. Long, *Ancient Rhetoric and Paul's Apology: The Compositional Unity of 2 Corinthians* (Cambridge: Cambridge University Press, 2004), 47. In particular, Long finds interesting the distinction that Quintilian makes between supernatural evidence (*divina testimonia*) and

divine arguments (*divina argumenta*): "When such arguments [appealing to the gods] are inherent in the case itself they are called supernatural evidence; when they are adduced from without they are styled supernatural arguments." Technically, Long points out, "When analyzing a speech, it is difficult to determine whether evidence is external or internal to the case; the inclusion of the former would technically fall under artificial proof" and he references (Carey 1994, 95–96) on these ambiguities. "The most important evidence that Paul mustered in his defense is divine. I have already noted his reliance on the Spirit as evidence of the efficacy of his ministry. Paul had also called God to witness against him in 1.23 in anticipation of the covenantal exhortation in 5.11–7.1. However, Paul argued throughout 2 Corinthians explicitly and implicitly that God approved of him." Especially noteworthy is that Cicero (*Part. Or.* 2.6) lists types of divine evidence (*testiominia*) that includes oracles (*oracula*), auspices (*auspicia*), prophecies (*vaticinationes*), and answers of priests, augurs, and diviners (*responsa sacerdotum, haruspicum, coniectorum*).

20. Jaroslav Pelikan in *Divine Rhetoric: The Sermon on the Mount as Message and as Model in Augustine, Chrysostom, and Luther* (Crestwood, NY: St. Vladimir's Seminary Press, 2001) emphasizes, like Kennedy, the continuities from classical Athenian rhetoric (primarily Aristotle) to the Hellenistic environment of early Christianity. A contrary and very helpful perspective is Carol Poster, "*Ethos*, Authority, and the New Testament Canon," in Thomas H. Olbricht and Anders Eriksson, *Rhetoric, Ethic, and Moral Persuasion in Biblical Discourse* (New York: Continuum, 2005), 118–37. Poster argues that early Christian rhetoric— including the distinction between extrinsic and intrinsic proof—cannot be understood in the tradition of Aristotle; instead, it must be more closely associated with Hellenistic handbooks such as those of Dionysius of Halicarnassus and Anonymous Seguerianus, who composed with different courtroom settings in mind. First, "[t]he tendency for handbooks to shift their emphasis from intrinsic to extrinsic *ethos* and from *logos* (reasoning which is part of the orator's art) to *pragmata* (extrinsic evidence) reflects a shift in judicial procedures, from classical Athenian and Republican Roman ones, which emphasized fine speeches with elaborate rhetorical flourishes, to Greco-Roman courtrooms, which emphasized facts and detailed knowledge of the law" (130). Then, early Christian arguments over authority exhibit the same preferences, Poster argues, whereby "extrinsic connection with Jesus and apostolic succession were among the strongest arguments for the authority of a person or text" (136–37). Relevant primary sources include Seguerianus Anonymus and Apsines. See Mervin R. Dilts and George A. Kennedy, *Two Greek Rhetorical*

Notes / 209

Treatises from the Roman Empire: Introduction, Text, and Translation of the Arts of Rhetoric, Attributed to Anonymous Seguerianus and to Apsines of Gadara (Leiden, Netherlands: Brill, 1997); especially Apsines 6; Anon. Seg. 145. Also *Julius Victor* 21.19 and 44.2–13; *Fortunatianus* 2.23–25.

21. R. W. Serjeantson, "Testimony: The Artless Proof," in *Renaissance Figures of Speech*, ed. Sylvia Adamson, Gavin Alexander, and Katrin Ettenhuber (Cambridge: Cambridge University Press, 2007).

22. As early as 1597 Francis Bacon had published a mixed commonplace book under the title *Essays, Religious Meditations, Places of perswasion and disswasion*. See Plett and Moss. As opposed to the cento that tended toward formal unity in the poetic tradition, a commonplace book tended toward types of organization including occasional, alphabetical, encyclopedic, and others.

23. See the introductory article by Marie Okáčová, "Centones: Recycled Art or the Embodiment of Absolute Intertextuality?" in *Laetae segetes iterum*, 2007. Also see George Hugo Tucker, "Justus Lipsius and the *Cento* Form," in Erik De Bom, *(Un)masking the Realities of Power: Justus Lipsius and the Dynamics of Political Writing in Early Modern Europe* (Leiden, Netherlands: Brill, 2011).

24. For a discussion, see Mirhady, "Non-Technical Pisteis in Aristotle and Anaximenes."

25. Thomas Wilson, *The Rule of Reason, Conteinying the Arte of Logique* (London: Richard Grafton, 1551).

Of the place called authoritie, otherwise named sentences of the sage [:] AL suche testimonies maie be called sentences of the sage, whiche are brought to confirme anye thyng, either taken out of olde authours, or els suche as haue bene vsed in this commune life. As the sentences of noble men, ye lawes in anie realme, quicke saiynges, prouerbes, that either haue bene vsed heretofore, or bee nowe vsed. Histories of wise philosophers, the iudgementes of learned men, the commune opinion of the multitude, olde custome, auncient fashions, or anie suche like. Testimonies, are two waies considered. For either they are such as pertayne to God, or els to man. Those authorities which come from God, and are spoken by the holy ghost, are vndoubtedly true, neither can they be false: therefore we ought moste reuerentlie to receiue the worde of God, & agre to such textes as are writen & spoken, euen as though we heard God him selfe speake, with liuely voice vnto vs. Mans autority hath no such great force, although noble men, learned Philosophers, and stoute capitaines haue pronounced manie thynges moste wiselie.... Hereunto myght be added all suche sentences as by the lawe of nature are graffed in man. As these folowyng. Do as thou wouldest be done vnto. Be thankefull to hym, that doth the a pleasure. Honoure thy father, & thy mother. Know there is a God. He that hath not these opinions naturally fastened in his hart, he maie iustely bee thought rather a beast, then man endued with reason.

See also discussion in Serjeantson, "Testimony: The Artless Proof," 180.

26. Thomas Wilson, *The Art of Rhetoric*, ed. Peter E. Medine (University Park: Pennsylvania State University Press, 1994), 45. In his *Art of Rhetoric* Wilson juxtaposes the terms "artificial" and "plain," as he explains scriptural exegesis: "Notwithstanding, the ancient fathers, because they did only expound the Scriptures for the most part, made no artificial narration but used to follow such order as the plain text gave them" (141).

27. See also for example, Richard Sherry, *A Treatise of Schemes and Tropes* (London: 1550), where the discussion falls in the section on "Figures of Sentence": "So when proposicions be found, remaineth argumentacion or proues, called in Greke *Pistis*, because they make suretye of a doutefull thyng. Of proues some be artificiall, some vnartificial. Vnartificial be, foreiudgementes, rumoures, tormentes, tabelles, othe, wytnesses, diuinacion, oracles. To these be referred whych the Greekes cal *Symeia* or sygnes: For they also commonlye are not set by the wytte of hym that disputeth, but are ministred otherwyse. They be called signes properlye, whyche rysynge of the thynge it selfe that is in question come vnder the sences of menne"; John Rainolds, *John Rainolds's Oxford Lectures on Aristotle's "Rhetoric,"* ed. Lawrence D. Green (Newark: University of Delaware Press, 1986): "But all of these [teach, delight, move] are achieved using proofs arising from the case itself as well as proofs extrinsic to the case. How can this be denied? Does not Justin Martyr teach, when he proves that God is one, by using only the testimonies of pagan men?" (171).

28. "What is an Artificial Argument? That which argueth of it self" (2). In Thomas Hobbes (anonymous publication), *A compendium of the art of logick and rhetorick in the English tongue. Containing all that Peter Ramus, Aristotle, and others have writ thereon: with plaine directions for the more easie understanding and practice of the same.* Includes: Robert Fage, *The Art of Persuasion, or a Compendium of Logick* [a reprint of Fage, *Peter Ramus ... his Dialectica in two bookes*, 1632]; Dudley Fenner, *The Art of Rhetorick plainly set forth, by a concealed author* [a reprint of Fenner, *The artes of logike and rhethorike*, 1548, bk. 2]; Thomas Hobbes, *A brief of the art of rhetorick* [1637]; "Sophistry" [an extract from Fenner, *The artes of logike and rhethorike*, 1548, bk. 3]. See Lawrence D. Green and James J. Murphy, *Renaissance Rhetoric Short-Title Catalogue 1460–1700* (Aldershot, UK: Ashgate, 2006).

29. John Morgan, *Godly Learning: Puritan Attitudes towards Reason, Learning, and Education, 1560–1640* (Cambridgeshire: Cambridge University Press, 1986), 107. Perry Miller, *The New England Mind: The Seventeenth Century* (Cambridge, MA: Harvard University Press, 1954). Miller writes about Ramus at Harvard:

"Although Peripatetics found this distinction absurd, for the Ramists it provided a place in logic for such arguments as could not be established by demonstration, particularly for revealed theology, which was the supreme example of the argument inartificial" (130).

30. Christopher Marlowe, *The Massacre at Paris with the Death of the Duke of Guise*, in *The Complete Works of Christopher Marlowe*, vol. 5, ed. Edward J. Esche (Oxford: Clarendon Press, 1998), 334, but adopting all of Dyce's emendations and further emending the Octavo's reading *"ipsi dixi"* according to Serjeantson, above.

31. By way of contrast, see Leon Howard, "'The Invention' of Milton's 'Great Argument': A Study of the Logic of 'God's Ways to Men,'" *Huntington Library Quarterly* 9, no. 2 (1946): 149–73.

> What Milton wanted illumined in him was his dark vision of the complex nature of that "great argument"—the cause—which was so absolutely coupled with its effect of death and woe and loss of Paradise. He was aware of many "inartificial" arguments related to that effect in the form of divine and human testimony; but although he had a profound faith in divine testimony, having frequently used it as the final argument in his controversial prose writings, the purpose he had set for himself was the discovery of a higher argument which had the power of proof within itself. "When the deepest truth *or nature* of things is carefully sought out," his logic had taught him, "testimony has little force for proof" (p. 281). "And divine testimony," he added, "affirms or denies that a thing is so and brings about that I believe; it does not prove, it does not teach, it does not cause me to know or understand why things are so, unless it also brings forward reasons" (p. 283).

32. Giambattista Vico, *The New Science of Giambattista Vico* (Ithaca, NY: Cornell University Press, 1968). For a fuller account of this historiography see Daniel M. Gross, "Metaphor and Definition in Vico's New Science," *Rhetorica: A Journal of the History of Rhetoric* 14, no. 4 (1996): 359–81.

33. Important works in philosophy on these lines include David Chalmers, foreword to *Supersizing the Mind: Embodiment, Action, and Cognitive Extension* by Andy Clark (Oxford: Oxford University Press, 2008); Michael Wheeler, *Reconstructing the Cognitive World: The Next Step* (Cambridge, MA: Harvard University Press, 2005); and Evan Thompson, *Mind in Life: Biology, Phenomenology, and the Sciences of Mind* (Cambridge, MA: Harvard University Press, 2007).

34. Sigmund Freud, *Group Psychology and the Analysis of the Ego: The Standard Edition* (New York: W. W. Norton, 1975), 86.

35. Sigmund Freud, *Totem and Taboo: Some Points of Agreement between the Mental Lives of Savages and Neurotics: The Standard Edition* (New York: W. W. Norton, 1950), 141.

36. Maclean, *Interpretation and Meaning in the Renaissance* (78n42). "It would, of course, be argued by many today that there is no such thing as a *probatio inartificialis* or unmediated, brute fact."

37. We also find the term in Sigmund Freud, *Jokes and Their Relation to the Unconscious: The Standard Edition* (New York: W.W. Norton, 1989): "Words are disfigured by particular little additions being made to them, their forms are altered by certain manipulations [*Veranstaltung*] (e.g., by reduplications or '*Zittersprache*'), or a private language may even be constructed for use among playmates. These attempts are found again among certain categories of mental patients" (153). And in *Group Psychology:* "We may further emphasize, as being specially instructive, the relation that holds between the contrivance [*Veranstaltung*] by means of which an artificial group is held together and the constitution of the primal horde. We have seen that with an army and a Church this contrivance [*Veranstaltung*] is the illusion that the leader loves all of the individuals equally and justly. But this is simply an idealistic remodelling of the state of affairs in the primal horde, where all of the sons knew that they were equally *persecuted* by the primal father, and *feared* him equally" (72).

38. For instance, Richard Weaver, in *Language Is Sermonic* (Baton Rouge: Louisiana State University Press, 1985), acknowledged that logic alone was not enough to persuade a human being, who is "a pathetic being, that is, a being feeling and suffering" (205). He felt that societies that placed great value on technology often became dehumanized. Like a machine relying purely on logic, the rhetorician was in danger of becoming "a thinking robot" (207). Hence Weaver writes about language as "suprapersonal" (35).

39. See also Kenneth Burke on administrative rhetoric in *A Rhetoric of Motives* (Berkeley: University of California Press, 1962), 158–66: "[T]he point to note for our purposes is that in both cases the rhetoric includes a strongly 'administrative' ingredient. The persuasion cannot be confined to the strictly verbal; it is a mixture of symbolism and definite empirical operations.... We might put it thus: the nonverbal, or nonsymbolic conditions with which both lover and ruler must operate can themselves be viewed as a kind of symbolism having persuasive effects. For instance, military force can persuade by its sheer 'meaning' as well as by its use in actual combat" (161). For a sustained treatment of Freud and Burke on identification, see Davis, *Inessential Solidarity*, ch. 1.

40. Kenneth Burke, *Attitudes toward History* (Berkeley: University of California Press, 1984), 47.

41. Kenneth Burke, *Permanence and Change: An Anatomy of Purpose* (Berkeley: University of California Press, 1984): "a statement is an attitude rephrased in

accordance with the strategy of revision made necessary by the recalcitrance of the materials employed for embodying this attitude" (255). See also Lawrence J. Prelli, Floyd D. Anderson, and Matthew T. Althouse, "Kenneth Burke on Recalcitrance," *Rhetoric Society Quarterly* 41, no. 2 (2011): 97–124.

42. In *The Philosophy of Literary Form: Studies in Symbolic Action* (Berkeley: University of California Press, 1974), Burke writes: "Magic, verbal coercion, establishment or management by decree, says, in effect: 'Let there be'—and there was. And men share in the magical resources of some power by speaking 'in the name of' that power" (3).

43. Sigmund Freud, *Dora: An Analysis of the Case of Hysteria* (New York: Collier, 1963), 53. "It follows from the nature of the facts which form the material of psycho-analysis that we are obliged to pay as much attention in our case histories to the purely human and social circumstances of our patients as to the somatic data and the symptoms of the disorder" (12). See also (71) on hysteria cured by marriage and normal sexual intercourse (112) on Dora "reclaimed once more by the realities of life."

44. Fritz Lang's *Nibelungen* (1924) to *Triumph of the Will* (1934): "These patterns collaborate in deepening the impression of Fate's irresistible power. Certain specific *human ornaments* in the film denote as well the omnipotence of dictatorship." Quoted in Karsten Witte, "Introduction to Siegfried Kracauer's 'The Mass Ornament,'" *New German Critique* 5 (1975), 61. With the aid of the radios, the living room is transformed into a public place, mythical powers of the mass are exploited for the appearance of elevation (62). Lundberg, in *Lacan in Public*, is correct that this psychoanalytic tradition has typically focused on the imaginary register; in this chapter I focus on the objectivity of something like Kracauer's living room scene building an argument about irreducible historicity.

45. Greek κοινωνία (koinonia) in 1 Corinthians 10:16; The King James Version has "The cup of blessing which we bless, is it not the *communion* of the blood of Christ? The bread which we break, is it not the *communion* of the body of Christ?"

46. Giorgio Agamben, *The Sacrament of Language: An Archaeology of the Oath* (Stanford, CA: Stanford University Press, 2011), 12: "In the human sciences, beginning at the end of the nineteenth century, the idea that explaining a historical institution necessarily means tracing it back to an origin or context that is sacred or magico-religious is so strong." Agamben's point about our bogus historiography recalls Jacqueline de Romilly's characterization of Gorgias in *Magic and Rhetoric in Ancient Greece* (Cambridge, MA: Harvard University Press,

1975): "Sacred magic rested on faith; Gorgias' magic rests on the notion that all truth is out of reach. Sacred magic was mysterious; Gorgias' magic is technical. He wants to emulate the power of the magician by a scientific analysis of language and of its influence. He is the theoretician of the magic spell of words" (16). Agamben's point is that this technical tour de force takes advantage of a recurring structural opportunity instead of marking a decisive historical turning point.

CHAPTER FOUR

1. See Cicero, *De oratore* 18.59 and *De officiis* 1.128–30 on masculine deportment. Meanwhile *De oratore* 97 (as discussed by Connolly) characterizes the grand style as a tool for manipulation designed "to pull minds, to push them in every possible way," while begging the question of how one listens to the grand style. Joy Connolly, "Virile Tongues: Rhetoric and Masculinity," in *A Companion to Roman Rhetoric*, ed. William J. Dominik and Jon Hall (Oxford: Blackwell, 2007), 83–97. Passages from Seneca and Soranus are discussed in Maud W. Gleason, *Making Men: Sophists and Self-Presentation in Ancient Rome* (Princeton, NJ: Princeton University Press, 1995), 92–96; Lucian in Erik Gunderson, *Staging Masculinity: The Rhetoric of Performance in the Roman World* (Ann Arbor: University of Michigan Press, 2000), 174. See Connelly for a brief bibliography on the topic and Roisman on masculinity in the Attic orators. Joseph Roisman, *The Rhetoric of Manhood: Masculinity in the Attic Orators*, (Berkeley: University of California Press, 2005).

2. The definitive work on this topic is forthcoming from Samuel McCormick, *The Chattering Mind: A Conceptual History of Everyday Talk* (Chicago: University of Chicago Press, 2020).

3. Peter Elbow, *Writing without Teachers* (New York: Oxford University Press, 1973), 6.

4. Peter Elbow, *Writing with Power* (New York: Oxford University Press, 1981), 300.

5. June Jordan, "Nobody Mean to Me Than You: And the Future Life of Willie Jordan," in *Landmark Essays on Voice and Writing*, ed. Peter Elbow (Mahwah, NJ: Hermagoras Press, 1994), 64.

6. In *Landmark Essays*, xxiv–xxxviii, Elbow distinguishes among a family of related meanings: (1) audible voice or intonation in writing; (2) dramatic voice in writing; (3) recognizable or distinctive voice in writing; (4) voice with authority, "having a voice"; (5) resonant voice or presence. And though we will

see how Elbow occasionally collapses a discussion of grammatical voice into these quasi-ethical categories, he is more careful about this collapse than many compositionists critiqued by Zwicky. In *Everyone Can Write*, for example, Elbow advises: "Talking about ineffective writing in terms of voice tends to bring about quicker improvements than talking in terms of, say, heavy nominalization, passive voice, or *ethos*." *Everyone Can Write: Essays Toward a Hopeful Theory of Writing* (New York: Oxford University Press, 2000), 227.

7. For those who want to see a publication along these lines, see Liberman and Pullman, where passive voice and bias in Reuters headlines is discussed in a chapter on "Some Disastrously Unhelpful Guidance on Usage." Mark Liberman and Jeffrey K. Pullman, *Far from the Madding Gerund and Other Dispatches from Language Log* (Wilsonville, OR: William, James & Co., 2006), 191.

8. Jay Fliegelman, *Declaring Independence: Jefferson, Natural Language, and the Culture of Performance* (Palo Alto, CA: Stanford University Press, 1993), 188.

9. "While active voice helps to create clear and direct sentences, sometimes writers find that using an indirect expression is rhetorically effective in a given situation, so they choose passive voice. Also, writers in the sciences conventionally use passive voice more often than writers in other discourses. Passive voice makes sense when the agent performing the action is obvious, unimportant, or unknown or when a writer wishes to postpone mentioning the agent until the last part of the sentence or to avoid mentioning the agent at all. The passive voice is effective in such circumstances because it highlights the action and what is acted upon rather than the agent performing the action" (accessed August 28, 2008).

10. For a richer history see Miriam Brody, *Manly Writing: Gender, Rhetoric, and the Rise of Composition* (Carbondale: Southern Illinois University Press, 1993).

11. Paul de Man, *Allegories of Reading: Figural Language in Rousseau, Nietzsche, Rilke, and Proust* (New Haven, CT: Yale University Press, 1982). For a related perspective in composition studies see Laura R. Micciche, "Making a Case for Rhetorical Grammar," *College Composition and Communication* 55, no. 4 (2004): 716–37; Martha Kolln, "Rhetorical Grammar: A Modification Lesson," *English Journal* 85, no. 7 (1996): 25–31.

12. In his *Handbook of Morphology*, written with Andrew Spencer, Zwicky defines voice simply as "a category of morphosyntactic properties distinguishing the various thematic relations that may exist between a verb and its subject," including the passive voice where the subject is the *theme* rather than the agent of the verb. Andrew Spencer and Arnold M. Zwicky, eds., *The Handbook of Morphology* (Oxford: Blackwell, 1998), 29.

13. Building on influential work of Emile Benveniste, Philippe Eberhard shows us how one latent alternative emerges from the history of grammar categories including the middle voice, which is an ancient construction persisting in English when an intransitive verb appears active but expresses a passive event, as in June Jordan's preferred grammar where "get" appears syntactically active but semantically passive ("the love she get from starin at the tree"). Though he doesn't share my rhetorical framework, Eberhard similarly explores how we "listen to language and the Word." Philippe Eberhard, *The Middle Voice in Gadamer's Hermeneutics: A Basic Interpretation with Some Theological Implications* (Tübingen: Mohr Siebeck, 2004), 1.

14. M. H. Klaiman, *Grammatical Voice* (Cambridge: Cambridge University Press, 1991), 3.

15. Lizbeth A. Bryant, *Voice as Process*, forward by Peter Elbow (Portsmouth, NH: Boynton/Cook, 2005); David G. Holmes, *Revisiting Racialized Voice: African-American Ethos in Language and Literature* (Carbondale: Southern Illinois University Press, 2004).

16. Quintilian 6.2.1–2: "Thus we have still before us a subject which both offers the most powerful means of securing our aims, and is much more difficult than anything we have discussed above: I mean the business of affecting the judges' minds, shaping them to our wishes, and, one might say, transfiguring them."

17. See, for instance, Rickert's discussion of Lester Faigley's influential effort to articulate within postmodern composition a "broad theory of agency that would lead directly ... to political action" (*Fragments*, 39). Thomas Rickert, *Acts of Enjoyment: Rhetoric, Žižek, and the Return of the Subject* (Pittsburgh: University of Pittsburgh Press, 2007), 73. Lester Faigley, *Fragments of Rationality: Postmodernity and the Subject of Composition* (Pittsburgh: University of Pittsburgh Press, 1992).

18. Mladen Dolar distinguishes the divine voice as a positivity that would relegate the subject to a passive stance of carrying out orders from "the voice as a pure call which commands nothing specific and offers no guarantee. In one and the same gesture it delivers us to the Other and to our own responsibility." *A Voice and Nothing More* (Cambridge, MA: MIT Press, 2006), 98. Also noteworthy is Dolar's discussion of the living voice (*mündlich*; *de vive voix*) that grounds written testimony in German and French Civil Code (108) much as rhetorical speech (e.g., authorial voice) serves as a guarantor, we might observe, of written composition.

19. Sebastian Franck, *280 Paradoxes and Wondrous Sayings* (Lewiston, NY: Edwin Mellen, 1986), 414–15.

20. Richard Boyd, "Writing without Teachers, Writing against the Past?" in *Writing with Elbow*, ed. Pat Belanoff (Logan: Utah State University Press, 2002), 9.

21. Finally, we should remember Elbow's skillful listener who acts not so much as a judge, but rather as a psychoanalyst uncovering "the gap that speakers are trying to hide" (*Landmark*, xlii).

WORKS CITED WITH ADDITIONAL SUGGESTED READINGS

Adorno, Theodor W. "On the Fetish-Character in Music and the Regression of Listening." In *Essays on Music: Theodor W. Adorno*, edited by Richard Leppert, 288–317. Berkeley: University of California, 2002.

———. "On Popular Music: Theory about the Listener." *Studies in Philosophy and Social Science* 9 (1941): 17–48.

Agamben, Giorgio. *Homo Sacer: Sovereign Power and Bare Life*. Stanford, CA: Stanford University Press, 1998.

———. *The Sacrament of Language: An Archaeology of the Oath*. Stanford, CA: Stanford University Press, 2011.

Ahmed, Sara. *Queer Phenomenology: Orientations, Objects, Others*. Durham, NC: Duke University Press, 2006.

Al-Kassim, Dina. *On Pain of Speech: Fantasies of the First Order and the Literary Rant*. Berkeley: University of California Press, 2010.

Alexander, Jonathan, Susan C. Jarratt, and Nancy Welch, eds. *Unruly Rhetorics: Protest, Persuasion, and Publics*. Pittsburgh: University of Pittsburgh Press, 2018.

Arendt, Hannah. *The Life of the Mind*. New York: Harcourt Brace Jovanovich, 1978.

Aristotle. *Movement of Animals*. In *The Complete Works of Aristotle*, rev. ed., edited by Jonathan Barnes, 1087–96. Princeton, NJ: Princeton University Press, 1984.

———. *Nicomachean Ethics*. Translated by H. Rackham. Cambridge, MA: Harvard University Press, 1926.

———. *Parts of Animals*. In *The Complete Works of Aristotle*, rev. ed., edited by Jonathan Barnes, 994–1086. Princeton, NJ: Princeton University Press, 1984.

———. *Physics*. In *The Complete Works of Aristotle*, rev. ed., edited by Jonathan Barnes. Princeton, NJ: Princeton University Press, 1984.

———. *Poetics*. In *The Complete Works of Aristotle*, rev. ed., edited by Jonathan Barnes, 2316–40. Princeton, NJ: Princeton University Press, 1984.

———. *Politics*. In *The Complete Works of Aristotle*, rev. ed., edited by Jonathan Barnes, 1986–2129. Princeton, NJ: Princeton University Press, 1984.

———. *Rhetoric*. In *The Complete Works of Aristotle*, rev. ed., edited by Jonathan Barnes, 2152–269. Princeton, NJ: Princeton University Press, 1984.

———. *On Rhetoric: A Theory of Civic Discourse*. Translated by George A. Kennedy. New York: Oxford University Press, 1991.

Attali, Jacques. *Noise: The Political Economy of Music*. Minneapolis: University of Minnesota Press, [1977] 1985.

Augstein, Rudolf, Georg Wolff, and Martin Heidegger. "Nur noch ein Gott kann uns retten." *Der Spiegel*, May 31, 1976: 193–219.

Augustine. *On Christian Doctrine*, The City of God, Confessions.

———. *The City of God*. Translated by William Chase. Cambridge, MA: Harvard University Press, 1960.

———. *Confessions*. Translated by Carolyn J. B. Hammond. Cambridge, MA: Harvard University Press, 2014.

Bachmann, Ingeborg. *Frankfurter Vorlesungen: Probleme zeitgenössischer Dichtung*. Munich: Piper, 1982.

Bagchee, Joydeep. Review of *Basic Concepts of Aristotelian Philosophy*, translated by Robert D. Metcalf and Mark B. Tanzer, *Bryn Mawr Classical Review* 10 (2010).

Baker, Nicholson. *Vox*. New York: Vintage, 1993.

Barnes, Jonathan, ed. *The Cambridge Companion to Aristotle*. Cambridge: Cambridge University Press, 1995.

Barthes, Roland. "Listening." In *The Responsibility of Forms: Critical Essays on Music, Art, and Representation*, 245–60. Oxford: Basil Blackwell, 1986.

Baxter, Leslie A., and Dawn O. Brathwaite, eds. *Engaging Theories in Interpersonal Communication: Multiple Perspectives*. Los Angeles: Sage, 2008.

Bearn, Gordon C. F. "Sounding Serious: Cavell and Derrida." *Representations* 63 (1998): 65–92.

Bender, John, and David E. Wellbery. *The Ends of Rhetoric: History, Theory, Practice*. Stanford, CA: Stanford University Press, 1990.

Benjamin, Walter. *The Arcades Project.* Cambridge MA: Harvard University Press, 1999.
Bennett, Jane. *The Enchantment of Modern Life: Attachments, Crossings, and Ethics.* Princeton, NJ: Princeton University Press, 2001.
Berman, Morris. *The Reenchantment of the World.* Ithaca, NY: Cornell University Press, 1981.
Bernstein, Charles, ed. *Close Listening: Poetry and the Performed Word.* New York: Oxford University Press, 1998.
Berwald, Olaf. *Philipp Melanchthons Sicht der Rhetorik.* Wiesbaden: Harrassowitz, 1994.
Bickford, Susan. *The Dissonance of Democracy: Listening, Conflict, and Citizenship.* Ithaca, NY: Cornell University Press, 1996.
Biesecker, Barbara. "Rethinking the Rhetorical Situation from within the Thematic of 'Différance.'" *Philosophy and Rhetoric* 22, no. 2 (1989): 110–30.
Biess, Frank, and Daniel M. Gross, eds. *Science and Emotion after 1945: A Transatlantic Perspective.* Chicago: University of Chicago Press, 2014.
Bitzer, Lloyd F. "The Rhetorical Situation." *Philosophy and Rhetoric* 1, no. 1 (1968): 1–14.
Bizzell, Patricia, and Bruce Herzberg, eds. *The Rhetorical Tradition: Readings from Classical Times to the Present,* 2nd ed. New York: Bedford/Saint Martin's, 2000.
Bloom, Gina. "Fortress of the Ear: Shakespeare's Late Plays, Protestant Sermons, and Audience." In *Voice in Motion: Staging Gender, Shaping Sound in Early Modern England.* 111–59. Philadelphia: University of Pennsylvania Press, 2007.
Blumenberg, Hans. "An Anthropological Approach to the Contemporary Significance of Rhetoric." In *After Philosophy: End or Transformation?,* edited by Kenneth Baynes, James Bohman, and Thomas McCarthy. Cambridge, MA: MIT Press, 1987.
———. *Wirklichkeiten, in denen wir leben. Aufsätze und eine Rede.* Stuttgart: Reclam, 1981.
Borch-Jacobsen, Mikkel. "Analytic Speech: From Restricted to General Rhetoric." In *The Ends of Rhetoric: History, Theory, Practice,* edited by John Bender and David E. Wellbery, 127–39. Stanford, CA: Stanford University Press, 1990.
———. *The Emotional Tie: Psychoanalysis, Mimesis, and Affect.* Stanford, CA: Stanford University Press, 1992.
Boyd, Richard. "Writing without Teachers, Writing against the Past?" In *Writing with Elbow,* edited by Pat Belanoff. Logan: Utah State University Press, 2002.

Brathwaite, Richard. *Essaies upon the Five Senses.* London: E. Griffin, 1620.
Breton, André. "Manifesto of Surrealism." In *Surrealism,* edited by Patrick Waldberg. New York: Oxford University Press, 1965.
Breymayer, Reinhard. "Bibliographie zum Thema 'Luther und die Rhetorik.'" *Linguistica Biblica* 21–22 (1973): 39–44.
Brody, Miriam. *Manly Writing: Gender, Rhetoric, and the Rise of Composition.* Carbondale: Southern Illinois University Press, 1993.
Brown, Allen, and David Taylor, eds. *Gabr'l Blow Sof': Sumter County, Alabama, Slave Narratives.* Livingston: University of West Alabama Press, 1997.
Bryant, Lizbeth A. *Voice as Process.* Portsmouth, NH: Boynton/Cook, 2005.
Buck-Morss, Susan. *The Dialectics of Seeing: Walter Benjamin and the Arcades Project.* Cambridge, MA: MIT Press, 1989.
Bull, Michael, and Les Black, eds., *The Auditory Culture Reader.* New York: Berg, 2003.
Bultmann, Rudolf. *Faith and Understanding.* Philadelphia: Fortress Press, 1971.
Burley-Allen, Madelyn. *Listening: The Forgotten Skill.* Hoboken, NJ: John Wiley & Sons, 1982.
Burke, Kenneth. *Attitudes toward History.* Berkeley: University of California Press, 1984.
———. *Permanence and Change: An Anatomy of Purpose.* Berkeley: University of California Press, 1984.
———. *The Philosophy of Literary Form: Studies in Symbolic Action.* Berkeley: University of California Press, 1974.
———. *A Rhetoric of Motives.* Berkeley: University of California Press, 1962.
Burke, Peter. *The Art of Conversation.* Cambridge: Polity, 1993.
Burroughes, Jeremiah. *Gospel-Worship, 1. Hearing the Word.* London: P. Cole and R. W., 1647.
Butler, Judith. "Gender Is Extramoral," *MR Zine.* Interview by Fina Birulés. May 16, 2009, http://mrzine.monthlyreview.org/2009/butler160509.html.
———. *Giving an Account of Oneself.* New York: Fordham University Press, 2005.
Butler, Shane. *The Ancient Phonograph.* New York: Zone, 2015.
Callender, Christine, and Deborah Cameron. "Responsive Listening as Part of Religious Rhetoric: The Case of Black Pentecostal Preaching." In *Reception and Response: Hearer Creativity and the Analysis of Spoken and Written Texts,* edited by Graham McGregor and R. S. White, 160–78. London: Routledge, 1990.
Cantril, Hadley. "Social Psychology of Everyday Life." *Psychological Bulletin* 31 (1934), 297–330.

Carey, Christopher. "'Artless' Proofs in Aristotle and the Orators." In *Oxford Readings in the Attic Orators*, edited by Edwin Carawan. Oxford: Oxford University Press, 2007.

Catano, James V. "The Rhetoric of Masculinity: Origins, Institutions, and the Myth of the Self-Made Man." *College English* 52, no. 4 (1990): 421–36.

Caussinus, Nicolaus. *Eloquentia sacrae et humaneae parellela libri XVI*. Paris: Sebastian Chappelet, 1619.

Ceraso, Steph. *Sounding Composition: Multimodal Pedagogies for Embodied Listening*. Pittsburgh: University of Pittsburgh Press, 2018.

Chalmers, David. Foreword to *Supersizing the Mind: Embodiment, Action, and Cognitive Extension*, by Andy Clark. Oxford: Oxford University Press, 2008.

Chion, Michel. *Sound: An Acoulogical Treatise*. Durham, NC: Duke University Press, 2016.

Chow, Rey, and James A. Steintrager. "In Pursuit of the Object of Sound: An Introduction." Special issue, *Differences: A Journal of Feminist Cultural Studies* 22, nos. 2–3 (2011): 1–9.

Cicero, Marcus Tullius. *De inventione*. Translated by H.M. Hubbell. Cambridge, MA: Harvard University Press, 1949.

———. *De officiis*. Translated by Walter Miller. Cambridge, MA: Harvard University Press.

———. *De oratore*. Translated by E.W. Sutton. Cambridge, MA: Harvard University Press, 1979.

———. *De partione oratoriu*. Translated by H. Rackham. Los Altos, CA: Packard Humanities Institute, 1991.

——— [attributed]. *Rhetorica ad Herennium*. Translated by Harry Caplan. Cambridge, MA: Harvard University Press, 1954.

———. *Topica*. Translated by Tobias Reinhardt. Oxford: Oxford University Press, 2003.

Classen, Constance, ed. *A Cultural History of the Senses*, vols. 1–6. London: Bloomsbury Academic, 2014.

Cmiel, Kenneth. *Democratic Eloquence: The Fight over Popular Speech in Nineteenth-Century America*. New York: William Morrow, 1990.

Conley, Thomas. *Rhetoric in the European Tradition*. Chicago: University of Chicago Press, 1990.

Connolly, Joy. "Virile Tongues: Rhetoric and Masculinity." In *A Companion to Roman Rhetoric*, edited by William J. Dominik and Jon Hall, 83–97. Oxford: Blackwell, 2007.

Connor, Steven. *Dumbstruck: A Cultural History of Ventriloquism*. Oxford: Oxford University Press, 2004.

———. "The Modern Auditory I." In: *Rewriting the Self: Histories from the Renaissance to the Present*, edited by Roy S. Porter, 203–23. London: Routledge, 1997.

Corbin, Alain. "The Auditory Markers of the Village." In *The Auditory Culture Reader*, edited by Michael Bull and Les Back, 117–25. New York: Berg, 2004.

Corbett, Edward P. J., and Robert J. Connors. *Classical Rhetoric for the Modern Student*. Oxford: Oxford University Press, 1965.

Crockett, Bryan. "'Holy Cozenage' and the Renaissance Cult of the Ear." In *The Play of Paradox: Stage and Sermon in Renaissance England*, 50–70. Philadelphia: University of Pennsylvania Press, 1995.

Crowley, Sharon, and Debra Hawhee. *Ancient Rhetoric for Contemporary Students*, 5th ed. London: Longman, 2011.

Currid, Brian. *A National Acoustics: Music and Mass Publicity in Weimar and Nazi Germany*. Minneapolis: University of Minnesota Press, 2006.

Davis, Bret W. *Heidegger and the Will: On the Way to Gelassenheit*. Evanston, IL: Northwestern University Press, 2007.

Davis, Diane. *Inessential Solidarity: Rhetoric and Foreign Relations*. Pittsburgh: University of Pittsburgh Press, 2010.

de Man, Paul. *Allegories of Reading: Figural Language in Rousseau, Nietzsche, Rilke, and Proust*. New Haven, CT: Yale University Press, 1982.

de Romilly, Jacqueline. *Magic and Rhetoric in Ancient Greece*. Cambridge, MA: Harvard University Press, 1975.

Deming, Richard. *Listening on All Sides: Toward an Emersonian Ethics of Reading*. Stanford, CA: Stanford University Press, 2007.

Department of Communication Studies. "Research." The University of Iowa. Accessed March 28, 2019. http://clas.uiowa.edu/commstudies/research.

Derrida, Jacques. *The Ear of the Other: Otobiography, Transference, Translation; Texts and Discussions with Jacques Derrida*. Edited by Christie McDonald. Lincoln: University of Nebraska Press, 1988.

———. *Of Spirit: Heidegger and the Question*. Translated by Geoffrey Bennington and Rachel Bowlby. Chicago: University of Chicago Press, 1989.

Dewey, John. *Democracy and Education*. New York: Macmillan, 1916.

Dilthey, Wilhelm, and Georg Misch. *Weltanschauung und Analyse des Menschen seit Renaissance und Reformation; Abhandlungen zur Geschichte der Philosophie und Religion*. Leipzig: B.G. Teubner, 1914.

Dilts, Mervin R., and George A. Kennedy, eds. *Two Greek Rhetorical Treatises from the Roman Empire: Introduction, Text, and Translation of the Arts of Rhetoric,*

Attributed to Anonymous Seguerianus and to Apsines of Gadara. Leiden, Netherlands: Brill, 1997.
Dobson, Andrew. *Listening for Democracy: Recognition, Representation, Reconciliation.* Oxford: Oxford University Press, 2014.
Dockhorn, Klaus. "Luthers Glaubensbegriff und die Rhetorik." *Linguistica Biblica* 21–22 (1973): 19–39.
———. Review of *Wahrheit und Methode*, by Hans-Georg Gadamer. *Göttingische Gelehrte Anzeigen* 218 (1966): 169–206.
———. "Rhetorica movet: Protestantischer Humanismus und karolingische Renaissance." In *Rhetorik: Beiträge zu ihrer Geschichte in Deutschland vom 16.–20. Jahrhundert*, edited by Helmut Schanze. Frankfurt am Main: Athenaion, 1974.
Dolar, Mladen. *A Voice and Nothing More.* Cambridge, MA: MIT Press, 2006.
Donne, John. *Holy Sonnets.* London: Hague and Gill, 1938.
Donoso Cortés, Juan. *Ensayo sobre el catolicismo, el liberalismo, y el socialismo considerados en sus principios fundamentales.* Madrid: M. Rivadeneyra, 1851.
Doxtader, Erik. "The Rhetorical Question of Human Rights: A Preface." *Quarterly Journal of Speech* 96, no. 4 (2010): 353–79.
Düring, Ingemar. *Aristotle in the Ancient Biographical Tradition.* Stockholm: Almqvist & Wiksell, 1957.
———. *Aristoteles: Darstellung und interpretation des Denkens.* Heidelberg: C. Winter, 1966.
Eberhard, Philippe. *The Middle Voice in Gadamer's Hermeneutics: A Basic Interpretation with Some Theological Implications.* Tübingen: Mohr Siebeck, 2004.
Edbauer, Jenny. "Unframing Models of Public Distribution: From Rhetorical Situation to Rhetorical Ecologies." *Rhetoric Society Quarterly* 35, no. 4 (2005): 5–24.
Elbow, Peter. *Everyone Can Write: Essays Toward a Hopeful Theory of Writing.* New York: Oxford University Press, 2000.
———. *Writing with Power.* New York: Oxford University Press, 1981.
———. *Writing without Teachers.* New York: Oxford University Press, 1973.
Egerton, Stephen. *The boring of the eare.* London: Printed by William Stansby, 1623.
Erlmann, Veit, ed. *Hearing Cultures: Essays on Sound, Listening and Modernity.* Oxford: Berg, 2004.
———. *Reason and Resonance: A History of Modern Aurality.* New York: Zone, 2010.
Esposito, Robert. *Bíos: Biopolitics and Philosophy.* Minneapolis: University of Minnesota Press, 2008.
Faigley, Lester. *Fragments of Rationality: Postmodernity and the Subject of Composition.* Pittsburgh: University of Pittsburgh Press, 1992.

Feld, Steven. *Sound and Sentiment: Birds, Weeping, Poetics, and Song in Kaluli Expression*. Philadelphia: University of Pennsylvania Press, 1982.

Fiumara, G. Corradi. *The Other Side of Language: A Philosophy of Listening.* London: Routledge, 1990.

Flacius Illyricus [Flacius, Matthias]. *Clavis Scripturae Sacrae, seu de Sermone Sacrarum Literarum*, 2 vols. Basel: Johannes Oporinus and Eusebius Episcopium, 1567.

Fliegelman, Jay. *Declaring Independence: Jefferson, Natural Language, and the Culture of Performance*. Palo Alto, CA: Stanford University Press, 1993.

Flügel, John C. *The Psychology of Clothes*. London: Hogarth, 1930.

Folkerth, Wes. *The Sound of Shakespeare*. London: Routledge, 2002.

Foucault, Michel. *The Government of Self and Others: Lectures at the Collège de France, 1982–1983*. Basingstoke, UK: Palgrave Macmillan, 2010.

———. *The History of Sexuality Volume 1: An Introduction*. New York: Vintage, 1980.

———. *The Order of Things: An Archaeology of the Human Sciences*. New York: Vintage, [1966] 1970.

———. *Security, Territory, Population: Lectures at the Collège de France, 1977–1978*. Basingstoke, UK: Palgrave Macmillan, 2007.

———. *Technologies of the Self: A Seminar with Michel Foucault*. Amherst: University of Massachusetts Press, 1988.

Franck, Sebastian. *280 Paradoxes and Wondrous Sayings*. Lewiston, NY: Edwin Mellen, 1986.

Freud, Sigmund. *Dora: An Analysis of a Case of Hysteria*. New York: Collier, 1963.

———. *Group Psychology and the Analysis of the Ego: The Standard Edition of the Complete Psychological Works of Sigmund Freud*, edited by James Strachey. New York: W. W. Norton, 1975

———. "Jokes and Their Relation to the Unconscious." In *The Standard Edition of the Complete Psychological Works of Sigmund Freud*, edited by James Strachey. New York: W.W. Norton, 1989.

———. "Psychical (or Mental) Treatment." In *The Standard Edition of the Complete Psychological Works of Sigmund Freud*, vol. 7, edited by James Strachey. London: Hogarth Press, 1953.

———. "Recommendations to Physicians Practicing Psycho-Analysis." In *The Standard Edition of the Complete Psychological Works of Sigmund Freud*, vol. 12, edited by James Strachey, 109–20. London: Hogarth Press, 1953.

———. *Totem and Taboo: Some Points of Agreement between the Mental Lives of Savages and Neurotics*. In *The Standard Edition of the Complete Psychological Works of Sigmund Freud*, edited by James Strachey. London: Hogarth Press, 1953.

Fromm, Erich. *The Art of Listening.* New York: Continuum, 1994.
Fuss, Diane. *The Sense of an Interior: Four Writers and the Rooms That Shaped Them.* New York: Routledge, 2004.
Gadamer, Hans-Georg. "The Significance of the Humanist Tradition for the Human Sciences." In *Truth and Method*, 2nd rev. ed., 3–42. New York: Crossroad, 1989.
———. *Wahrheit und Methode: Grundzuge einer philosophischen Hermeneutik.* Tübingen: Mohr, 1960.
Gaonkar, Dilip Parameshwar. "Rhetoric and Its Double: Reflections of the Rhetorical Turn in the Human Sciences." In *The Rhetorical Turn: Invention and Persuasion in the Conduct of Inquiry*, edited by Herbert W. Simons, 341–66. Chicago: University of Chicago Press, 1990.
Garsten, Bryan. *Saving Persuasion: A Defense of Rhetoric and Judgment.* Cambridge, MA: Harvard University Press, 2006.
Garver, Eugene. *Aristotle's "Rhetoric": An Art of Character.* Chicago: University of Chicago Press, 1994.
Gehrke, Pat J., Susan C. Jarratt, Bradford Vivian, and Arthur E. Walzer. "Forum on Arthur Walzer's '*Parrēsia*, Foucault, and the Classical Rhetorical Tradition.'" *Rhetoric Society Quarterly* 43, no. 4 (2013): 355–81.
Gell, Alfred. "The Language of the Forest: Landscape and Phonological Iconism in Umeda." In *The Anthropology of Landscape: Perspectives on Place and Space*, edited by Eric Hirsch and Michael O'Hanlon, 232–54. Oxford: Oxford University Press, 1995
Gerald, Amy Spangler. "An Uneasy Relationship: Feminist Composition and Peter Elbow." *Composition Studies* 31, no. 2 (2003): 73–90.
Glassius, Salomon [Glaß, Salomon]. *Philologiae sacrae, qua totius sacrosanctae, Veteris et Novi Testamenti, scripturae, tum stylus et literatura, tum sensus et genuinae interpretationis ratio expenditur; Libri quinque: Quorum I. II. Generalia de Scripturae Sacra stylo & sensu; III. IV. Grammatica Sacra; V. Rhetorica Sacra, comprehensa.* Jena: Steinmann, [1623] 1668.
Gleason, Maud W. *Making Men: Sophists and Self-Presentation in Ancient Rome.* Princeton, NJ: Princeton University Press, 1995.
Glenn, Cheryl. *Unspoken: A Rhetoric of Silence.* Carbondale: Southern Illinois University Press, 2004.
Glenn, Cheryl, and Krista Ratcliffe, eds. *Silence and Listening as Rhetorical Arts.* Carbondale: Southern Illinois University Press, 2011.
Goodale, Greg. *Sonic Persuasion: Reading Sound in the Recorded Age.* Urbana: University of Illinois Press, 2011.

Gordon, Peter. *Continental Divide: Heidegger, Cassirer, Davos*. Cambridge, MA: Harvard University Press, 2010.
Gould, Timothy. *Hearing Things: Voice and Method in the Writing of Stanley Cavell*. Chicago: University of Chicago Press, 1999.
Gouk, Penelope, Michael Fend, and Charles Burnett. *The Second Sense: Studies in Hearing and Musical Judgement from Antiquity to the Seventeenth Century*. London: Warburg Institute, University of London, 1991.
Green, Lawrence D., and James J. Murphy, eds. *Renaissance Rhetoric Short-Title Catalogue 1460–1700*. Aldershot, UK: Ashgate, 2006.
Green, Reina. "'Ears Prejudicate' in *Mariam* and *Duchess of Malfi*." *SEL Studies in English Literature 1500–1900* 43, no. 2 (2003): 459–74.
Greenblatt, Stephen. *Renaissance Self-Fashioning: From More to Shakespeare*. Chicago: University of Chicago Press, 1980.
Gross, Alan G., and Arthur E. Walzer, eds. *Rereading Aristotle's "Rhetoric"*. Carbondale: Southern Illinois University Press, 2000.
Gross, Daniel M. "Caussin's Passion and the New History of Rhetoric." *Rhetorica: A Journal of the History of Rhetoric* 21, no. 2 (2003): 89–112.
———. "Foucault's Analogies, or How to Be an Historian of the Present without Being a Presentist." *Clio: A Journal of Literature, History and the Philosophy of History* 31, no. 1 (2001): 57–82.
———. "Metaphor and Definition in Vico's *New Science*." *Rhetorica: A Journal of the History of Rhetoric* 14, no. 4 (1996): 359–81.
———. *The Secret History of Emotion from Aristotle's "Rhetoric" to Modern Brain Science*. Chicago: University of Chicago Press, 2006.
Gross, Daniel M., and Ansgar Kemmann, eds. *Heidegger and Rhetoric*. Albany: State University of New York Press, 2005.
Gross, Kenneth. *Shakespeare's Noise*. Chicago: University of Chicago Press, 2001.
Gunderson, Erik. *Declamation, Paternity, and Roman Identity: Authority and the Rhetorical Self*. Cambridge: Cambridge University Press, 2003.
———. *Staging Masculinity: The Rhetoric of Performance in the Roman World*. Ann Arbor: University of Michigan Press, 2000.
Gusdorf, Georges. *Introduction aux sciences humaines : Essai critique sur leurs origines et leur développement*. Paris: Les Belles Lettres, 1960.
Habermas, Jürgen. *Between Naturalism and Religion*. Translated by Ciaran Cronin. Cambridge: Polity, 2008.
———. *Zwischen Naturalismus und Religion*. Frankfurt am Main: Suhrkamp, 2005.
Hacking, Ian. "Making People Up." *London Review of Books* 28, no. 16 (2006): 23–26.

———. *Rewriting the Soul: Multiple Personality and the Sciences of Memory.* Princeton, NJ: Princeton University Press, 1995.

Halberstam, Jack [Judith]. *The Queer Art of Failure.* Durham, NC: Duke University Press, 2011.

Hardt, Michael. "Militant Life." *New Left Review* 64 (2010): 151–60.

Harrison, Carol. *The Art of Listening in the Early Church.* Oxford: Oxford University Press, 2013.

Harrison, William. *A plaine and profitable exposition, of the parable of the sower and the seede: wherein is plainly set forth, the difference of hearers, both good and bad.* London: Printed for William Bladen, 1625.

Hartfelder, Karl. *Philipp Melanchthon als Praeceptor Germaniae.* Nieuwkoop, Netherlands: Graaf, 1964.

Hauser, Gerald A. *Introduction to Rhetorical Theory,* 2nd ed. Long Grove, IL: Waveland, 2002.

Hawk, Byron. *Resounding the Rhetorical: Composition as a Quasi-Object.* Pittsburgh: University of Pittsburgh Press, 2018.

Heidegger, Martin. *Basic Concepts of Aristotelian Philosophy.* Translated by Robert Metcalf and Mark B. Tanzer. Bloomington: University of Indiana Press, 2009.

———. *Being and Time.* New York: Harper & Row, 1962.

———. "Building Dwelling Thinking." In *Poetry, Language, Thought,* translated by Albert Hofstadter. New York: Harper Colophon Books, 1971.

———. *Grundbegriffe der aristotelischen Philosophie: Marburger Vorlesung Sommer Semester 1924.* Gesamtausgabe, vol. 18. Frankfurt am Main: Klostermann, 2002.

———. *History of the Concept of Time. Prolegomena.* Bloomington: Indiana University Press, 1992.

———. *An Introduction to Metaphysics.* New Haven, CT: Yale University Press, 1959.

———. *Nietzsche,* vol. I. New York: Harper & Row, 1979.

———. *Parmenides.* Bloomington: Indiana University Press, 1992.

———. *Pathmarks.* Cambridge: Cambridge University Press, 1998.

———. "Phänomenologische Interpretationen zu Aristoteles: Anzeige der hermeneutischen Situation." In *Phänomenologische Interpretation ausgewählter Abhandlungen Aristoteles zu Ontologie und Logik.* Frankfurt am Main: Vittorio Klostermann, 2005.

———. *The Phenomenology of Religious Life.* Translated by Matthias Fritsch and Jennifer Anna Gosetti-Ferencei. Bloomington: Indiana University Press, 2010.

———. *Plato's Sophist*. Bloomington: Indiana University Press, 2003.
———. *Ponderings: Black Notebooks*. Bloomington: Indiana University Press, 2016.
———. *Supplements: From the Earliest Essays to "Being and Time" and Beyond*. Albany: State University of New York Press, 2002.
Herbert, George. *The Works of George Herbert*. Chestnut Hill, MA: Adamant Media, 2006.
Hirschkind, Charles. *The Ethical Soundscape: Cassette Sermons and Islamic Counterpublics*. New York: Columbia University Press, 2009.
Hitler, Adolf. *Mein Kampf*, vol. 2. Munich: Verlag Franz Eher Nachfolger, 1927.
Holmes, David G. *Revisiting Racialized Voice: African-American Ethos in Language and Literature*. Carbondale: Southern Illinois University Press, 2004.
Howard, Leon. "'The Invention' of Milton's 'Great Argument': A Study of the Logic of 'God's Ways to Men.'" *Huntington Library Quarterly* 9, no. 2 (1946): 149–73.
Hume, David. *A Treatise of Human Nature*. Oxford: Clarendon Press, [1738] 1888.
Hunt, Arnold. *The Art of Hearing: English Preachers and Their Audiences, 1590–1640*. Cambridge: Cambridge University Press, 2010.
Hyde, Michael J. *The Call of Conscience: Heidegger and Levinas, Rhetoric and the Euthanasia Debate*. Columbia: University of South Carolina Press, 2001.
Ihde, Don. *Listening and Voice: A Phenomenology of Sound*. Athens: Ohio University Press, 1976.
Isakower, Otto. "On the Exceptional Position of the Auditory Sphere." *The International Journal of Psychoanalysis* 20 (1939): 340–48.
Jaeger, Werner. *Aristotle: Fundamentals of the History of His Development*. Oxford: Clarendon Press, [1923] 1934.
James, Heather. "Dido's Ear: Tragedy and the Politics of Response." *Shakespeare Quarterly* 52, no. 3 (2001): 360–82.
Jarratt, Susan C. "Feminism and Composition: The Case for Conflict." In *Contending with Words: Composition and Rhetoric in a Postmodern Age*, edited by Patricia Harkin and John Schilb, 105–23. New York: Modern Language Association, 1991.
———. *Rereading the Sophists: Classical Rhetoric Refigured*. Carbondale: Southern Illinois University Press, 1991.
Jay, Martin. *Downcast Eyes: The Denigration of Vision in Twentieth-Century French Thought*. Berkeley: University of California Press, 1993.
Johnson, Kevin E. "Burke's Lacanian Upgrade: Reading the Burkean Unconscious through a Lacanian Lens." *KB Journal: The Journal of the Kenneth Burke Society*, 6, no. 1 (2009).

Jonas, Hans. *Gnosis und spätantiker Geist*. Göttingen: Vandenhoeck and Ruprecht, 1934.

———. *The Phenomenon of Life: Toward a Philosophical Biology*. New York: Harper and Row, 1966.

Jordan, June. "Nobody Mean to Me Than You: And the Future Life of Willie Jordan." In *Landmark Essays on Voice and Writing*, edited by Peter Elbow, 59–72. Mahwah, NJ: Hermagoras Press, 1994.

Jütte, Robert. *A History of the Senses: From Antiquity to Cyberspace*. Cambridge: Polity, 2005.

Kaes, Anton, Martin Jay, and Edward Dimendberg. *The Weimar Republic Sourcebook*. Berkeley: University of California Press, 1994.

Kahn, Douglas. *Noise, Water, Meat: A History of Sound in the Arts*. Cambridge, MA: MIT Press, 1999.

Kant, Immanuel. *Critique of Judgment*. Indianapolis: Hackett, [1790] 1987.

Kaplan, Leonard V., and Rudy Koshar. *The Weimar Moment: Liberalism, Political Theology, and Law*. Lanham, MD: Lexington, 2012.

Keller, Evelyn Fox. *Reflections on Gender and Science*. New Haven, CT: Yale University Press, 1985.

Kelley, Donald R. "*Altera natura*: The Idea of Custom in Historical Perspective." In *New Perspectives on Renaissance Thought: Essays in the History of Science, Education and Philosophy*, edited by John Henry and Sarah Hutton. London: Duckworth, 1990.

———. *History, Law, and the Human Sciences*. London: Variorum, 1984.

Kisiel, Theodore. *The Genesis of Heidegger's "Being and Time."* Berkeley: University of California Press, 1995.

———. "Rhetorical Protopolitics in Heidegger and Arendt." In *Heidegger and Rhetoric*, edited by Daniel M. Gross and Ansgar Kemmann, 131–60. Albany, NY: State University of New York Press, 2005.

Kittler, Friedrich A. *Discourse Networks 1800/1900*. Translated by Michael Metteer and Chris Cullens. Stanford, CA: Stanford University Press, 1990.

Kittler, Friedrich A., Thomas Macho, and Sigrid Weigel. *Zwischen Rauschen und Offenbarung: zur Kultur- und Mediengeschichte der Stimme*. Berlin: Akademie Verlag, 2008.

Klaiman, M. H. *Grammatical Voice*. Cambridge: Cambridge University Press, 1991.

Kleinberg-Levin, David M. *The Listening Self: Personal Growth, Social Change, and the Closure of Metaphysics*. London: Routledge, 1989.

Kolln, Martha. "Rhetorical Grammar: A Modification Lesson." *English Journal* 85, no. 7 (1996): 25–31.

Kopperschmidt, Josef. *Heidegger über Rhetorik*. Munich: W. Fink, 2009.
———, ed. *Rhetorische Anthropologie: Studien zum Homo rhetoricus*. Munich: Fink, 2000.
Krause, Peter D., ed. "Rhetorik und Anthropologie." Special issue, *Rhetorik: Ein internationales Jahrbuch* 23 (2004).
Kristeller, Paul Oskar. "The Dignity of Man." In *Renaissance Concepts of Man and Other Essays*. New York: Harper and Row, 1972.
Kusukawa, Sachiko. *The Transformation of Natural Philosophy: The Case of Philipp Melanchthon*. Cambridge: Cambridge University Press, 1995.
Lacan, Jacques. *The Seminar of Jacques Lacan: Book I, Freud's Papers on Technique, 1953–1954*. Edited by Jacques-Alain Miller and translated by John Forrester. Cambridge: Cambridge University Press, 1988.
Lacoue-Labarthe, Philippe. "The Echo of the Subject." In *Typography: Mimesis, Philosophy, Politics*, 139–207. Stanford, CA: Stanford University Press, 1998.
Landshut, Siegfried. *Kritik der Soziologie und andere Schriften zur Politik*. Berlin: Luchterhand, 1969.
Landy, Joshua, and Michael Saler, eds. *The Re-Enchantment of the World: Secular Magic in a Rational Age*. Palo Alto, CA: Stanford University Press, 2009.
Lea, Mary R., and Brian V. Street. "Student Writing in Higher Education: An Academic Literacies Approach." *Studies in Higher Education* 23, no. 2 (1998): 157–72.
Leader, Darian. "The Voice as Psychoanalytic Object." *Analysis* 12 (2003): 70–82.
Lee, Jerry Won. *The Politics of Translingualism: After Englishes*. New York: Routledge, 2018.
Lerner, Gerda. *The Creation of Patriarchy*. Oxford: Oxford University Press, 1986.
Liberman, Mark, and Jeffrey K. Pullman. *Far from the Madding Gerund and Other Dispatches from Language Log*. Wilsonville, OR: William, James & Co., 2006.
Lipari, Lisbeth. *Listening, Thinking, Being: Toward an Ethics of Attunement*. University Park: Pennsylvania State University Press, 2014.
Long, Fredrick J. *Ancient Rhetoric and Paul's Apology: The Compositional Unity of 2 Corinthians*. Cambridge: Cambridge University Press, 2004.
Lothane, Zvi. "The Art of Listening: A Critique of Robert Langs." *Psychoanalytic Review* 67, no. 3 (1980): 353–64.
———. "Listening with the Third Ear as an Instrument in Psychoanalysis: The Contributions of Reik and Isakower." *Psychoanalytic Review* 68, no. 4 (1981): 487–503.
Lovejoy, A. O. *The Great Chain of Being: A Study of the History of an Idea*. New York: Harper and Row, 1965.

Lucian of Samosata. "Rhetorum praeceptor." In *Lucian*, vol. 4, translated by A. M. Harmon. New York: Macmillan, 1925.
Luckyj, Christina. *"A Moving Rhetoricke": Gender and Silence in Early Modern England*. Manchester: Manchester University Press, 2002.
Lundberg, Christian. *Lacan in Public: Psychoanalysis and the Science of Rhetoric*. Tuscaloosa: University of Alabama Press, 2012.
Luther, Martin. *Dr. Martin Luthers Werke, kritische Gesamtausgabe*, vol. 40/3. Weimar: Böhlau, 1883–1987.
Lyons, John. *Introduction to Theoretical Linguistics*. Cambridge: Cambridge University Press, 1968.
Lyotard, Jean-François. "Jewish Oedipus." In *Driftworks*, edited by Roger McKeon, 35–56. Los Angeles: Semiotext(e), 1984.
Maclean, Ian. *Interpretation and Meaning in the Renaissance: The Case of Law*. Cambridge: Cambridge University Press, 1992.
Mader, Gottfried. "Foresight, Hindsight, and the Rhetoric of Self-Fashioning in Demosthenes' Philippic Cycle." *Rhetorica: A Journal of the History of Rhetoric* 25, no. 4 (2007): 339–60.
Mainberger, Gonsalv K. *Rhetorica II: Spiegelungen des Geistes, Sprachfiguren bei Vico und Lévi-Strauss* (Problemata 116–117). Stuttgart-Bad Cannstatt: Frommann-Holzboog, 1987–1988.
Marlowe, Christopher. "The Massacre at Paris with the Death of the Duke of Guise." In *The Complete Works of Christopher Marlowe*, vol. 5, edited by Edward J. Esche. Oxford: Clarendon Press, 1998.
Marshall, David. *Vico and the Transformation of Rhetoric in Early Modern Europe*. Cambridge: Cambridge University Press, 2010.
Marx, Karl. *Economic and Philosophic Manuscripts of 1844*. Translated by Martin Milligan. Moscow: Foreign Languages Publishing House, 1959.
Mazzio, Carla. *The Inarticulate Renaissance: Language Trouble in an Age of Eloquence*. Philadelphia: University of Pennsylvania Press, 2009.
McCormick, John P. *Carl Schmitt's Critique of Liberalism: Against Politics as Technology*. Cambridge: Cambridge University Press, 1997.
McCormick, Samuel. *The Chattering Mind: A Conceptual History of Everyday Talk*. Chicago: University of Chicago Press, 2020.
McKeon, Richard. "Aristotle's Conception of Moral and Political Philosophy." *Ethics: An International Journal of Social, Political, and Legal Philosophy* 51, no. 3 (1941).
———. *The Basic Works of Aristotle*. New York: Random House, 1941.
Melanchthon, Philipp. "De corrigendis adolescentiae studiis." In *Melanchthons Werke in Auswahl: Studienausgabe*, edited by R. Stupperich. Gütersloh: Bertelsmann, 1963.

———. "Elementorum rhetorices libri II." In *Corpus Reformatorum Philippi Melanthonis Opera quae Supersunt Omnia*, vol. 13, edited by C. B. Bretschneider and H. E. Bindseil. Halle: C. A. Schwetschke, 1846.

———. "Liber de anima." In *Corpus Reformatorum Philippi Melanthonis Opera quae Supersunt Omnia*, vol. 13, edited by C. B. Bretschneider and H. E. Bindseil. Halle: C. A. Schwetschke, 1846.

———. "Praefatio in officia Ciceronis." In *Corpus Reformatorum Philippi Melanthonis Opera quae Supersunt Omnia*, vol. 11, edited by C. B. Bretschneider and H. E. Bindseil. Halle: C. A. Schwetschke, 1846.

Metzger, Stefan, and Wolfgang Rapp, eds. *Homo inveniens: Heuristik und Anthropologie am Modell der Rhetorik*. Tübingen: Narr, 2003.

Meyer-Kalkus, Reinhart. *Stimme und Sprechkünste im 20. Jahrhundert*. Berlin: Akademie Verlag, 2001.

Micciche, Laura R. "Making a Case for Rhetorical Grammar." *College Composition and Communication* 55, no. 4 (2004): 716–37.

Mill, John Stuart. *System of Logic, Ratiocinative and Inductive, Being a Connected View of the Principles of Evidence, and the Methods of Scientific Investigation*. London: John W. Parker, 1843.

Miller, Perry. *The New England Mind: The Seventeenth Century*. Cambridge, MA: Harvard University Press, 1954.

Mirhady, David. "Non-Technical Pisteis in Aristotle and Anaximenes." *The American Journal of Philology* 112, no. 1 (1991): 5–28.

Moraux, Paul. *Les listes anciennes des ouvrages d'Aristote*. Louvain: Ed. Universitaires, 1951.

Morgan, John. *Godly Learning: Puritan Attitudes Towards Reason, Learning, and Education, 1560–1640*. Cambridgeshire: Cambridge University Press, 1986.

Morhof, Daniel Georg. *Polyhistor literarius philosophicus*, rev. ed. Lubeck: Petri Bockmanni, 1714.

Moss, Ann. *Printed Commonplace-Books and the Structuring of Renaissance Thought*. Oxford: Clarendon Press, 1996.

Most, Glenn W. "Heidegger's Greeks." *Arion: A Journal of Humanities and the Classics* 10, no. 1 (2002): 83–98.

Müller, Adam H., Dennis R. Bormann, and Elisabeth Leinfellner. *Adam Müller's Twelve Lectures on Rhetoric: A Translation with a Critical Essay*. Ann Arbor, MI: Published for University of Nebraska Press by University Microfilms International, 1978.

Muther, T. *Die Wittenberger Universitäts- und Facultäts-Statuten vom Jahre 1508*. Halle: Buchhandlung des Waisenhauses, 1867.

Nancy, Jean-Luc. *Listening.* New York: Fordham University Press, 2007.
Nelson, John S. "Approaches, Opportunities and Priorities in the Rhetoric of Political Inquiry: A Critical Synthesis." In *The Recovery of Rhetoric: Persuasive Discourse and Disciplinarity in the Human Sciences,* edited by Richard H. Roberts and James M.M. Good, 164–90. Charlottesville: University of Virginia Press, 1993.
Newman, John, B. Grosvenor, Thomas Bradbury, Jabez Earle, William Harris, and Thomas Reynolds. *Practical Discourses Concerning Hearing the Word; Preach'd at the Friday Evening-Lecture in Eastcheap.* London: Printed by J. Darby, 1713.
Ngũgĩ wa Thiong'o. *Decolonizing the Mind: The Politics of Language in African Literature.* London: James Curry, 1986.
Nichols, Michael P. *The Lost Art of Listening: How Learning to Listen Can Improve Relationships.* New York: Guilford, 1996.
Nicholson, Catherine. *Uncommon Tongues: Eloquence and Eccentricity in the English Renaissance.* Philadelphia: University of Pennsylvania Press, 2014.
Noland, Carrie. "Phonic Matters: French Sound Poetry, Julia Kristeva, and Bernard Heidsieck." *PMLA* 120, no. 1 (2005): 108–27.
Norberg-Schulz, Christian. *Genius Loci: Towards a Phenomenology of Architecture.* London: Academy Editions, 1980.
Nuttall, A.D. *Overheard by God.* London: Methuen, 1980.
Okáčová, Marie. "Centones: Recycled Art or the Embodiment of Absolute Intertextuality?" In *Laetae segetes iterum,* 2007, http://www.kakanien-revisited.at/beitr/graeca_latina/MOkacova1.pdf.
Pelikan, Jaroslav. *Divine Rhetoric: The Sermon on the Mount as Message and as Model in Augustine, Chrysostom, and Luther.* Crestwood: St. Vladimir's Seminary Press, 2001.
Perelman, Chaïm, and Lucie Olbrechts-Tyteca. *The New Rhetoric: A Treatise on Argumentation.* Translated by John Wilkinson and Purcell Weaver. South Bend, IN: University of Notre Dame Press, 1971.
Peters, John Durham. *Speaking into the Air: A History of the Idea of Communication.* Chicago: University of Chicago Press, 1999.
Philo of Alexandria. *The Contemplative Life, The Giants, and Selections.* Translated by David Winston. New York: Paulist Press, 1981.
Picker, John M. *Victorian Soundscapes.* New York: Oxford University Press, 2003.
Plett, Heinrich F. "Rhetoric and Intertextuality." *Rhetorica: A Journal of the History of Rhetoric* 17, no. 3 (1999): 313–29.

Plutarch. "On Listening to Lectures." In *Moralia*, vol. 1, translated by Frank Cole Babbitt. Cambridge, MA: Harvard University Press, 1927.
Pollard, Tanya. "Vulnerable Ears: Hamlet and Poisonous Theater." In *Drugs and Theater in Early Modern England*, 123–43. New York: Oxford University Press, 2005.
Porter, James I. *The Origins of Aesthetic Thought in Ancient Greece: Matter, Sensation, and Experience*. Cambridge: Cambridge University Press, 2010.
Poster, Carol. "*Ethos*, Authority, and the New Testament Canon." In *Rhetoric, Ethic, and Moral Persuasion in Biblical Discourse*, edited by Thomas H. Olbricht and Anders Eriksson, 118–37. New York: Continuum, 2005.
Prelli, Lawrence J., Floyd D. Anderson, and Matthew T. Althouse. "Kenneth Burke on Recalcitrance." *Rhetoric Society Quarterly* 41, no. 2 (2011): 97–124.
Quintilian. *The Orator's Education*. Edited and translated by Donald A. Russell. Cambridge, MA: Harvard University Press, 2002.
Rainolds, John. *John Rainolds's Oxford Lectures on Aristotle's "Rhetoric."* Edited and translated by Lawrence D. Green. Newark: University of Delaware Press, 1986.
Rancière, Jacques. *The Ignorant Schoolmaster: Five Lessons in Intellectual Emancipation*. Palo Alto, CA: Stanford University Press, 1991.
Rapp, Christof, and Klaus Corcilius. *Aristoteles-Handbuch: Leben, Werk, Wirkung*. Stuttgart: Metzler, 2011.
Ratcliffe, Krista. *Rhetorical Listening: Identification, Gender, Whiteness*. Carbondale: Southern Illinois University Press, 2005.
Ratzinger, Joseph, and Angelo Amato. "Letter to the Bishops of the Catholic Church on the Collaboration of Men and Women in the Church and in the World." May 31, 2004.
Rebhorn, Wayne. *The Emperor of Men's Minds*. Ithaca, NY: Cornell University Press, 1995.
Reik, Theodor. *Listening with the Third Ear*. New York: Farrar, Straus, 1949.
Rhodes, Neil. *Shakespeare and the Origins of English*. Oxford: Oxford University Press, 2004.
Rickert, Thomas. *Acts of Enjoyment: Rhetoric, Žižek, and the Return of the Subject*. Pittsburgh: University of Pittsburgh Press, 2007.
———. *Ambient Rhetoric: The Attunements of Rhetorical Being*. Pittsburgh: Pittsburgh University Press, 2013.
Rivers, Nathaniel, and Ryan Weber. "Ecological, Pedagogical Public Rhetoric." *College Composition and Communication* 63, no. 2 (2011): 187–218.
Roberts, Hugh. *The Day of Hearing*. London: J. Barnes, 1600.
Robinson, Robert. *The Art of Pronunciation*. Menston, UK: Scolar Press, [1617] 1969.

Rogers, Carl R. *A Way of Being.* Boston: Houghton Mifflin, 1995.
Rogers, Carl R., and Richard Evans Farson. *Active Listening.* Chicago: Industrial Relations Center, University of Chicago, 1957.
Roisman, Joseph. *The Rhetoric of Manhood: Masculinity in the Attic Orators.* Berkeley: University of California Press, 2005.
Rosen, Stanley. "Phronesis or Ontology: Aristotle and Heidegger." In *The Impact of Aristotelianism on Modern Philosophy*, edited by Riccardo Pozzo, 248–65. Washington, DC: Catholic University of America Press, 2004.
Rosenfeld, Sophia. "AHR Forum on Being Heard: A Case for Paying Attention to the Historical Ear." *American Historical Review* 116, no. 2 (2001): 316–34.
Rowe, Aimee Carrillo. *Power Lines: On the Subject of Feminist Alliances.* Durham, NC: Duke University Press, 2008.
Santner, Eric, Kenneth Reinhard, and Slavoj Žižek. *The Neighbor: Three Inquiries in Political Theology.* Chicago: University of Chicago Press, 2005.
Schafer, Murray. "Open Ears." In *The Auditory Culture Reader*, edited by Michael Bull and Les Back, 25–39. New York: Berg, 2004.
Schafer, R. Murray. *The Soundscape: Our Sonic Environment and the Tuning of the World.* Rochester, VT: Destiny Books, [1977] 1994.
Scheible, Heinz. *Melanchthon: Eine Biographie.* Munich: Beck, 1997.
Scheurl, C. *Briefbuch, ein Beitrag zur Geschichte der Reformation und ihrer Zeit.* Edited by F. von Soden and J. K. F. Knaake. Aalen: Zeller, 1962.
Schmidt, Leigh Eric. *Hearing Things: Religion, Illusion, and the American Enlightenment.* Cambridge, MA: Harvard University Press, 2000.
Schmitt, Carl. *The Concept of the Political.* New Brunswick, NJ: Rutgers University Press, 1976.
———. *The Crisis of Parliamentary Democracy.* Translated by Ellen Kennedy. Cambridge, MA: MIT Press, 1985.
———. *Political Romanticism.* Translated by Guy Oakes. Cambridge, MA: MIT Press, 1986.
———. *Political Theology.* Translated by George Schwab. Chicago: University of Chicago Press, 1985.
Serjeantson, R. W. "Testimony: The Artless Proof." In *Renaissance Figures of Speech*, edited by Sylvia Adamson, Gavin Alexander, and Katrin Ettenhuber. Cambridge: Cambridge University Press, 2007.
Sexton, Jared. "The Social Life of Social Death: On Afro-Pessimism and Black Optimism." *InTensions* 5 (2011): 1–47.
Sheehan, Thomas. *Heidegger: The Man and the Thinker.* Piscataway, NJ: Transaction Publishers, 1981.

Shepard, Thomas. *Subjection to Christ in all his ordinances and appointments: The best means to preserve our liberty: Together with a treatise of ineffectual hearing the word . . .: With some remarkable passages of His life*, 2nd ed. London: Printed for John Rothwell, 1652.
Sherry, Richard. *A treatise of schemes and tropes*. London: 1550.
Shuger, Debora K. *Sacred Rhetoric: The Christian Grand Style in the English Renaissance*. Princeton, NJ: Princeton University Press, 1988.
Siisiäinen, Lauri. *Foucault and the Politics of Hearing*. London: Routledge, 2013.
Silverman, Kaja. *The Acoustic Mirror*. Bloomington: Indiana University Press, 1988.
Sloan, Thomas, ed. *Encyclopedia of Rhetoric*. Oxford: Oxford University Press, 2001.
Smith, Bruce R. *The Acoustic World of Early Modern England: Attending to the O-Factor*. Chicago: University of Chicago Press, 1999.
Smith, Mark M. *Hearing History: A Reader*. Athens: University of Georgia Press, 2004.
——— . "Listening to the Heard Worlds of Antebellum America." In *The Auditory Culture Reader*, edited by Michael Bull and Les Back, 137–63. New York: Berg, 2004.
——— . *Listening to Nineteenth-Century America*. Chapel Hill: University of North Carolina Press, 2001.
Smith, Roger. *The Norton History of the Human Sciences*. New York: W. W. Norton, 1997.
Spencer, Andrew, and Arnold M. Zwicky, eds. *The Handbook of Morphology*. Oxford: Blackwell, 1998.
Spivak, Gayatri. "Can the Subaltern Speak? Speculations on Widow-Sacrifice." *Wedge* 7–8 (1985): 120–30.
Steintrager, James A., and Rey Chow, eds. *Sound Objects*. Durham, NC: Duke University Press, 2019.
Sterne, Jonathan. *The Audible Past: Cultural Origins of Sound Reproduction*. Durham, NC: Duke University Press, 2003.
——— . "Medicine's Acoustic Culture: Mediate Auscultation, the Stethoscope and the 'Autopsy of the Living.'" In *The Auditory Culture Reader*, edited by Michael Bull and Les Back, 191–219. New York: Berg, 2004.
——— . *MP3: The Meaning of a Format (Sign, Storage, Transmission)*. Durham, NC: Duke University Press, 2012.
———, ed. *The Sound Studies Reader*. London: Routledge, 2012.
Stewart, Garrett. *Reading Voices: Literature and the Phonotext*. Berkeley: University of California Press, 1990.

Stoever, Jennifer Lynn. *The Sonic Color Line: Race and the Cultural Politics of Listening.* New York: New York University Press, 2016.
Strauss, Leo. *What Is Political Philosophy? And Other Studies.* Chicago: University of Chicago Press, 1959.
Strecker, Ivo. "The *Genius Loci* of Hamar." *Northeast African Studies* 7, no. 3 (2000): 85–118.
Struever, Nancy. "Garin, Camporeale and the Recovery of Renaissance Rhetoric." *Modern Language Notes* 119, no. 1 (2004): 47–55.
Sullivan, Ceri. "The Art of Listening in the Seventeenth Century." *Modern Philology* 104, no. 1 (2006): 34–71.
Szendy, Peter. *Listen: A History of Our Ears.* New York: Fordham University Press, 2008.
Tannen, Deborah. *You Just Don't Understand: Women and Men in Conversation.* New York: Ballantine, 1990.
Taylor, Thomas. *The Parable of the Sower and of the Seed.* London: T. Purfoot, 1634.
Thompson, Evan. *Mind in Life: Biology, Phenomenology, and the Sciences of Mind.* Cambridge, MA: Harvard University Press, 2007.
Tracy, Karen, James P. McDaniel, and Bruce E. Gronbeck. *The Prettier Doll: Rhetoric, Discourse, and Ordinary Democracy.* Tuscaloosa: University of Alabama Press, 2007.
Trinkaus, Charles. *The Scope of Renaissance Humanism.* Ann Arbor: University of Michigan Press, 1983.
Tucker, George Hugo. "Justus Lipsius and the *Cento* Form." In *(Un)masking the Realities of Power: Justus Lipsius and the Dynamics of Political Writing in Early Modern Europe*, edited by Erik De Bom. Leiden, Netherlands: Brill, 2011.
Ueding, Gert, and Bernd Steinbrink. *Grundriss Der Rhetorik: Geschichte, Technik, Methode.* Stuttgart: Metzler, 1986.
Vendler, Helen Hennessy. *Invisible Listeners: Lyric Intimacy in Herbert, Whitman, and Ashbery.* Princeton, NJ: Princeton University Press, 2005.
Vickers, Brian. *In Defence of Rhetoric.* Oxford: Oxford University Press, 1988.
Vico, Giambattista. *The New Science of Giambattista Vico.* Ithaca, NY: Cornell University Press, 1968.
Vidal, Fernando. *The Sciences of the Soul: The Early Modern Origins of Psychology.* Chicago: University of Chicago Press, 2011.
Volpi, Franco. *Heidegger e Aristotele.* Padua: Daphne Editrice, 1984.
Walker, Jeffrey. *Rhetoric and Poetics in Antiquity.* Oxford: Oxford University Press, 2000.

Wall, John N. "Shakespeare's Aural Art: The Metaphor of the Ear in *Othello.*" *Shakespeare Quarterly* 30, no. 3 (1979): 358–66.
Walzer, Arthur E. "*Parrēsia*, Foucault, and the Classical Rhetorical Tradition." *Rhetoric Society Quarterly* 43, no. 1 (2013): 1–21.
Warner, Marina. *Phantasmagoria: Spirit Visions, Metaphors, and Media into the Twenty-First Century.* Oxford: Oxford University Press, 2006.
Waters, William. *Poetry's Touch: On Lyric Address.* Ithaca, NY: Cornell University Press, 2003.
Weaver, Richard. *Language Is Sermonic.* Baton Rouge: Louisiana State University Press, 1985.
Wellbery, David E. Foreword to *Discourse Networks 1800/1900.* Translated by Michael Metteer and Chris Cullens. Stanford, CA: Stanford University Press, 1990.
Wheeler, Michael. *Reconstructing the Cognitive World: The Next Step.* Cambridge, MA: Harvard University Press, 2005.
Wichelns, Herbert A. "The Literary Criticism of Oratory." In *Studies in Rhetoric and Public Speaking in Honor of James Albert Winans*, edited by Alexander Magnus Drummond. New York: Century Co., 1925.
Wilkinson, Robert. *A sermon of hearing, or, jewell for the ear.* London: T. Orwin, 1593.
Wilson, Thomas. *The Art of Rhetoric*, edited by Peter E. Medine. University Park: The Pennsylvania State University Press, [1553] 1994.
———. *The Rule of Reason, Conteinying the Arte of Logique.* London: Richard Grafton, 1551.
Witte, Karsten. "Introduction to Siegfried Kracauer's 'The Mass Ornament.'" *New German Critique* 5 (1975).
Wolf, Eric R. *Anthropology.* New York: W. W. Norton, [1964] 1974.
Woods, Marjorie Curry. *Classroom Commentaries: Teaching the Poetria nova across Medieval and Renaissance Europe.* Columbus: Ohio State University Press, 2010.
Woolgar, C. M. *The Senses in Late Medieval England.* New Haven, CT: Yale University Press, 2013.
Zammito, John H. *Kant, Herder, and the Birth of Anthropology.* Chicago: University of Chicago Press, 2002.

INDEX

affectability, 32, 39, 47, 104–5, 206n11
Afro-pessimism, 93
Agamben, Giorgio, 65, 92–93, 121, 213–14n46. *See also* biopower
agency, 71, 76–77, 84, 107, 117, 127, 131–33, 135; political, 1, 216n17; rhetorical, 9, 109, 121; vocal, 8, 13, 97, 130. *See also* democracy; voice
apathy, 1, 137
Arendt, Hannah, 2–4, 31–32, 184n4
Aristotle: *bios* (life), 92; Corpus Aristotelicum, 36–46; *Nicomachean Ethics*, 33, 35, 48, 191n9, 193n22; "practical sciences," 74, 193n23, 202n24; *Rhetoric*, 21, 35, 100–101, 106, 131, 192n16, 210n27 (*see also* Heidegger, Summer Semester 1924 lecture course); rhetorical tradition of, 208–9n20
atechnoi pisteis (unartful or artless means of persuasion): Aristotle on, 101, 106, 121, 206n12; Demosthenes's use of, 106–7; in Freud, 114–21; Quintilian on, 108, 111, 113–14, 207n17; Ramus on, 112–13; in the Renaissance, 110–14; in sacred rhetoric, 109–10; tradition of, 95, 97;
Vico on, 113–14. *See also* communication, extrapersonal
attunement, 189n29
audiology, 32, 58. *See also* Speech Pathology and Audiology Department at the University of Iowa
audition, 2, 12
auditor, 4, 12, 47, 68–69, 81, 84, 123, 128, 131
auditory culture, 82–83
Augustine, 69, 92–93, 122; *The City of God*, 13–14; *Confessions*, 135; *De doctrina Christiana* (*On Christian Doctrine*), 134–135

babble, 40, 46, 52, 56, 124
Bacon, Francis, 209n22
Bagchee, Joydeep, 193n22
Baxter, Leslie A., and Dawn O. Brathwaite, 97
being-against-one-another. See *Gegeneinandersein*
being-moved, 1, 13, 15, 30, 35–36, 40, 42–45, 58, 62, 89, 91, 134–35, chapter 2
being-there. See *Dasein*

241

being-with. See *Mitsein*
being-with-one-another. See
 Miteinandersein
Bekker, August Immanuel, 41–43
Benjamin, Walter, 7, 12, 188n23
Bernstein, Charles, 85–86
Bickford, Susan, 187n16
biopolitics. *See* biopower. *See also*
 Foucault, Michel; Hacking, Ian;
 Hardt, Michael
biopower, 59, 65–66, 91–94, 199–200n11,
 204n46. *See also* Foucault, Michel
Bitzer, Lloyd F. *See* rhetorical situation
Black English, 125–26. *See also* Jordan,
 June
Blumenberg, Hans. *See* rhetorical
 anthropology
body politic, 47, 58, 62
Borch-Jacobsen, Mikell, 101, 104, 187n19,
 206n11
Breton, André, 11
Buck-Morss, Susan, 188n23, 197n43
Bultmann, Rudolph, 30, 39, 49
Burke, Kenneth: Freudian influence,
 101, 205n6; magic and power, 213n42;
 on recalcitrance, 117–18, 213–14n41; *A
 Rhetoric of Motives*, 117–18; 212n39
Burley-Allen, Madelyn, 18, 21–24
Burroughes, Jeremiah, 84, appendix

capacity. See *dunamis*
Carey, Christopher, 206n12, 207–8n19
Caussin, Nicholas, 73, 114, 119
Cicero: Augustine on, 134–35;
 Ciceronian tradition, 3, 12, 38,
 185n7, 198–99n8; ideal orator, 6,
 123; Melanchthon on, 67, 200n15;
 Quintilian on, 207–8n19; Wilson
 on, 112
Clement of Alexandria, 124
Cmiel, Kenneth, 183n1
communication: extrapersonal, 12, 16,
 49–50, 87, 96–97, 99–100, 103, 121;
 face-to-face, 7, 12, 16, chapter 3;
 interpersonal, 23, 27, 58, 81, 86,

95–101, 104–5, 114, 204n2, 205n4;
studies, 7, 19–27, 97–98, 205n4;
transactional model of, 21–22,
98–100, 99*fig.*, 110
confession, 23, 25
Conley, Thomas, 38, 46–47

Dasein (being-there), 33–35, 40, 45, 48,
 52–53, 96–97, 196n38
Davis, Diane, 206n11, 212n39
decisionism, 122, 132
demagoguery, 10–11, 38, 47, 50
de Man, Paul. *See* grammar
Deming, Richard, 85–86
democracy: conditions of, 7, 183n1,
 185–186n12; deliberative, 31, 50–51,
 54–55; ear of, 1–2, 10; liberal, 10–11,
 30, 55–56; modern, 52; movements,
 196–97n41; voice of, 1, 12, 16, 30;
 Western democratic traditions, 4
Demosthenes, 106–7, 206–207n13
Derrida, Jacques, 195n36
Dewey, John, 7, 183n1, 185–86n12. *See also*
 public
Dilthey, Wilhelm, 37, 39, 46, 79, 91
disciplinary formation, 3–4, 6–7, 10, 14,
 57–58, 59–67, 69, 72, 74, 76, 79–80,
 86, 90–92, 94, 96–97, 184n3, 189n29,
 199–200nn9–11, 204n2. *See also*
 human sciences
Dobson, Andrew, 185n7
Dolar, Mladen, 5, 216n18
Donne, John, 72, 85, 136
Donoso Cortés, Juan, 51, 195–96n37
dunamis (capacity), 13, 34–36, 45, 55, 60,
 71–73, 77, 112, 190–91n7
Düring, Ingemar, 41
dyad: active/passive, 9, 66, 82, 128, 130;
 agent/patient, 9, 66; eye/ear, 9;
 masculine/feminine, 9, 130; voice/
 ear, 66, 130. *See also* voice

ear: of democracy (*see* democracy);
 open, 5; virtuoso, 6. *See also* hearing
Eberhard, Philippe, 216n13

Egerton, Stephen, 83, 85
Elbow, Peter, 122, 124–26, 128, 130, 135–37, 214–15n6, 217n21
eloquence, 71, 134, 207n17
enchantment: dis-, 102, 104–5, 118–20, 188n23; re-, 11–12, 102–4, 118–20, 188n23, 205n9. *See also* sacred rhetoric
Enlightenment: critique of, 4; early, 60, 75; post-, 42, 88
entechnoi pisteis (artful means of persuasion): Aristotle on, 97, 106; in canons of rhetoric, 107; Quintilian on, 207n17; Wilson on, 112. *See also* Aristotle, *Rhetoric*; *atechnoi pisteis*
epistemology, 61, 65, 87–88, 184n3, 198–99nn7–8, 204n45
epithetoi pisteis (supplemental proofs), 111
Erasmus, 72, 202n21
eudaimonia (human flourishing), 48
Expressivism. *See* Elbow, Peter
extrahuman, 99, 101
eye. *See* seeing

factical life, 39, 47
fashion, 52, 119–20. *See also* self-fashioning
feeling, 10, 19, 35, 50, 81, 96, 115, 212n38
Feld, Steven, 81–82
Fiumara, Gemma, 4
Fliegelman, Jay, 128
Flügel, J. C., 5–8, 185n10
Foucault, Michel, 3, 12–14, 20, 57–66, 74, 76, 89–90, 92–94, chapter 2, 198n4. *See also* human sciences
Franck, Sebastian, 71–72, 136
free speech, 1, 10, 50–51, 196–97n37
Freud, Sigmund, 11, 23, 78, 101–102, 205n6; *Dora: An Analysis of a Case of Hysteria*, 6, 21, 118, 120, 213n 43; "magic words," 100–101, 104, 117; post-Freudian, 206n11; "Psychical Treatment," 119–20, 187n19; "Recommendations to Physicians Practicing Psycho-Analysis," 21;

Veranstaltungen (persuasive adjuncts or contrivances), 16, 95, 101, 105, 114–17, 212n37

Gadamer, Hans-Georg, 21, 32–34, 44
Galen, 67, 72, 200n15, 202n21
Gaonkar, Dilip Parameshwar, 78
Garsten, Bryan, 3–4, 185n7
Garver, Eugene, 192n16
Gegeneinandersein (being-against-one-another), 48, 55, 194n31
Gegeneinandersprechens (speaking-against-one-another), 48
Geisteswissenschaft/Naturwissenschaft (human science/natural science), 42–43, 74, 91
gender, 20, 80, 82, 123–25, 131–33, 135–136. *See also* dyad; Gleason, Maud; voice
genealogy, 5, 10, 12–13, 15–16, 20, 65, 80, 91–93, 95, 98, 122, 129, 132, 184n3
genius loci, 80–82
Gleason, Maud, 123–24, 131, 137
Glenn, Cheryl, 9, 27
"good man speaking well," 4–5, 8, 16, 31, 50, 90–91, 124. *See also* gender; voice
Gordon, Peter, 194n32
grammar, 19, 24, 67, 107, 123, 126, 128–30, 135, 214–15n6, 216n13
grand style, 73, 214n1
Greenblatt, Stephen. *See* self-fashioning
Gregory Nazianzen, Saint, 90
Gross, Kenneth, 83
Gunderson, Erik, 124, 131, 137

Habermas, Jürgen, 10, 54–55, 196–97n41. *See also* democracy; public
Hacking, Ian, 204n45. *See* Foucault, Michel
Hardt, Michael, 93, 204n46
Hauser, Gerald A., 107, 207n15
hearing: *akouein* (hearing), 33; *audire* (to hear), 7, 49; faculty of, 3, 26,

hearing *(continued)*
184n4; group hearing, 25; in Heidegger, 33–34, 55–56, 191n8; "mere hearing," 53; not-hearing, 34; overhear, 21, 25; in the scientific sense, 22, 24, 27, 58, 95; true hearing, 53; unheard, 9; the Word of God, 2, 21, 49, 83–85, appendix
Heidegger, Martin: *Being and Time*, 13, 32–34, 42, 54, 95–97, 190–91n7, 193n26, 196n38; Black Notebooks, 55; on metaphysics, 36, 41–42, 53–56, 87, 197n44; Summer Semester (SS) 1924 lecture course ("Aristoteles, Rhetorik II"), 4–5, 13, 15–16, 28, 32, 35–36, 40–41, 43–45, 48, 56, 91, chapter 1
Heraclitus, 47, 52–53, 189n29
Herbert, George, 85–88
Hercules Gallicus, 28, 29*fig.*, 36, 83
hermeneutics, 40–41, 53, 68, 74–75, 78, 97, 108, 193n22
Hilliard, Kevin F., 80
historicity, 12, 39, 50, 116, 213n44
historiography, 9–10, 59, 74, 76, 89–94, 109, 113, 118–119, 121
history: aural, 4; cultural, 26, 202–203n30; of the human sciences (*see* human sciences); intellectual, 32, 198n6; of the senses, 15, 203n39; social, 26–27
Hobbes, Thomas, 197n43
homiletics, 134
humanities, 2, 20, 85–86
"human ornament," 118, 213n44
human sciences, 3–6, 10, 12–16, 39, 57–67, 72–75, 84, 89–93, 184n3, 198n7, 199nn10–11, 204n45, 213–14n46
Hume, David, 75

"ideal orator," 6, 123–24, 133–134. *See also* Cicero; Seneca the Elder
identification, 6, 31, 116, 123, 205n6, 212n39
Ihde, Don, 4

Jaeger, Werner, 43. *See also* Heidegger, Summer Semester 1924 lecture course
Jarratt, Susan C., 9, 125
Jay, Martin, 26
Jesuit rhetoric, 73
Jewish God, 2–3. *See also* Philo of Alexandria
Jonas, Hans, 3–4, 32
Jordan, June, 125–28, 130–31, 135, 216n13. *See also* agency
judgment: aesthetic, 2; dispositions of, 3; moved to, 4, 10, 111, 132; practical judgment, 3, 185n7

Kant, Immanuel, 10, 78, 87
Keller, Evelyn Fox, 9
Kelley, Donald R., 66
Kennedy, George A., 206n12
kinēsis (motion), 42–43
Kisiel, Theodore, 28–29, 32, 190–191n7
Kittler, Friedrich A., 8, 183n13. *See also* psychoanalytic theory
Kleinberg-Levin, David Michael, 4
Kopperschmidt, Josef, 77–79
Kracauer, Siegfried, 7, 118, 213n44
Kristeller, Paul Oskar, 64, 72, 198n6

Lacan, Jacques, 100–101, 116, 186n13
Landshut, Siegfried, 32, 194n31
Lerner, Gerda, 9
Lipari, Lisbeth, 189n29
Lippmann, Walter, 7, 9, 185–86n12
listening: active, 50, 131–32, 137, 162, 195n36; attentive, 1, 5, 9, 12, 68–69, 191n10; culture, 75–76, 81; deep, 133; empathic, 24; feminization of, 25 (*see also* dyad; gender); as finding oneself, 36; in the humanities, 2; inventive, 80; listener-as-judge, 83–84; models of, 24; -as-obedience, 49–50; obediently, 31, 47–56; to one another, 34; passive, 6, 50, 123, 131–32; -as-patience, 133; rhetorical, 17, 122; rhetoric of, 134; rituals of, 25; sacred

arts of, 15, 49, 58; as a skill, 24; for
subtext, 25; strategies, 24;
technologies, 6; across time, 24–25;
unconscious, 24; to yourself, 25
logon echon (speaking-being), 33, 48, 52
logos: per Heidegger, 33–34, 45, 48, 53;
means of persuasion, 106, 111,
208–9n20; in rhetorical
anthropology, 79; in sacred rhetoric,
69, 113, 135
Long, Frederick J., 207–8n19
Lucian, 123
Lundberg, Christian, 101, 213n44
Luther, Martin, 37, 39, 61, 69–72, 91,
201n17
Lyons, John, 129

"magic words." *See* Freud, Sigmund
Mainberger, Gonsalv K., 79
Marlowe, Christopher, 112–13
Marshall, David, 113
Marx, Karl, 15, 78, 189n27
masculinity, 5, 122–25, 128, 131, 133–34,
136, 187n17, 214n1. *See also* gender
McCormick, John P., 197n43
McKeon, Richard, 193n23, 202n24
media: apparatus, 185–86n12; mass,
1, 7, 30–31, 51, 194n31; studies, 100,
205n4
mediation, 110–11, 133
medicine, 66–67
Melanchthon, Philipp, 15, 37, 61, 66–69,
71–72, 74–75, 91, 200n15, 201–2n20
"mere ornamentation," 6, 123
metaphors: gendered, 125, 127; of
hearing, 2; of listening, 25, 84; of
oratory, 137; of sound, 81
mind, change of, 58, 123
miracle working, 115, 118, 120
Miteinandersein (being-with-one-
another), 33–34, 55
Mitsein (being-with), 48, 96
modernity, 53, 61, 64, 78, 92, 119, 188n23,
198n6
Morhof, Daniel Georg, 73

Most, Glenn W., 192–93n21
Müller, Adam, 28, 51–52
Mulvey, Laura, 9

National Socialism, 54, 196–97n41
Natorp, Paul, 40. *See also*
neo-Kantianism
Nazism, 6, 48, 50, 52–53
Nelson, John S., 184n3
neo-Kantianism, 33–34, 40
Ngũgĩ wa Thiong'o, 8, 186n14
Nietzsche, Friedrich, 11–12, 20, 47, 107, 128
noise, 15, 23–25, 34, 98
nonhuman, 12, 44
nonliving, 44
Norberg-Schulz, Christian. *See genius
loci*
nous (mind), 45, 184n4. *See also* mind,
change of; public

obedience, 1–3, 13, 30–31, 33, 35, 37, 49–51,
130, 191nn8–9. *See also* listening
obediently
object petit-a. *See* transference
ontology, 15, 32, 44, 61
Origen, 133
original sin, 49, 91, 205n6.

Parable of the Sower, 21, 99, 133,
appendix. *See also* sacred rhetoric
paraklēsis (incitement), 33
Parmenides, 47, 55
parrēsia (frank speech), 59, 63, 94. *See
also* Foucault, Michel
passion: -action, 35, 132; of Christ, 39, 71;
great, 47; Heidegger on, 35–37, 47;
human, 32, 69–71, 128, 137, 190n5;
phenomenology of, 91; rhetoric of,
38–39, 42; of the soul, 4; passivity, 3,
17, 68, 82, 127–28, 133–35
pastoral, 58, 62–63, 90
pathologies, 6, 66, 73, 93, 104,
196–197n41
pathos, 30, 39, 43–45, 48, 67, 77, 79, 106,
111, 113, 196–97n41

patience, 70–71, 132, appendix
Paul, the Apostle, 49, 68–69, 108–9, 120–21, 207–8n19
Pelikan, Jaroslav, 208–9n20
Perelman, Chaïm, 55, 78, 194n30
Peters, John Durham, 18, 98–100, 205n4
phantasm, 5, 8
phantasmagoria, 5, 9, 185–86n12, 197n43
phenomenology, 2, 4, 12, 19, 39, 87–88, 91, 191n8
Philo of Alexandria, 2, 89, 133
philology, 31, 59–60, 62
phōnē (sound), 53, 129
pilgrimage, 101–2, 116–17, 119
Plato, 2, 39–41, 63, 89, 198–99n8
Plutarch, 21, 123–24
poetics, 42, 53, 64, 71, 85–89
politics, discipline of, 9, 14, 50, 64–65, 97
Porter, James I., 190n6
Poster, Carol, 208–209n20
practical arts, 64–66, 72, 74
prayer, 69, 73, 79, 84, 88, appendix
preaching/preacher, 102
probatio inartificialis, 212n36. *See* Quintilian, on supernatural evidence
Project on Rhetoric of Inquiry (POROI), 20, 184n3
propaganda, 7, 52, 99. *See also* media; publicity
psychagogy, 36, 63–64
psychoanalysis, 23, 104, 118, 120, 187n19, 217n21. *See also* Freud, Sigmund; psychoanalytic theory
psychoanalytic theory, 4–10, 87, 101, 213n44
psychology: field of, 4, 23, 37, 184n3; group, 104, 116, 212n37; manipulative, 39; physiological, 80; politics and pedagogy, 14–15, 57, 62, 65–66, 76; popular, 27; rational, 80; scientific, 81. *See also* Freud, Sigmund
psychophysiology, 38. *See also* psychagogy

public: arena, 6, 102; culture, 9; debate, 1, 10, 183n1; discourse, 8; ear, 18, 58, 83–85; education, 7; mind, 7; opinion, 194n31; space, 21, 25, 27, 196; sphere, 10, 55, 84, 122, 131, 196
publicity, 7, 82. *See also* media

Quintilian: on Aristotle's proofs, 207n17; on the art of rhetoric, 67, 70, 216n16; on supernatural evidence, 108, 110–11, 113, 116, 119, 207n18, 207–8n19

Ramus, Peter, 112–13, 210–11n29
Ratcliffe, Krista, 19, 27, 122, 132
ratio atque oratio (reason and speech), 38–39, 45
reason: irrationality, 6, 11, 81, 191n9; political, 3; practical, 11; rational actor, 6, 11; rationality, 4, 11, 103, 188n23, 194–95n32, 196–97n41; state, 4, 14, 31
Reformation, European, 16, 61–62, 66–69, 72–73, 75, 82. *See also* Luther, Martin; Melanchthon, Philipp
Renaissance: classical revival, 38; drama and literature, 83, 88–89; humanism, 60, 65, 198–99n8; orator, 28; philosophy, 72, 198nn6–7; sacred arts of listening, 58, 136; self-fashioning, 199n9. *See also atechnoi pisteis* in the Renaissance
reputation, 120–21
responsibility: Heidegger on, 196n38; irresponsibility and passivity, 127–28; personal, 23; social 51, 85, 132
rhetoric: affective, 38; as architectonic, 57, 67, 75, 199n10; as a discipline, 3, 15, 19, 32, 39–41, 44, 75, 78, 90–91, 108–10, 123–24, chapter 4; encomiastic (of praise and blame), 14, 20, 33, 35, 91; genres of (deliberative, forensic, epideictic), 48, 107; Gothic, 5, 12; instrumental, 13, 40;

as meta-practical, 62, 65, 84 (*see also* practical arts); motivistic rhetoric, 36–38, 46; sacred, 11–13, 16, 45, 62, 69, 71–75, 83–85, 91–92, 98–99, 101–4, 108–9, 133–36 (*see also* public ear); triumphal, 28–36

rhetorical: anthropology, 8, 75–82; situation, 81, 119, 202–3n30; theology, 198–199n8; theory, 50, 91, 101, 132, 137, 193n24

Rhodes, Neil, 83
Rickert, Thomas, 193n24, 216n17
Rogers, Carl R., 99
Ross, David, 40
Royster, Jacqueline Jones, 132

sacrament, 119–20
Schmitt, Carl, 31, 48–53, 55, 196–97n41
Scripture, 18, 55, 66, 68, 84, 111, 134, appendix, 210n26
seeing: bodily eye, 4, 7–9, 118; faculty of, 2–3, 23, 26, 81, 184n4; in Heidegger, 33–34; in Luther, 70; vision in poetics, 85–89
self-fashioning, 199n9, 207–208n13
Seneca the Elder, 124, 131. *See also* Gleason, Maud
Seneca the Younger, 130
senses, 4, 15, 26, 30, 34, 85, 88, 189n27, 197n43, 203n39
sensorium, 12, 15
Sexton, Jared. *See* Afro-pessimism
Sherry, Richard, 210n27
silence, 9, 23
Silverman, Kaja, 5, 9, 187n17
Smith, Bruce, 26, 86
social sciences, 2, 12–13, 27, 75, 84, 92
sōma (body), 45
sophists: in Heidegger's lecture course, 48, 52; rhetoric-as-sophistry, 51–52; second sophistic, 89, 134–35; sophistic literature, 198–199n8
Soranus, 123
souls: "government of" (*regimen animarum*), 90; movement of, 4,

6, 14–15, 57–58, 63–76, 91, 100, 104–5; preparing those of the auditors, 68

soundscape, 22–26
sound studies, 2, 15, 86, 188–89n26
Speech Pathology and Audiology Department at the University of Iowa, 18, 24
Spivak, Gayatri, 9
Sterne, Jonathan, 6, 15, 21, 26, 188–89n26
Strauss, Leo, 3, 32, 190n5
Strecker, Ivo. See *genius loci*
Struever, Nancy, 198n7
Strunk, William, 127, 129
subject: male, 6–7; subjectivity, 1, 3–4, 6, 8–9, 93–94; writing, 8
subjection, 3, 6, 87, 89, 123, 130, 132
suffering, 25, 71, 115, 123–24, 136–37, 212n38. *See also* passivity; patience

Tannen, Deborah, 18, 132–33
Taylor, Thomas, 85, appendix
technē (an art or technology), 34, 63. See also *entechnoi pisteis*
technologies of the self, 89, 133
theology, 13, 42, 46, 67–69, 72–73, 85, 210–11n29; political, 31; rhetorical (*see* rhetorical theology)
transference, 104, 116, 118
transferential object. *See* transference
Trinkaus, Charles, 198–99n8

Vendler, Helen, 86–88
Vickers, Brian, 38
Vico, Giambattista, 113–14
vision. *See* seeing
voice: active, 126, 129–30, 132, 134, 215n9, 216n13; audible vs. in writing, 83; of authority, 30; in composition studies, 16, 122; disembodied, 5, 23; divine, 13, 22, 111, 135, 140, 144, 149–50, 157–59, 172, 216n18; of the friend or enemy, 34, 55; human, 23; masculine, 5, 122–25, 131;

voice *(continued)*
  mediopassive, 127; middle-, 1, 30, 137, 216n13; passive, 19, 30, 123, 127, 129–30, 132, 134–35, 215n7, 215n9, 215n12; personal, 1, 6, 25, 88, 126, 128; as political subjectivity, 1, 12, 133; in rhetorical tradition, 93, 97; *vox*, 129

Waters, William, 87, 203n39
Weaver, Richard, 119, 212n38

Weber, Max, 12, 102, 188n23
Weimar Germany, 10–11, 16, 30–31, 51–52, 55, 118, 195n35
Wichelns, Herbert A., 7–8
Wilson, Thomas, 83, 111–12, 209–210n25, 210n26
Wolf, Eric R., 202n25

Zammito, John H., 80
Zwicky, Arnold, 127–29, 215n12

Founded in 1893,
UNIVERSITY OF CALIFORNIA PRESS
publishes bold, progressive books and journals
on topics in the arts, humanities, social sciences,
and natural sciences—with a focus on social
justice issues—that inspire thought and action
among readers worldwide.

The UC PRESS FOUNDATION
raises funds to uphold the press's vital role
as an independent, nonprofit publisher, and
receives philanthropic support from a wide
range of individuals and institutions—and from
committed readers like you. To learn more, visit
ucpress.edu/supportus.

www.ingramcontent.com/pod-product-compliance
Lightning Source LLC
Chambersburg PA
CBHW030537230426
43665CB00010B/925